MOTHERGUILT

Ita Buttrose, AO, OBE, is one of Australia's most prominent women. She has enjoyed a long and distinguished career in the Australian media and is currently Editor of *Highlife* magazine and Editor-at-Large for *OK!* magazine. She has twice been voted Australia's 'Most Admired Woman' and was awarded a Centenary Medal in 2003 for service to Australian society in business leadership. Over the years she had been the confidante of thousands of Australian mothers who have written to her at the leading magazines and newspapers she has edited including *Cleo*, *The Australian Women's Weekly*, *ITA* magazine and the Sydney *Daily* and *Sunday Telegraph*s. She has drawn on some of the letters she had received for *Motherguilt*. The author of six books, *How Much is Enough? Your Financial Roadmap to a Happy Retirement*, *What is Love?*, *A Word to the Wise*, *A Passionate Life*, *Every Occasion: The Guide to Modern Etiquette* and *Early Edition: My First Forty Years*, Ita is one of Australia's busiest public speakers, is chair of the National Breast Cancer Advisory Network and President of Arthritis Australia. Ita has two children.

Dr Penny Adams, graduated from the University of New South Wales in 1982 with first-class honours and the University Medal. She worked at Royal North Shore Hospital for several years before leaving to establish a General Practice in Mosman, where she has practised for the last twenty years. She subsequently gained her Fellowship in General Practice, being awarded the Kent Hughes Medal for topping the nation in the exams. While the diversity of General Practice is its main attraction, Penny's special interests include women and children's health, adolescent medicine, sexual health and preventative health and screening. With a passion for health promotion, Penny is a frequent guest speaker for charities, and has made regular appearances on shows such as *Beauty and the Beast*, *Mornings with Kerri-Anne* and *Good Health Television*. She has a reputation, not only with her patients but also media audiences, for her caring nature and a lively sense of humour. Penny is married to Dr Ian Stevenson, an anaesthetist, and has three children: Diana, a university student, and Tom and Olivia, who are at school.

AUSTRALIAN
WOMEN REVEAL
THEIR TRUE
FEELINGS ABOUT
MOTHERHOOD

Ita Buttrose and Dr Penny Adams

MOTHER GUILT

VIKING
an imprint of
PENGUIN BOOKS

VIKING

Published by the Penguin Group
Penguin Group (Australia)
250 Camberwell Road
Camberwell, Victoria 3124, Australia
(a division of Pearson Australia Group Pty Ltd)
Penguin Group (USA) Inc.
375 Hudson Street, New York, New York 10014, USA
Penguin Group (Canada)
10 Alcorn Avenue, Toronto, Ontario, Canada, M4V 3B2
(a division of Pearson Penguin Canada Inc.)
Penguin Books Ltd
80 Strand, London WC2R ORL, England
Penguin Ireland
25 St Stephen's Green, Dublin 2, Ireland
(a division of Penguin Books Ltd)
Penguin Books India Pvt Ltd
11, Community Centre, Panchsheel Park, New Delhi -110 017, India
Penguin Group (NZ)
Cnr Airborne and Rosedale Roads, Albany, Auckland, New Zealand
(a division of Pearson New Zealand Ltd)
Penguin Books (South Africa) (Pty) Ltd
24 Sturdee Avenue, Rosebank, Johannesburg 2196, South Africa

Penguin Books Ltd, Registered Offices: 80 Strand, London WC2R ORL, England

First published by Penguin Group (Australia), a division of Pearson Australia Group Pty Ltd, 2005

1 3 5 7 9 10 8 6 4 2

Design by Sandy Cull © Penguin Group (Australia)
Cover photograph by Chris Kapa Photography
Author photographs by Vicki Skarratt (Penny Adams) and Robert Morehead (Ita Buttrose)
Typeset in 11.75/16 pt Granjon by Post Pre-press Group, Brisbane, Queensland
Printed and bound in Australia by McPherson's Printing Group, Maryborough, Victoria

National Library of Australia
Cataloguing-in-Publication data:

Buttrose, Ita, 1942– .
Motherguilt: Australian women reveal their true feelings about motherhood.

ISBN 0 670 04151 3.

1. Motherhood – Australia. 2. Mother – Australia – Attitudes.
I. Adams, Penny. II. Title.

306.8743

www.penguin.com.au

I

Contents

Introduction   1

Chapter 1
Pregnancy and childbirth: the guilt begins   16

Chapter 2
Why does guilt attack mothers and not fathers?   33

Chapter 3
Breastfeeding can be a cow of a job!   52

Chapter 4
When things go wrong: the not-so-perfect child   67

Chapter 5
When mothers go out to work   84

Chapter 6
The agony and ecstasy of childcare   102

Chapter 7
Giving up work: Wendy Harmer's quantum leap   122

Chapter 8
Stay-at-home mums work full-time too   132

Chapter 9
Our son has two mothers   149

Chapter 10
Anything your child can do mine can do better   160

Chapter 11
Different cultures, different times   177

Chapter 12
Tackling the teen years – triumphantly   199

Chapter 13
When a mother gives up her child   220

Chapter 14
Is sex ever the same after children?   237

Chapter 15
Why doesn't Mum love Dad any more?   254

Chapter 16
Stepmothers are seldom wicked   270

Chapter 17
Learning to live with the loss of a child   288

Chapter 18
Like mother, like daughter – the unbreakable bond   304

Chapter 19
Like mother, like son – the resilient relationship   320

Chapter 20
Motherguilt has no place in the twenty-first century   339

With love and thanks to my children, Kate and Ben,
for always allowing me to wear the title of 'Mother' with pride.

ITA BUTTROSE

To my mother Pamela, who has taught me so much about
being a mother, and my children, Diana, Thomas and Olivia,
who continue to teach me more, and my husband, Ian.

PENNY ADAMS

Acknowledgements

This book would not have been possible without the contribution of the many women and men around Australia who have shared their stories with us. We have valued their confidences and thank them all very much indeed.

We are grateful to Jennifer Bouda for her invaluable assistance with some of the interviews, research and proofing. Many thanks also to researcher Denby Browning.

Finally, our sincere thanks to Julie Gibbs, Executive Publisher of Penguin Australia, for her enthusiastic support and belief in this book.

Introduction

This is a book about guilt. Not the ordinary everyday kind of guilt a person might feel when they have done something wrong, but a guilt so powerful and so uniquely related to motherhood that it has a name all of its own – Motherguilt. Just about all mothers acknowledge its existence but few of them can offer any rational explanation as to why they suffer from it. And suffer they do! Motherguilt can make even the most competent woman doubt her mothering ability. It slinks into her life when she least expects it and anything and everything can cause an outbreak.

If mothers are working full-time in the paid workforce, they feel guilty that they are not at home. When they are at home full-time, women feel guilty that they are not earning an income or fulfilling their career potential, and if working part-time, they feel guilty because they are not doing either job properly. Mothers also mentally accuse themselves of all kinds of 'crimes'. Did I drink too much when I was pregnant? Did I do enough exercise? Did I do too much exercise? I should have had a vaginal delivery. I should have had a Caesarean. Am I being a good mother? Am I being too good a mother? Motherguilt goes on and on.

As mothers themselves, the authors know how Motherguilt operates and how easily it can shatter a woman's confidence. 'I used to think it must be only me who felt this way,' Ita says, 'but once I started writing about my motherhood experiences in *The Australian Women's Weekly*, which I edited as a young mother with two kids, other women wrote to me relieved – almost delighted in fact – to find that someone else suffered from guilt just like they did.'

'It is probably the "dark thoughts" women have about motherhood that catch them off guard,' Penny says. 'They don't expect to have such negative thoughts because motherhood is always talked about in glowing terms. Unlike my own *very* honest mum, many mothers fail to tell the truth although they know what their daughters soon discover – creating life and shaping a child into a useful human being *is* rewarding and satisfying but there are times when being a mother is tedious, frustrating and stressful. There are days when the drudgery of her role makes a woman want to scream. She feels ashamed and guilty for having such thoughts but keeps them to herself because she is scared of being labelled a bad mother, causing people to think she doesn't love her children.

'I have been speaking to mothers in the safe and confidential confines of my surgery for almost twenty years now. When I have seen that familiar tortured look on the weary face of a fellow Motherguilt sufferer and shared with her some of my "dark thoughts", the look of relief on her face has provided me with some of my most satisfying experiences, both as a doctor and a mother. The healing goes *both* ways and with it comes relief knowing we are both "normal".'

The simple truth of the matter is that mothers are finding it increasingly difficult to live up to society's expectations of them and are worn out from striving to be like others would have them be. This does not mean women want to turn back the clock or give up having 'choices' but they do need more help to carry out their mothering role. Children are a nation's future and their wellbeing should be of national concern. We live in a society where women are expected to work, and Australia's high cost of living means many women are unable to stop work for long, if at all, after having children. Many families today need the money a mother can earn!

It was probably easier to be a mother back in the days when most girls accepted that motherhood was the main reason for their existence and unquestioningly looked forward to the day when they would marry and start raising a family. Such thinking changed almost overnight when the 'choices' fuelled by the advent of the Pill and Women's Liberation transformed women's lives in the late 1960s and early 1970s. At last women could choose whether or not to have children and, perhaps more importantly, *when* to have them. This gaining of 'control' meant that women were able to make decisions about their life direction, and one of their new options included combining paid employment and motherhood. However, if anything went wrong as a result of juggling so many roles, women blamed themselves and, secretly, felt guilty.

As usual, they rarely discussed the way they felt – not even with other women – fearing that guilt might be seen as letting down the side. Women had waited a long time for the independence that came with readily available, effective contraception and had enthusiastically embraced the concept of 'having it all'. No one was brave enough (yet) to admit that 'liberation' had flaws. But, as women continued to clamber over the barricades and climb every mountain, the unrealistic expectations placed on them became intolerable. It was not enough that women were required to be perfect wives, perfect daughters, perfect sisters, perfect friends and perfect workmates – they had to be perfect mothers too. Instead of rejecting such an impossible task, however, women endeavoured to do what was expected of them. The age of Superwoman had arrived!

It is the authors' belief that Motherguilt, as we know and understand it in the twenty-first century, can be directly attributed to the gaining of 'choices' at the time of Women's Liberation. By adding part of the financial responsibilities for raising a family to their job of mother, women have had to shoulder the burden of guilt that comes from trying to overcome their natural nurturing instincts and combine conflicting roles. One part of a woman wants never to let her baby out of her sight, the other misses the satisfaction of using her brain and skills in the workplace and the financial independence that comes with paid employment. No matter how hard she might try to rationalise her behaviour, both sides of her continually compete against each other in an emotionally wearing struggle. Guilt is the natural consequence. With more women and mothers in the Australian workforce now than at any other time in our history, it is hardly surprising that Motherguilt has grown to epidemic proportions.

The subject certainly cropped up frequently in letters from viewers who wrote to the popular television show *Beauty and the Beast*, where the authors first met as panellists. But it wasn't only a problem of viewing mothers – all the 'beauties' had first-hand knowledge of Motherguilt, too! This simply confirmed the authors' belief that few women are immune to it. They are convinced, however, that Motherguilt can be conquered and their aim in writing this book is to help women set themselves free from guilt.

≈

'These days I have little guilt,' says Ita, 'because both my children are adults and I can see the results of my mothering. They have turned out well and I am proud of them. Over the years there were times when I blamed myself for all sorts of things that weren't really my fault at all, but I can see no evidence now that my being a working mother, and whatever shortcomings I might have had, has been to my children's detriment. Once I was divorced the choice of staying at home was never an option. I had to work to support my children and pay for their schooling and while I always felt exhausted I don't remember any massive attacks of Motherguilt, but that doesn't mean I've had a guilt-free passage through motherhood.

'There were aspects of being a mother that bored me witless – like school concerts and sports days for instance – not that I told anyone. However, I don't feel guilty for thinking like that. If they're honest about it, few parents want to watch other people's children perform, once their own child has been on. I did feel guilty about not doing canteen duty – it's odd how children see having a parent do this chore as some kind of status symbol – but my kids' schools had me opening art shows, performing as quiz mistress at trivia nights, and giving motivational speeches to teachers. It occasionally crossed my mind that canteen duty would be an easier option.

'When I left school at fifteen, my plan was to work for a few short years and retire when I married and had children. I never thought my life would turn out the way that it has and as a teenager I never considered the "having it all" approach, which is how my life's journey has panned out. Not long before I married at twenty-one, I asked my mother and my aunt if they thought I'd be bored if I gave up work when I had kids. They both assured me that looking after my children would keep me so busy that boredom would be kept at bay. They fibbed!

'By the time I was twenty-five, my career was forging ahead but there were no signs of any children – not by choice, I just hadn't managed to get pregnant. My GP referred me to an eminent Sydney gynaecologist and obstetrician, who "examined" me while – much to my embarrassment – his nurse, a stern-looking woman, watched. He delivered his verdict bluntly. I was sub-fertile and might never have children. He offered me no hope. I was devastated. The possibility I might not be able to have children was something that had never crossed my mind. I slunk off to see one of my closest girlfriends, who was at home with her three children, and sobbed my heart out. I was a failure as a woman.

'Two years later when I was living and working in London, I proved that stuffy doctor wrong – much to my satisfaction. I became pregnant! In 1968 my daughter Kate was born. She was so pink and beautiful I couldn't take my eyes off her and I've never forgotten the incredible look of joy on my husband's face when he came into the ward and saw her for the first time. Husbands were not "allowed" to be involved in the birth process back then, they were "confined" to the waiting room.

'After ten days we took her home to Wadhurst, a charming village in the Sussex countryside where few people except the shopkeepers spoke to me because we had not been introduced. I discovered how lonely a new mother can be and the uncertainties that come with looking after your first baby. My immediate family and my husband's parents were in Australia and if it hadn't been for my husband's splendid Aunt Audrey who lived in Surrey, I don't know what I would have done. She was a godsend, especially when it came to breastfeeding and weaning – like many other women I soon learned that doing such things well does not automatically come with being a mother. Later, when Kate was beginning to walk, Aunt Audrey gave me a piece of advice that has become family folklore: "Treat them like dogs, duckie. Tell them to sit and stay. If they don't, smack them on the nose!"

'In spite of my lack of knowledge and, it must be said, occasional stupidity, Kate thrived and when she was three months old and my first-time-mother insecurities were beginning to calm down I began to enjoy getting to know my baby. I would take her for long walks in the country lanes in the afternoons, she would watch me garden, and I would clean the house and cook delicious dinners for my husband when she napped during the day. I loved being a mother and the garden became a kind of work project – my raspberries were sensational! I was happy but I knew that this kind of life was not enough. I wanted my career back. I had sixteen months at home with Kate, during which time we came back to Australia and I accepted Sir Frank Packer's offer to return to his company Australian Consolidated Press and resume the position I had held before going overseas.

'I have never felt guilty about making this choice, not then and not now. Like motherhood my career was something I *had* to do. I was determined to achieve my ambition to become Editor of *The Australian Women's Weekly* – then the top job for a woman journalist in Australia – but the first few months back at work just about killed me. Combining motherhood and a job was harder than I thought it would be and although my husband was supportive there was no way I would confess, even to him, how much I was struggling to do all that was expected of me. I hate to admit this now but I did think I was Superwoman. What a joke. There were so many responsibilities to juggle that after a day that combined cooking breakfast for everyone, looking after Kate, making beds and doing household chores including the ironing, plus working at the office I was completely pooped when I got home in the evening. Superwoman? Hardly!

'Most of my salary was spent on paying two women who came to our home (two days a week each) to look after Kate when I wasn't there. As Women's Editor of the Sydney *Daily Telegraph* and *Sunday Telegraph* – which Sir Frank then owned and later sold to Rupert Murdoch and News Ltd in 1972 – I worked shifts from Tuesday to Saturday and had Sundays and Mondays off. A couple of days a week I worked from two in the afternoon until eleven at night, so I was able to have the mornings with Kate while my husband looked after her at night and on Saturdays. It was a good arrangement that worked well for us. Working mothers with toddlers were a rarity in those days. Other mothers often asked me, somewhat disapprovingly, "And *who* is looking after your daughter?" Men used to ask the same question and were equally reproachful. Such questions not only managed to make me feel guilty but also damned angry.

'The first day I went back to work close to Kate's lunchtime. One of her carers, Mrs Ratcliffe (much to her chagrin, later nicknamed "Ratty"), was about to give her the lunch that I had prepared. As I said goodbye, Kate began to cry and after I closed the front door her wails got louder. I walked to the bus stop feeling awful. Then I began to worry. Had she stopped crying? Was she eating her lunch? Would she be all right without me? Motherguilt gnawed away at me.

'The next day, Ratty assured me that Kate had stopped crying within seconds of me leaving, had eaten all her lunch and played happily all afternoon but, even so, when she cried on my leaving for the second day, Motherguilt struck again! Of course, as all mothers know, toddlers often cry when they are left behind for whatever reason. Kate's tears had nothing to do with my going to work; she just liked having me around. Looking at my delightful daughter today I know that my career did not come between us or harm the love we have for one another. At thirty-six, she is a successful architect, a hard-working, decent and tolerant young woman of whom any mother would be proud.

'It took me four and a half years to become pregnant again and give Kate a brother. Once again my gynaecologist – not the abrupt one of earlier years but a kinder, more understanding doctor – said that getting pregnant might be difficult for me. My husband and I tried everything. We had charts, thermometers, books . . . all in an effort to work out the best times when we would be most likely to conceive. This kind of 'productive' lovemaking leaves much to be desired! We were just about to try fertility drugs when I discovered I was pregnant. I had often thought it would be nice to have twins, but not quadruplets, which can happen when taking fertility drugs. Motherguilt multiplied by four would have been too much to bear.

'My pregnancy coincided with a major career opportunity. Sir Frank had asked me to become Founding Editor of *Cleo* magazine, the first mass-market magazine for women to be introduced in Australia for some years. It was a substantial investment for Australian Consolidated Press and a great deal was riding on its success. The year was 1972 and Women's Liberation was well underway. Women were being told they should make choices and not apologise for any of them. The message fell on receptive ears. Anything was possible, women *could* have it all. It was heady stuff. The new progressive women at whom *Cleo* was aimed had arrived and I was one of them. Life was exciting.

'With the help of loose-fitting jackets, I kept my pregnancy a secret for almost four months even though I had the most ghastly morning sickness and regularly disappeared to the women's loo for the first few months. No one noticed, which doesn't say much for observant journalists. When I could no longer hide my condition I gave Sir Frank's son Kerry the news. He was kind and sweet and seemed genuinely pleased for me but I heard afterwards that he had ranted and raved about "silly bloody women" who got themselves pregnant. Because he found the new progressive woman difficult to comprehend and, I suspect, didn't approve of her either, Sir Frank had given Kerry the responsibility for the success of the new magazine. Back in those dark ages women usually resigned when they became pregnant and I think Kerry was worried that I might do exactly that, leaving him without an Editor. Later that day he rang to tell me that he and his father wanted to know why I hadn't paid more attention to an article in the first issue of *Cleo* – "How Much Do You Know About Contraception?"

'He probably would have been in a state of shock if he had known I did not use contraceptives. Why would I? I wanted to have a baby and becoming a mother again was more important to me than anything else in the world. I was sure I would be able to still successfully edit *Cleo* and look after my new baby and my family and, as it turned out, I did. Once again I did not feel guilty about taking this decision.

'I was twenty-seven when I had Kate and thirty-one when I had Ben. Having children was never a hindrance to my career; if anything it was a help. Readers of the magazines I edited – in particular *The Australian Women's Weekly* – were able to identify with me as a mother. I became a role model and showed women that it was possible to combine motherhood with working and, at the same time, enjoy life. That is one of the big differences between the way so many women (and men) work now and then. When I was a young working mother the workplace *was* fun. Today it seems to be a somewhat grim and earnest place with not much laughter in it. People have allowed work to dominate their lives, leaving them little time to enjoy life and relationships.

'In the last few years the argument that having children will be detrimental to their career path has often been used as an excuse by ambitious young women of child-bearing age who say they are not prepared to take this risk. Work is so paramount in their lives that they would prefer to forego having children. I have no problem with women having ambition – I'm all for it – but, as they get older, I believe many women will regret not having children. In the scheme of things, work is only a small part of our lives while children are forever. Other career-conscious females say they intend to wait until they are well established in their chosen profession before having children. Sounds good, but the fact is that a woman's fertility declines as she grows older. Ovaries don't care about a woman's career; they age. Women who try to become pregnant in their late thirties or early forties often find they are unable to do so or, if they do, miscarry.

'There does come a time in most women's lives when work loses its significance and the value of human relationships – especially with children, family and friends – becomes more important. It is relationships that sustain us through life, not work. When our relationships are going well we feel invigorated and alive. We like being at work. We like being at home. Most importantly, we like ourselves. When today's successful career women are older and sitting in their rocking chairs I doubt many of them will be thinking of major coups in yesteryear's boardroom. I know I won't be. I will be counting my blessings and by that I mean my children.

'I've never regretted having children or combining motherhood with my career. The years have flown by and every now and then I wish my kids were still at home with me because I enjoyed their company so much. We've had such great times – we have travelled, played, laughed, learned and grown together – and have shared much fun. I still enjoy being with them and our relationship has changed and matured. Of course there were some trying times but nothing bad enough to ever make me wish I wasn't a mother. And while I've had a fabulous career, as far as I am concerned it pales into insignificance beside my children. They have enriched my existence and mean the world to me and I know that without them I would have felt my life was pointless. Through my children – and as long as their progeny procreate – I will have eternity because a little piece of me will go on being created in future generations. I love the idea of that.'

Penny has been a doctor for twenty-two years, and her eldest child, Diana, is twenty-one. 'I'm at a different stage to Ita in my "mothering career" and I still frequently battle my Motherguilt. I left university with my Medical Degree, First Class Honours and the University Medal. I was going to conquer the medical world and "Professor of Medicine" sounded good to me. But life rarely goes according to plan. Like Ita, fertility turned out to be a problem for me too – however, in my case, the problem was *too much* fertility. I had married my first husband, Michael, when I was in my final year at university and as a result of a contraceptive failure, I found myself pregnant. I was an intern and devastated. Michael was delighted. Pregnancy as an intern was not considered a great career move. This was my first experience with Motherguilt. I felt so guilty that I wasn't delighted to be pregnant. Instead, I was horrified! Now I love the fact that I am a relatively young mother for my daughter.

'I finished my intern year, gave birth and took ten months off work. I had all the usual problems with breastfeeding, lack of sleep and not really knowing what I was doing – a medical degree teaches you how to be a doctor, *not* how to be a mother. My own mother was brilliant; I asked her about absolutely everything and she always had the answers.

'Then it was time to go back to work as a resident doctor at Sydney's Royal North Shore Hospital. It was horrendous. I felt tortured leaving my baby at childcare and at the same time, I felt guilty that I enjoyed being back at work. I was chronically tired. In those days, resident doctors worked ten-hour days, one night a week until midnight and one weekend in three. Eventually, something had to give and, sadly, it was my marriage.

'I decided to leave the hospital system, take stock, and work part-time in general practice. My plan was to do this for a short time while working out the best way to get my career and life back on track. At least, that is what I thought I was going to do. That was nineteen years ago and I am still a GP. Quite accidentally I had found my calling. I love my work and consider it an honour to treat my patients and be involved in their lives.

'During this time, I met and married my husband Ian, an anaesthetist. He loved Diana from the moment he met her and is an amazing stepfather whom she calls "Poppy". Of course, my Motherguilt continued, compounded by my fears that my marriage break-up would harm my daughter – she saw her dad all the time as we had remained friends, but still I worried that she might be affected somehow. Ian and I had two more children: Tom, who is now fourteen, and twelve-year-old Olivia. More guilt potential! But even though Ian met me as a working mum, once our children arrived he suddenly became very 'traditional' and wanted me to become a stay-at-home mother. There was no way I was going to agree to that, and some interesting "battles" followed. My compromise was to work part-time.

'I work three days per week at my surgery. While they are my "official" hours, it's a rare weekend when a patient doesn't pop around to my home for some medical advice. Over the years, I have shared my medical expertise with girlfriends and their families as my contribution to the "sisterhood bartering" that women do so well. If I'm caught up late at the surgery, I can always find a girlfriend to pick up my kids from sports training. And when their child has a sore ear on a Sunday, I check them out. The system works well. True sisterhood members don't keep score; they just help each other. I also do some media work and public speaking. When it comes to the home front, I don't do any washing or ironing. I don't bake cakes and my house is often rather messy – not dirty though, I have a cleaner. This arrangement seems to work for my family although I never sit still, something that drives my husband nuts.

Whenever I feel that I have finally achieved the "right balance" some new project turns up and off I go while my husband rolls his eyes. I love the hustle and bustle of being a working mum, but on the rare occasions that I am "home alone" it is bliss. The thought has occurred to me more than once – and has been often suggested to me by my husband and my mother – that I might finally learn to offload Motherguilt when I learn to sit still!

'In a medical context, I have found the concept of Mother-guilt intriguing, as do the other GP mothers in our practice. They all suffer from it and school holiday rosters are a nightmare. I love my three children and I know they love me, so why the guilt? Being a mother is not only the best thing I have ever done, it is also the most tiring, the most frustrating and the most rewarding – the most everything, including the most guilt ridden. As I sit here writing *during the school holidays*, having just sent my younger two to hire some DVDs, I can feel the pangs of Motherguilt creep-ing in.

'I did find being at home with small children unbelievably boring. I can't stand playing board games and cards. Playgrounds and theme parks are torture and at times I have wanted space to just be me. These thoughts and feelings, when looked at in an objective way, are really quite understandable and yet they made me feel so guilty. I used to wonder if I could ever admit them to other mothers. I finally decided to "come clean" and talk openly to other moth-ers, not only about my Motherguilt but my perceived shortcomings as a mother. My pet subject was the Motherguilt "minefield" of teenagers, and the more I confessed to being tortured by my own adolescents the more mothers would bring their teenagers to see me. I now have a special interest in this area of medicine and see many of my medical colleagues' kids. Honesty has a curative power all of its own.'

In talking with the many women who have contributed to this book the authors have concluded that mothers are too critical of themselves and need to learn to love themselves as much as they love their children. Over the centuries women have learned from each other by sharing their stories and the authors are indebted to the many women who have opened their hearts and minds – the good, the bad and the ugly – for this book. Some of the mothers are well known; others for obvious reasons have chosen to be anonymous, however that does not matter. It is their true stories that are important because immense learning and healing occurs when women share their real experiences.

This is not just a 'feel good' theory; there is a scientific basis to the value of sisterhood sharing. When women share a special bond through whatever means, their oxytocin levels rise, producing feelings of calmness, contentment and wellbeing. Interestingly, oxytocin is present in high levels during breastfeeding.

We have much to learn from each other, so read on and let the healing begin.

I

Pregnancy and childbirth: the guilt begins

Getting pregnant is big news these days. Women's magazines are besotted with celebrity mums. A March 2004 *Woman's Day* cover offered a pregnancy smorgasbord of headlines: 'Brooke Shields' deadly IVF gamble', 'Madonna's last-ditch fertility treatment' and 'Clucky Catherine puts Michael on a sex diet'. Brooke, Madonna and Catherine are already mums, but are anxious to have more children and prepared to do whatever it takes to fall pregnant again.

This 'mumsy' issue of the magazine is not an isolated one. Celebrities and their babies or babies-in-production frequently feature in its pages and those of other publications like *New Idea* and *The Australian Women's Weekly,* whose Editor-in-Chief Deborah Thomas made baby headlines of her own in 2002 when she had her first child at forty-six. Although Deborah's pregnancy took her completely by surprise – at first she thought the menopause had arrived early! – she now says, 'Having a baby late in life wasn't something that I planned. I'm very glad it happened. I can't believe I nearly missed out on motherhood. It's the best thing that's ever happened in my life.' Her son Oscar, who is adorable, regularly features in the *Weekly* and has appeared on television with his mother.

The reason why fertility has become so fashionable in the twenty-first century probably has much to do with the fact that babies are in short supply. Fertility rates have dropped worldwide and Australia's fertility rate is at an all-time low. Bureau of Statistics figures show our fertility rate is currently 1.7 babies per woman and expected to continue to drop. But women are not only having fewer babies, they are having them later and, as a result, babies have become precious commodities. In certain circles a baby is seen as a 'fashion accessory', a symbol of privilege and power and just another item on a woman's shopping list.

In early 2004, the *Australian Financial Review Magazine* examined the media's baby mania. In the article, Natasha Cica, a lecturer in media ethics at the University of Canberra's School of Professional Communication, warned about what she called the 'baby trophy syndrome' that was 'in danger of widening painfully the gulf between women who are "partnered and pregnant" and those who are not. But perhaps the saddest thing about society mistaking a baby for a handbag is that the child will suffer most. Claudia Keech, the Managing Director of *motherInc*, the online magazine for twenty-first century mothers, says, 'It's now normal for couples to save up to have a child just as they do for a house, a car or a holiday.'

Babies go everywhere these days. They are 'accessories' on the fashion catwalk; they star in television commercials; go out to lunch and dinner; see all the latest movies; go to the office with their mothers; attend meetings; and are breast- and bottle-fed in public on trains, planes, in restaurants, the boardroom and even parliament. Sometimes they are a bloody nuisance wailing with boredom – poor little things would probably prefer to be sleeping in their cots – interrupting the peace and driving people to distraction, but in these politically correct times no one would dream of saying such a thing out loud. 'But they sure as hell think it,' Ita says. Babies are not only a fashionable item they are big business. The Australian economy now includes the 'baby sector' and in 2003 it was worth $1.23 billion! Twenty-first century parents want the best for their babies and are willing to pay for it.

Sooner or later the current magazine frenzy with mothers and babies will end – the media's attention span is always a short one. But one dubious consequence of their current fixation is the influence these magazines have on the way women view their post-pregnancy bodies and motherhood in general. Articles wax lyrical about the celebrity mums who get their figures back in record time, usually by following eating plans that should never be published. The magazines never question whether it is in the best interests of the woman's health to shed her maternal weight so rapidly. There is no mention either of the housekeepers, trainers, nannies and other helpers that make celebrity motherhood nothing like the 'normal' experiences of most other women. If celebrity mums do get up in the middle of the night to feed their babies no one hears about it, nor is there any suggestion they might occasionally feel wretchedly tired or that they experience any difficulties with breastfeeding. In magazine land having a baby is such a breeze! But this kind of fantasy reporting merely creates unrealistic role models for non-celebrity mums, for whom pregnancy and motherhood are very different.

For example, remember the photograph of confident and glowingly pregnant Cate Blanchett in a regal claret-coloured gown at the 2004 Academy Awards? It is impossible to imagine anyone daring to approach her to offer unsolicited advice on how she should behave during her pregnancy. However, when Joy Smithers, another Australian actor but not world famous like Cate, was expecting, she was shocked at the behaviour of the 'pregnancy police' who seem to consider it their 'right' to inflict guilt on a pregnant woman.

'I was seven months pregnant and walking in downtown Bali eating a chocolate Paddle Pop when some guy came up, all upset with me, claiming I was harming my baby eating cocoa and preservatives! What right does pregnancy give other people, especially someone you don't know, to impose their beliefs on you?' asks Joy.

'It amazes me how such interfering do-gooders come out in force when you're expecting a baby. What I hated most was the way their hands came out when I was really big and popping – absolute strangers thought nothing about touching my stomach! But the horror stories were the worst. On learning I was five months pregnant a woman I'd never met before volunteered that she had lost her second child at five months and that the baby had suffered from brain damage. She terrified me.'

Most mothers-to-be have their first brush with guilt during pregnancy. This is not full-blown Motherguilt, however, but rather guilt 'growing pains' felt as women cope with the transitions and adjustments that come with pregnancy and tackle a myriad fluctuating feelings, many of which come attached with guilt. Do I want the baby? Is this the right time? Have I made the correct decision? Will I be a good mother? How will I know what to do? Most women are somewhat ignorant about the realities of motherhood but, having swallowed the myth that motherhood is something that comes naturally to all women, they naïvely expect everything to fall into place – *perfectly* – once their baby has arrived.

'I was so focused on the pregnancy and the birth experience, getting the cot and all the stuff that comes afterwards, that it didn't occur to me until about a week before my son was born that I was actually going to have a baby,' Rabbi Allison Conyer says. 'I was really terrified as to what to do.' Sometimes women are still searching for the answers when their baby is born. Mary-Lou, an academic, didn't prepare herself for motherhood, 'which is interesting from an academic point of view, because you always prepare yourself for the next stage of your career – whether it's as an undergrad preparing to get into a Masters program, so that you can get to a PhD, in order to get an academic appointment, etc. etc. But for motherhood, you just get pregnant. Once I was, I devoured every textbook on birthing and the stages of pregnancy, but now I realise I read nothing on mothering.'

Regardless of how many books a woman might read, Mother Nature delights in springing a surprise or two on a pregnant woman – and her unsuspecting partner – such as food cravings. It was a freezing evening in London when Ita told her husband she just *had* to have plum pudding. 'It was wet and miserable as only an English winter night can be, and my poor husband said, "What – *now?*" I did feel a little guilty because the rain was bucketing down. "Yes," I said, "I simply *must* have some." He sighed as he put on his duffle coat but he returned with a plum pudding and it was delicious. I felt so much better but instantly guilty for pigging out on something as calorie-ridden as plum pudding.'

During Penny's pregnancy, she suddenly developed a longing for Chinese chicken and sweet corn soup. 'It was probably full of awful chemicals like MSG and I felt guilty that I was OD-ing on the stuff and guilty that my poor husband was always looking for late-closing takeaway restaurants.'

Then there is the emotional turmoil that pregnancy generates – like crying for no good reason. 'The slightest thing makes me weep,' says 21-year old Brianna, who is three months pregnant. 'My husband is going mad. The other morning I burst into tears over something he said and I just couldn't stop. He finally walked out in exasperation. We made up later but I felt so guilty because it's his pregnancy too and I want him to be as happy as I am.'

Hard though it may be to believe in these enlightened

times, 50 per cent of pregnancies are unplanned, which means many women – blissfully unaware of their condition – carry on as usual, drinking, smoking and doing whatever else takes their fancy. On confirmation of their pregnancy, worried sick that they might have unintentionally done something to harm their baby, they suffer serious guilt. However, it is hard to fathom why women who should know better torment themselves like this. A Melbourne GP agonised over the fact that her son had been conceived when she was on holidays and had consumed a generous amount of red wine, even though as a doctor she knew it takes at least seventeen days before the embryo actually 'plugs in' to the maternal circulation. Why did she cause herself so much angst? There is no logical answer.

Rabbi Conyer required antibiotics for severe sinusitis during her second pregnancy and, although her GP assured her that they would not harm the baby, she later told her doctor that she had felt terribly guilty taking antibiotics. 'I called five of the doctors in my congregation to get a second opinion!' All of them concurred with her GP's recommendation, but that did not alleviate the Rabbi's guilt.

Work is another potential source of anxiety for the pregnant woman. On average, Australian women work until they are thirty-three weeks pregnant but half of them work for two weeks beyond that. The women who work the longest into pregnancy live in New South Wales and Canberra with 4 per cent working right up to week forty. In a national survey of 500 working pregnant women conducted by the magazine *Pregnancy and Birth* in 2003, almost 10 per cent felt they were being treated unfairly by their boss because they were pregnant, and 3 per cent said their bosses tried to give them the sack when they heard the news.

The fact that some women feel the need to apologise to their boss for becoming pregnant infuriates ABC broadcaster Sally Loane. When she gives workplace motivational lectures, she tells prospective mothers to, 'Never apologise. Go to the boss and say "I'm pregnant, I need time off, and this is what I see happening with my workload while I am away."'

But a friend of Ita's who took maternity leave from her position as personal assistant to the CEO of a large multinational insurance company returned to work as agreed after six months at home with her baby, only to find that she had been replaced and assigned another position. 'My boss wasn't pleased with me when I told him I was pregnant but I found a good temp to hold the fort while I was away and he seemed happy enough when I went off to have my baby.' When she protested about the situation her boss told her she could either like it or lump it. She took legal action instead and won a handsome settlement.

Financial needs are a major reason why women stay in the workforce both during and after pregnancy. Most of the women in the *Pregnancy and Birth* magazine survey said they worked because they needed the money; more than one-third admitted to working forty hours a week and more than 77 per cent said they were feeling quite exhausted. Given such time pressures it is understandable why so many women say they find pregnancy stressful. Carrying the baby is usually the least of their concerns; more often than not it is workplace attitudes and other people's expectations – such as working long hours – that cause them the greatest anxiety.

The motherhood urge is an exceptionally strong desire and capable of pushing a woman to extraordinary lengths to become pregnant. Some women miscarry time and time again and yet refuse to give up trying to conceive. Even though in Australia, one in three pregnancies results in a miscarriage and doctors constantly reassure women who miscarry that it had nothing to do with anything they might have done, women invariably feel not only despair and a great sense of loss, but also guilty. Was it something I did or ate? Did I work too hard? Should I have exercised more or had more rest?

Community nurse Diana Aspinall had two miscarriages, and a great deal of medical intervention and tests before she was able to carry a baby full term. 'I always used to ask myself did I cause the miscarriages. The guilt was awful. When I finally did give birth to a healthy baby, I realised how anxious I'd been throughout the entire nine months. In the beginning I felt very inadequate with my new son. My sister's four-month old baby was "perfect" while my son was difficult to feed and had colic. I always seemed to be trying out new things to fix it, never with much luck. It wasn't until he was eleven weeks old that I stopped listening to everyone's advice and did what I thought was right. From then on we never looked back.'

Symantha Perkins suffered three miscarriages in nine months. In January 2004 the thirty-year-old mother of two told *Woman's Day*, 'Miscarriage triggers so many emotions . . . You go from the sheer joy of being pregnant to feelings of guilt, despair, sadness and inadequacy . . . For a long time I thought it was all my fault.' At the time, Symantha said she and her Olympic swimming champion husband Kieran had given up their dream of having 'a whole tribe' of children and how, with counselling and by talking with other women who experienced losing a baby, she realised 'that no one was to blame – least of all myself.' But miracles do happen. In December 2004, Symantha publicly confirmed she was five months pregnant – clearly, no one should ever underestimate a woman's maternal determination!

The loss of a baby marks the end of a woman's dream and her subsequent guilt feelings often reflect her anger at not being able to make that dream come true. Jan Murray had five children when she became pregnant once more. 'I have serious guilt about the baby I lost. I had a termination because I had cervical cancer. I was a coward. Modern medical evidence suggests I could have gone full term with cancer but the doctors told me that one of us wouldn't see full term and, as I already had children, I opted to have the hysterectomy, which caused me to lose that baby. Thirty years later, it still upsets me. The doctors rushed me. They didn't tell you anything in those days.'

Early in 2004 Federal Health Minister Tony Abbott raised his concern about the high rate of abortions in Australia only to be howled down by university students, fellow politicians and other critics for trying to impose his morals on the nation. 'But perhaps these people missed the point Abbott was trying to make,' Ita says. As Tony Abbott pointed out, 'Even those who think that abortion is a woman's right should be troubled by the fact that 100 000 Australian women choose to destroy their unborn babies every year. What does it say about the state of our relationships and our values that so many women (and their husbands, lovers and families) feel incapable of coping with a pregnancy or a child?'

'Not much,' Ita says. 'Of course abortion must be a woman's choice but it shouldn't be used as a form of contraception, which is what I think is happening. And there needs to be much better family planning advice available to women. Abortion should be a woman's last option – however, we live in a world that places little value on human life. We have only to look at the suicide bombers in the Middle East who are prepared to sacrifice their lives and take those of others to know that.'

'Of course it is a tragedy that 100 000 Australian women choose to end their pregnancies, but the real national disgrace is the fact that they find themselves in this situation in the first place,' Penny says. 'I've counselled hundreds of women in my surgery who have, for many different reasons, needed an abortion. And it's not only younger women who choose to have abortions. That's just a popular myth. Older women, many of whom are already mothers, often decide they cannot continue with a pregnancy, citing financial, relationship and support issues as major contributors to their decision. These women suffer huge anguish and guilt, particularly if their religious beliefs are anti-abortion. It's *never* something they do lightly. They need tremendous *non-judgemental* support, both before and after their distressing medical ordeal.

'Project Rachel, a group under the auspices of the Catholic Church, runs weekend retreats where women who are overwhelmed by their grief and guilt following an abortion can off-load their guilt, and be emotionally cleansed. We need more of these groups, but, more importantly, prevention is better than cure. It is appalling that Australia has the second highest abortion rate in the western world, after the United States. Countries like the United Kingdom and Sweden have a much lower rate because contraception is free in these countries. There would be fewer abortions and a lot less guilt for women if Australia followed suit.'

One welcome development of changed societal attitudes has been the removal of the stigma 'illegitimate' for children born out of wedlock, something that in the past caused so much unhappiness (and guilt) for many families. Few unmarried mothers-to-be bother to hide their condition these days and many couples choose de facto relationships over marriage.

Back in the 1960s, attitudes were different. Unwanted pregnancies were considered shameful. Jan Murray was twenty, and four months pregnant, when she married. 'I was sixteen when I met John Brown. We were always going to get married but were going to wait until I was twenty-one.' In those days, 'nice' girls did not become pregnant before they were married and the couple's wedding was arranged hastily.

'Did I feel guilty about being pregnant on my wedding day? Oh my God yes! There was no way you could tell anybody. My husband was thirty-one and it took him until two weeks after we got back from our honeymoon to sit down with his mother and tell her. It was horrendous. Things are so different now – our daughter got married when our grandson was old enough to be her page boy!'

It is only to be expected that a woman will experience a mixture of sentiments as her pregnancy progresses, but because she is no longer in control of her body there are times when she feels insecure. While it is exciting and wonderful to feel a baby's first kick, to hear its heartbeat via a doctor's stethoscope, to see the baby taking shape in the womb on an ultrasound, it can be scary too. What if something goes wrong? Many a pregnant woman haunts herself with that question for the entire nine months! What if something she does, eats, or drinks harms her baby? This is the stuff of women's worst nightmares and a fertile breeding ground for guilt.

There are so many hurdles for a woman to clear before a baby is born, among them the regular check-ups and weighing. Some obstetricians – most of whom never give any practical nutritional advice about what a woman should eat during pregnancy – are martinets about weight gain. One woman was so afraid of her doctor's criticism about any weight gain that she would eat only carrots and tomatoes for two days before her weigh-in. Then she would spend the weeks in between feeling guilty about depriving her baby of proper nutrients even though she had kept her doctor happy.

'Helpful' comments from partners often make a woman

feel worse. During her second pregnancy, Jenny put on 22 kilograms. 'My husband said I looked like the nose cone of a 747.' Then there are stretch marks, swollen ankles, varicose veins, acne, and, of course, the dreaded haemorrhoids, which Rebecca Wilson of television's *The Fat* found out to her horror. 'I had one of those dream pregnancies and childbirths and then I got friggin' haemorrhoids – so much for the perfect childbirth. With the benefit of hindsight, what a lot of bunkum we put ourselves through.'

The actual birth can be a nerve-wracking prospect too – especially the first time. Will the birth be normal? Is a vaginal delivery better than a Caesarean? How will I react to labour? Will the contractions be very painful? What does *really* happen when my waters break? How will I know when it is time to push? This last question can be a real nail biter for many first-time mums and, sometimes, experienced mothers can be condescending when they try to allay their fears. 'Don't panic,' they say, 'you'll just *know* when to push.' That kind of reassurance is *no* help to a mother-to-be who still worries exactly how she will know! But few women, whether a first timer or an old hand, take childbirth for granted because things can go unexpectedly wrong and when they do, a mother blames herself.

Most women lead a programmed life because it is the only way they can handle the time constraints forced on them by their multiple roles, so naturally they want to 'program' their baby's birth too. They arrive at their doctor's surgery with an eight-page laminated birth plan, a kind of marketing chart that they are confident will give them an easy entry to motherhood. 'You have to feel sorry for them,' Penny says. 'Children are born with a program all of their own and when these women make this discovery they suffer massive guilt at what they consider is their failure to be in control.'

A Perth midwife had planned the ideal childbirth. 'I knew

all the facts, what to do, when to breathe. I was going to be totally in control of this process – mind over matter, no pain relief, and no stitches. After twenty-seven hours of labour, epidural, forceps and a large episiotomy, I wouldn't have cared if they hauled out a labrador just as long as they got the damn thing out and left me alone. Afterwards, despite my beautiful new bundle, I felt so guilty and such a failure.'

Everything about having a baby is streamlined today. Women are in and out of hospital in a few days, not always by choice – Australia's cash-strapped health system cannot afford to have them stay too long – and more women are having Caesarean deliveries than ever before. Obstetricians are often wrongly accused of encouraging Caesars so 'they don't have to get up at night'. The truth is that doctors are incredibly and exhaustingly used to getting up at night. The real impetus behind the increasing Caesar rate comes from women who are either fearful of a vaginal delivery – because they think it will be too painful and are worried about damage to their 'nether regions' – or who simply feel they need to plan the baby's arrival because of work and social commitments. Australia has one of the highest Caesarean rates in the world. The latest annual figures show that just over 23 per cent of babies were delivered by Caesarean, representing 59 051 births – well above the World Health Organization's (WHO) recommended rate of 15 per cent.

The increased number of older mothers has also had an influence on this figure. The average age of a woman having her first child is now twenty-nine, and one in ten women has her first baby at thirty-five or older. But having babies later is not without problems. Older women have a greater risk of having a baby with Down syndrome and a higher chance of having a low birth-weight baby. Still births are also more common and just getting pregnant in the first place is more difficult.

Now fifty-something, Barbara and her husband are both surgeons. Unable to conceive a child together when they were in their mid-thirties they opted for IVF using his sperm and her eggs. They had two sons this way. Both children have health problems. Barbara now wonders if perhaps 'nature was trying to tell us something by not letting us be natural parents'. She feels guilty that she 'pushed nature too hard. We fiddled with nature if you like. We sort of knocked around a gene or two.

'My guilt began when I went along with my doctor's advice to have a Caesar. I was told I was in premature labour even though my membranes hadn't ruptured. I wasn't given an option of lying in bed for a week or two and seeing how things went and I didn't question that as a possibility because there is nothing worse than a pain-in-the-butt "doctor-patient" who says I don't want to do what you are recommending. So when I was told, "You've got to have a Caesar," I did as I was told. My son was delivered at only thirty weeks.

'My next load of guilt happened one night in the hospital nursery. Once again I deliberately didn't interfere because of my medical background. I knew I'd have been considered a bloody nuisance if I interfered with any of the hospital's treatment of my baby. When my husband and I went in that particular night our son wasn't being monitored for apnoea (a common precaution in premature babies in case they stop breathing). We'd been out for an early dinner and rocked in on our way home to see him, and we could see he was having little apnoeas. We sat there watching him, thinking, "How much do we interfere?" We were so concerned that we actually told the on-duty nurse that we thought our son was having apnoeas. We left it at that and went home. Later that night our son had a significant apnoea, which is probably the one that caused him to develop cerebral palsy. It's something I know I can never change. I always think I should have interfered more.'

Self-employed publicist Sally Burleigh had her first baby at thirty-five. Scarlett was four weeks premature and when Sally went home her daughter had to stay in hospital for almost two weeks. 'I did feel responsible in some way for her early arrival and I felt awful and very empty without her. I had a fantastic pregnancy, was fit and healthy, kept my weight under control and did everything the doctor said. I had to go to Melbourne when I was thirty-five weeks and four days but only did so after checking with my doctor first. When I came back, I felt so tired and the following morning my waters broke. When I went into labour I did wonder if it was because I had been working so hard. The funny thing is, I didn't feel guilty about leaving Scarlett behind in hospital because I knew she was in good hands and the only reason she had to stay there was that she was just so little. What I did feel slightly guilty about was thinking how good it was that I didn't have to deal with a screaming baby like some other mothers do when they first get home! How bad am I?'

When Carolyn Hewson had her first child at forty, she was in no hurry whatsoever to return home. 'I was petrified, absolutely and utterly petrified. I stayed in hospital for nine days. My husband had three children from his first marriage and every day he'd come to see me and would ask, "Is today the day?" And I would say no. In the end, the doctor told me I had to leave! When we got home, it was fine but I still didn't go out for a month. I didn't pack up the baby and say, "Come on, let's go." My husband kept suggesting we go out to a restaurant for a meal. "When you have a baby you just pop it in a little bassinet under the table and it sleeps there," he said. Well, we never did that. Our daughter was just not that sort of baby or maybe I wasn't that sort of mother. I think my husband was shocked.'

Diana Aspinall, who has worked intensively with mothers and babies as a community nurse since 1989, believes that women having their first babies are sent home too early from hospital and before they are confident about managing their babies' needs. 'All mothers, especially those having their second and third child, need adequate rest to establish breastfeeding and to build up enough energy to care for themselves and their children. The amount of rest they get is reduced by the short stays in hospital. I know these days that fathers are much more involved both in the birth process and in helping out in the first few weeks a mother and baby are at home, but in my experience, fathers feel pretty helpless with a colicky baby and aren't sure how to help their partners through birth blues. When dads go back to work, the mother is left on her own with no one to talk to and often worries as to whether or not she is doing the right thing.

'Middle-class mothers with their degrees, careers and "can do it all" expectations have it the toughest. They are independent, usually living geographically away from their mothers and extended families. Often their mothers are working and not able to offer much practical help because of time constraints. Many mothers tell me they feel very isolated and lonely. Mothering does need to be taught and a brief three days in hospital is inadequate. Mothers need to be shown how to bring up a baby's wind for instance and it takes time to learn to do this properly. Hormonally driven post-natal blues usually occur around day four or five after delivery. I know that the mothers that I support don't get post-natal depression – they may have a down day, but with support that can be remedied.'

In spite of everything, however, nothing takes away from the miracle of birth. Beth was prepared for a long labour. 'Everyone told me that's what always happens with a first baby. My husband and I arrived at the hospital at 7 p.m., which was changeover time and we couldn't find anyone to help us. My husband was in a bit of panic and was tearing up and down the corridor. Finally a midwife turned up and I made some quip about probably being only 1 centimetre dilated. She took a look at me and said, "No dear, you're 9 centimetres – you'll want to push in a moment." "I want an epidural," I said. "No dear, you're past that."

'She gave me some gas and I took only two drags before she took it away from me. At that very moment, my doctor walked in and I yelled, "The fucking bitch took my gas away." I can't believe I said this now; I still feel dredged with guilt. The gas hadn't helped much but I liked having something to hang on to . . . My husband stayed with me for the birth and he kept saying, "Oh my God, oh my God, Beth, open your eyes and look." They had given me a mirror so I could watch but I didn't want to. My husband was insistent. "Beth, do look, it has dark curly hair." So I looked and it *was* amazing.'

'Being a mother makes me feel complete as a woman,' Sally Burleigh says. 'It's not just the love you feel but the fact that I've given my husband a baby, my parents a grandchild, my sister a niece. I have created a family.'

Each mother–baby relationship is unique. After a difficult, long labour, Polly eventually gave birth to a healthy baby girl. Within an hour of giving birth, she insisted on speaking to her own mother on the phone. As she lay in her hospital bed looking at her little miracle, Polly sobbed into the phone, 'Mum, I've just had the most beautiful little baby girl, and I don't know why, but I feel so guilty.' Her mother simply replied, 'Welcome to motherhood.'

2

Why does guilt attack mothers and not fathers?

Motherhood comes as something of a shock to most women because it is so different from what they imagine pre-birth. This is especially true for first-time mums. Once a new mother is 'home alone', the realisation that such a tiny human being is so utterly reliant on her can be overwhelming. She has to be seen to be in control but instead feels totally inadequate because there is so much she does not know about being a mother. The first few weeks of a baby's life can also be some of the toughest times of motherhood, with a new baby capable of reducing even the most competent of women to tears. The fact that a mother, even a first timer, is expected to be automatically good at everything – something that she also has been conditioned to expect of herself – does not help the situation.

During the early months, a mother is expected to be able to cope with chronic fatigue caused by endless sleepless nights, successfully breastfeed without a glitch, and 'gratefully' accept the advice of family, friends and other do-gooders who always presume to know better than she does what is best for baby. In their ignorance, some mothers try to take on board every suggestion given to them and simply exhaust themselves further. As if all this emotional wear and tear was not enough, the mother also has to run a household that now includes a great deal more washing. It is amazing how many changes of outfits a baby can get through in a week, but then the quantity of peeing, pooing and vomiting from something so small is astonishing. 'No one ever told me that babies poo while they are breastfeeding. If they had it would have made my life much easier,' Ita remarks. 'I used to think there was something wrong with my breast milk!'

The cry of a hungry baby in the middle of the night can be the worst sound in the world, but when a baby wants a feed it could not care less what the time is, often leaving a new mother yearning for a good night's sleep. Some women do resent having to get up night after night to feed their babies and Motherguilt soon sets in. Helen, a lawyer, went back to work when her son was three months old. 'He was still waking up several times each night to be fed. I would lie in bed and hear that squeaky noise that babies make as they work themselves up to a loud cry and I'd think, "Please, please don't wake up." I knew that by the time I fed him and settled him it would be an hour before I'd get back to sleep. He didn't sleep through the night until he was ten months old. I feel so guilty admitting it, but sometimes I just wanted someone – anyone – to take him away.'

Many women experience similar feelings – not that they would own up to them because the associated guilt is monumental. Mothers can have recurring 'black thoughts' or dreams in which they imagine doing something that could harm their baby. 'I can remember having them with my first baby,' Penny says. 'I would be standing near the back window, holding her, thinking, "I could just throw her out – it could be an accident – no one would know and even if they did, it could be post-natal depression." Of course, I *never* would do anything like that, but it used to horrify me that such thoughts would even enter my head. Sometimes they occurred to me when I was bathing my children as babies: "What if I just let go – they would drown." I never talked about this to anyone until a few years ago I spoke to a GP (female, of course) colleague who had done a lot of psychiatry training. I felt like an "axe murderer" confessing. "Oh," she said casually, as if we were talking about a urinary tract infection, "so many mothers have those sorts of thoughts – they're called Obsessional Doubt, a well-recognised medical phenomenon and very common."'

During these challenging first months a mother feels extraordinarily guilty at her shortcomings, constantly agonising that she might inadvertently do something to harm her child. However, being a mother is a lifetime calling – something that does not really cross a woman's mind when she is pregnant – and each developmental stage of a child's life will bring new challenges of its own.

Have you ever stopped to think how a typical job advertisement for a mum might read?

> WANTED: Person to work, often 24/7, in chaotic
> environment. The successful applicant must have outstanding
> communication and organisation skills and be proficient
> in all the following areas: counselling, events management,
> nursing, catering, teaching, home maintenance, odd job
> repair skills, transportation, sanitation and conflict resolution.
> No previous experience is required, as on-the-job training
> will occur on a continually exhausting basis. While no paid
> holidays, superannuation or stock options are offered, this
> job offers limitless opportunities for personal growth without
> remuneration.

Working for the dole seems a better option – but while the 'advertisement' might be a bit of a laugh, being a mother is not. Motherhood is a full-time job, which everyone, including mothers, is apt to forget. There is no doubt that the biological purpose for women is to become mothers and that many women feel the surge of libido mid cycle when they are ovulating. Mother Nature wants women to be mothers too, and women who have not entered motherhood by their mid-thirties notice the persistent ticking of their 'biological clock' – it is there in all women. But having followed their physiological destiny, women find that the society in which they live often doesn't play the game. Their bodies tell them motherhood is their most important job and yet the community deems it as just an 'add on' to women's numerous other roles.

Mothers now have no time for their relationships, for romance – what's that? – and, most importantly, none for themselves. Neroli, an anaesthetist, thought she could organise life with a baby in the same way she scheduled the rest of her life. 'The fact that I wasn't going off to work meant that I would have all this free time. I was going to have French lessons and tennis lessons and he would come along in his baby capsule. Little did I know I would be chronically exhausted. My first son never slept properly until he was eight!'

A mother doesn't even have time to be sick. All too often when she has a bad cold or a stomach upset, usually passed on by her infected offspring whom she has been nursing, a mum just battles on. Doctors do not give mothers medical certificates for being off their maternal job.

'Most people take female care-giving utterly for granted and the job of making a home for a child and developing his or her capabilities is often equated with "doing nothing",' says Ann Crittenden, author of *The Price of Motherhood: Why the Most Important Job in the World is Still the Least Valued*. 'Lack of respect and tangible recognition is part of every mother's experience. A mother's work is not just invisible; it can become a handicap. Raising children may be the most important job in the world, but you can't put it on a résumé,' says Ann, who believes 'the very definition of a mother is selfless service to another. We don't owe Mother for her gifts; she owes us. And in return for her bounty, Mother receives no lack of veneration. For instance, the Arabs have a poem declaring: "The mother is a school; if she is well reared, you are sure to build a nation."'

Girls grow up knowing what is expected of them when their time comes to have children. Mothers are not only revered and put on pedestals, but there is only one type of mother – the 'good' kind. Songs have been dedicated to mothers, they have inspired poets and authors – and the importance of perfection is a common theme. Motherguilt thrives on unrealistic expectations. There is no such thing as perfect mothering or a mother who never makes mistakes. Think about your own mother. Was she perfect? Human beings are not made that way. What needs to be remembered is that in spite of any imperfections mothers might have, most kids thrive and prosper nonetheless.

Sydney sociologist Dianne McKissock blames Women's Liberation for Motherguilt; it's the price women have paid for 'freedom'. 'More mothers are suffering from more guilt today than ever before because the expectations on women as human beings have increased. There is so much pressure on mothers these days to be everything – not only to be mothers and raise the family but to participate in the workforce and to share the financial obligations of buying a home.'

With all these new additional roles how much is the original one of motherhood valued? Could it be that men value women more if they contribute financially? What price, if any, do men and society in general put on mothering skills? Have we created a paradox where the more a mother takes on, the less her fundamental role of mothering is respected? Motherhood has become incredibly undervalued and yet a mother is expected to be the best possible carer for her child. Confused? Well, join the club!

~

While the increasing demands on mothers have resulted in their guilt growing to massive proportions, guilt is not something new. But what is it and why do women feel guilt the way they do? What, if any, purpose does it serve? Over the years many psychologists and therapists have tried to define and understand guilt but their research has not stopped people suffering from it. The dictionary defines guilt as 'the mental preoccupation with the idea of having done something wrong'. Freud believed that guilt was an emotion that signalled the presence of aggressive wishes, and in traditional psychoanalysis the term 'guilt' is most commonly used as a way of describing unconscious processes that may lead to neurotic actions.

In essence, guilt is an unpleasant feeling associated with unfulfilled wishes. In the most positive light, it can be a warning system that we have transgressed a boundary that we value. When a person feels guilty their body releases adrenaline, their heart rate increases, blood pressure goes up and their stomach churns, as blood is channelled to more important organs to enable a quick protective response. From an evolutionary point of view, it is an adaptive feature designed to enable people to escape from danger. But when guilt persists, the body remains in 'overdrive' and anxiety develops. It is this angst that ultimately stirs up Motherguilt in women.

Because women mother as they were mothered, many of them have inherited Motherguilt from their own mothers and their mothers before them. They have accepted the mandate that they must take responsibility for everything to do with their families and make everything right for their children. It is the female *raison d'être* to achieve perfection in this most important of biological roles, but when things go wrong, as they often do, they blame themselves and guilt is a natural reaction.

Motherguilt slinks into a woman's life when she least expects it, kindled by a belief that she has somehow failed in her responsibility to her children. This often occurs when a mother puts her own needs and desires first. Motherguilt does not discriminate – wherever mums are, guilt will find them. Even wealthy, gorgeous superstars like Nicole Kidman, who has two adopted children Isabella and Conor, admits to Motherguilt. 'There is a lot of guilt with motherhood because you always think you're doing everything wrong.'

'I wish I knew where the guilt comes from,' says bestselling author Di Morrissey. 'It seems to be more of a woman's burden, something that's passed down in our female genes. I try not to have regrets, to look backwards or to blame anyone, even myself, but there are times when a woman can't help but feel that dark blanket of "what ifs" and "if onlys" weighing her down. The knowledge of always being there for my children never leaves me.' There is no doubt our genes are tricky blighters and responsible for much of our physical and mental inheritance but could guilt possibly be genetic as Di suggests?

If there is a gene for this emotion it surely must be on the X chromosome, because women certainly have a double dose. But although the notion is an interesting one, it does not explain why men are not affected by guilt when they become fathers. 'What's there to feel guilty about?' asks Charles, a policeman and father of two. 'Guilty means you've done something wrong. What have I done wrong?' If only women could think in such a simple, but effective way.

Perhaps women are too complex for their own good, or could it be that the gene for 'rationalisation' is carried on the male-only Y chromosome? Maybe . . . But genes are tricky and we know very little about them or men's feelings of guilt as fathers, because nothing much has been documented. Men tend not to give voice to emotions – and this is universally accepted – but whether this has anything to do with guilt or false pride no one is sure. It probably has a lot do with the power relations of thousands of years old patriarchal societies that dictate a superior controlling male and inferior subservient female.

Although most men recognise Motherguilt in their wives and often laugh about it, the closest emotion fathers experience seems to be regret, usually related to not being able to spend more time with their children. Dr John D'Arcy is a GP, medical writer and media presenter, and married with four children, the youngest of whom is fourteen. 'Interestingly, there is an enormous level of guilt in mothers – constant and overpowering guilt,' he says. 'I saw it for years in the mothers who came to my surgery and I see it now in my media workplace. As a father, probably my only feeling of guilt comes from not having enough time with my kids but it's much easier to rationalise – men do that so well – because my role is accepted as the major breadwinner. The trade-off is that I miss out on the interaction with my kids that makes me closer to them, and I sometimes don't know what's going on in their heads. Mothers are much closer to their children but kids can be very manipulative and mothers seem much more vulnerable to that than fathers.' Dr D'Arcy also believes that when things go wrong fathers 'blame' whereas mothers feel guilty.

Fascinating though the workings of the male mind are the authors believe that male 'logic' is often questionable. Educationalist Agnes Czeiger, who tutors at the University of New South Wales, points out that as far as men are concerned there is such a thing as unconscious guilt, which is acted out by a person without knowing that it is guilt. 'Being unaware of it they are unable to identify it – whether it is through pride, vanity or ego, men will deny guilt because it has a negative valency to it. Negative thoughts interfere with their positive egos and false pride and the male ego must never be neglected. The male ego is always on the defensive. Freud wrote a lot of good and sensible material on defence mechanisms. If a man is attacked mentally and feels fear or threatened, then he extinguishes it from his system and does not allow it to happen. Hence no guilt.'

Mark, a father of three, has yet another point of view. 'Implicit in men's culture is that we are "in control" so we don't talk about guilt. Winning and accomplishment are bred into us and we don't allow guilt to happen because it's a negative emotion and a waste of emotional energy. Women tend to communicate much more openly with each other, so they explore their feelings and guilt becomes a greater focus, often overly so and kids try very hard to pull the "guilt strings". When our family is together I tend to "delegate" guilt to my wife!' Tongue in cheek though Mark's last remark may be, it does reinforce the fact that some men are bemused by their wives' apparent inability to control their emotions.

Could men and women's different emotional responses be explained by their different hormones? As a doctor, Penny believes this is part, but only part, of the story. 'We know from animal studies that testosterone is the hormone of aggression. Oestrogen is a much "softer" hormone. There have been no actual scientific studies to prove my theory but, when you think about it, Motherguilt starts virtually as soon as a woman becomes pregnant and that's when female oestrogen levels surge. Throughout a woman's reproductive cycles, her susceptibility to guilt varies and again this could be related to her oestrogen levels. After menopause, when oestrogen levels are very low, many women find that their guilt levels seem to lessen.'

As a mother a woman has many goals but her primary

one is to be thought of as 'a good mother' and *never* 'a bad mother'. 'I'd rather be called a slut then a bad mother,' says Ita. Penny agrees. How would a man react if he were called a bad father? Apparently he wouldn't react at all: to be called 'a bad provider' is far worse as, generally speaking, men still see that as their major role

John Cummine, a senior consultant doctor at a major teaching hospital and married with two daughters in their twenties, insists that 'guilt does not exist in men. Show me a man who feels guilt and I'll show you a woman. Guilt is inverted anger – anger directed inwards – which is what women do. Men show their anger in active ways such as rape, bullying, fighting, and with wars; or in passive ways by lying, cheating, pretending and frustrating. I *never* feel guilty as a father but I do feel angry. Women learn to internalise their anger from the moment they are born and I don't think it is possible for women *not* to feel guilt. It's too simplistic to say that it is just due to oestrogen. Women have a whole chromosome that is different to men. There are so many physical and emotional differences between them and the differences in behaviour are accepted and condoned by our society – the societal influence is huge.'

So could there be an evolutionary purpose for guilt? 'You can ask that question about *everything* that happens in our lives, but often we simply do not have an answer,' John says. 'Men's aggression has been an essential part of evolution. They have always been physically bigger and stronger and this was important for "survival of the fittest". Testosterone probably causes this, but society has always legitimised their conduct.

'Fathers will never be as close as mothers are to their children but guilt is the price women pay for part of that closeness. Men have compartmentalised minds, whereas women's minds are diffuse, which is why women are such good carers.' Are women financially punished for their intimacy with their children and their natural role as carers? John thinks they are. 'But society will eventually change this because we need carers. However "carer" is often seen as a dirty word because it is a soft word, it's not aggressive or powerful, but as the importance of physical strength is rendered almost negligible, men will have to readdress their roles, not just as partners but also as fathers.'

~

This is already happening. More men are accepting a role reversal where they stay home and mind the children while their partner carries out the role of main breadwinner. However, there is still a long way to go before househusbands and stay-at-home dads are universally accepted. Many men admit to finding it difficult to forsake their 'provider' role, while a lot of women have misgivings at what they see as a male invasion of a previously women-only role.

But, whether women like it or not, the role of men *is* changing. In 2004 the Australian Institute, an independent public policy research unit, predicted that a new breed of stay-at-home father is well on the way and that the number of dads taking an active role in child-rearing will double in the next five years. Those pioneering men who now stay at home to care for their kids claim they are enjoying the opportunity to spend quality time with their kids, although some of them are also honest enough to admit that they find housework boring. They complain, too, that as well as doing what has always been thought of as 'women's work' in the home, they also have to do 'the bloke things' like mowing the lawns, cleaning the swimming pool and taking out the garbage. 'Sometimes I feel tired at the end of the day,' Charles says, 'and when my wife comes home expecting dinner to be ready I know she sometimes thinks what *has* he been doing all day.' Goodness! Where have women heard that before? Maybe there is not all that much difference between men and women after all?

There is now an expectation of shared parenting and

Why does guilt attack mothers and not fathers?

'exploiting' this change in attitude has become a potential vote winner. Federal Labor leader Mark Latham won much approval from women in 2004 when he portrayed himself as a new-age dad who reads to his children. He quickly cashed in on such approval by providing the media with photo opportunities showing him reading to little boys and girls in school classrooms. This is not to say that Mr Latham does not do this as part of his role as a father or that dads have not been reading to their children for generations – they have and many have taken on the 'soft' role of caring parenting too. In the same way that women questioned their role back in the 1960s and 1970s many twenty-first century men are now doing the same. They not only want a better balance in their lives and to be able to spend more time with their families, men also want family-friendly workplaces as much as women do. If we ever bothered to ask them, no doubt kids would say they wanted the same thing too – but who ever asks them what they want?

Penny's husband Ian believes that in today's society men still have a defined role as 'provider' while 'women are plagued by choice and no choice is a perfect solution. Mothers suffer immense guilt because everything they do is a compromise between the demands of their career or just life generally and the extraordinary demands of raising children and trying to maintain a relationship with their partners.'

Sydney businessman Rob Douglass has been both father and mother to his daughter Katherine – 'KK' – for ten years following the severe illness and subsequent death of his wife. KK's situation has compelled him to try to think and feel like a mother and over the years, he says he has learned the guilt of mothers, especially working mothers.

'Men and women are different – they may be equal, but they *are* different in physiology and psychology,' Rob says. He feels that the patriarchal model created by men forced women to repress their feminine side and develop a masculine self when they were 'permitted' into the paid workforce. 'Ironically this occurred partly as a result of women being dragged into the economy because of man-made wars.' Not only did they have to fit into masculine-style relationships, they, had to acquire a male outlook. 'By that I mean women acted like men *because* that is the only way they were accepted by men, and in order to carry out their duties efficiently to their bosses' satisfaction they also were obliged to see everything from a male point of view. They had no other option.'

The fact that in 2004 women make up more than half the Australian workforce has not however eliminated their traditional role as 'domestic technologists', a description some women like to use to elevate themselves from the subservient title of home duties. Consequently, Rob believes working women developed a 'split personality' with the 'independent working woman' dominating their 'instinctive, sex-related self'. 'The old interdependent relationship between men and women in the home situation changed. They were no longer couples working as one yin and yang harmoniously for the wellbeing of themselves and their family, but instead, inevitably, if unconsciously, became separate, competing individuals.'

Agnes Czeiger has a different perspective. 'I wonder how many women really feel they are competing, or even want to compete, with men. In order to function in the male-dominated world of commerce, I believe women were compelled – they had no option – to take on male roles, not to compete but to succeed. This is perceived as competition only by men and very different from men competing with each other.'

Dianne McKissock believes that 'as mothers entered the workforce waving their "seventies feminist banners", they forgot to take their mothering skills with them. The very skills that could remould the workplace to make it family-friendly for mothers *and* fathers were dropped off at the daycare centre with the children.

Women felt they had to behave like men to compete in the work-place and it not only affected how they were at work but their relationships at home.'

Rob Douglass often asks himself, 'What is the quintessential role of mothers – the bit I don't have naturally? The one thing that mothers can give their children – and are physiologically and psycho-logically good at – is unconditional love. This is the most important element for the healthy growth of children. A child can be consciously or unconsciously reminded that if it does or does not do this or that "Mum will not love you". However, usually no one else gives a child as much acceptance and appreciation as its mother does and nobody can forgive children their mistakes like mothers can. As a trained lawyer, I often find myself qualifying my love for my daughter KK when what she needs and yearns for above all is unconditional love. I find this hardest to give. A child may be lucky enough to receive such an unconditional love from another person apart from its mother; however, it seems to me that, in general, a mother's love is relatively less conditional than love from any other person.

'But unfortunately since we mothers – and yes, I do include myself in that term – feel we *must* play the "all and every-thing" role, including nursing, teaching, guiding, tutoring, making friends, etc., in addition to our housewifely role with all its duties and chores and probably also an outside job, we are constantly so exhausted and therefore irritable that we are incapable of giving unconditional love because we haven't the strength or the patience. The most we can achieve is to have a well-trained, well-behaved, highly educated child who, in spite of all its brilliant qualities, lacks the most essential aspect of "being" – the feeling of happiness. Unconditional love is the only legitimate thing we can and should give our children.'

'Many people think that unconditional love is the sole ter-rain of women,' Agnes Czeiger says. 'But in fact, conditional love is not gender specific and the bond between baby/child and parent (or parent substitute) is dependent on caring and affection and nothing else. The natural or "birth" mother is not the only person who can "mother" a child; any one person can fulfil the role. Parenting is a different matter altogether. It is contingent on our past, which, with baggage and all, determines what kind of adult person we become.'

Rob Douglass married late, due mostly, he says, to his gypsy life as an international banker. 'But I always wanted to be a parent and I remember very clearly deliberately conceiving KK and in a spirit of joy. Parenting has opened a whole new world for me and, while not always without its problems, it has been a huge plus in my life and a wonderful learning experience. KK is a delight – well, mostly.

'I know that I have a tendency to overcompensate her for having no real mother, and I recognise this fault in myself and try to counteract it. There are circumstances where I let KK venture out onto the thin ice alone and break through it and struggle in the icy waters until she swims to shore. She is strengthened by the experience. There are occasions where I warn her and then let her go out on the ice, and there are times when I jump in and save her. Either way, it is a gut-wrenching decision – every time – and one feels guilt that perhaps some situations should have been handled differently. I ask myself what her mother would have done in such circumstances.

'The best guideline for anyone who wants to improve the world, including the way we raise children, is something I heard from a Buddhist guru,' Rob says. 'When faced with the question, "What should we *teach* our children?" the wise man replied, "Nothing. The one person you can and should work on is yourself. If you successfully teach yourself whatever you wish your child to learn, that will teach your child."

'It has taken me years to really understand the wisdom hidden in that simple sentence and I continually have to learn it over and over again. We are our children's role models – and if we are successful and happy doing whatever we do, the way we live will be imitated by them and therefore no further teaching is necessary. Only those words that come out of our hearts can penetrate into another person's heart – being happy is the best example we can give our children. That doesn't mean that limits on their behaviour shouldn't be set and adhered to, but this mustn't limit the love we give them. "No" can be a very loving word. When KK was fourteen she asked if she could go with her friends to a disco. I've never forgotten her sigh of relief when I said no.'

Pascal, the father of two sons aged nineteen and fourteen, comes from a French Jewish background, and took on the motherhood role a couple of years ago when he was abruptly retrenched from his job. 'The concept of a father in our society is still the "hunter" – the provider. I was working in a very pressured job in IT. I *never* felt guilty – in fact, sometimes I used to feel annoyed that my family didn't appreciate me and sometimes I'd say, "Hey, guys, I am working so hard to give you everything you want, give me some space." When I was suddenly unemployed, I found myself at home, taking on the role of househusband while my wife worked full-time. Ironically, although I was now spending more time than ever before with my sons, I felt guilty. Part of my guilt related to me feeling that I was not being a good role model to them – I was "a bad provider" – but it wasn't only that; my new role seemed to encourage me to feel guilty. I felt I was more in the mother's role. I watched my sons more, talked with them more, analysed them more, worried about them more and felt guilty more.'

The authors believe it significant that once Rob and Pascal took on a mothering role they 'felt' guilt, which suggests that motherhood and guilt go together and that perhaps women can't have one without the other. However, there are always exceptions to the rule. Kathryn Greiner was astonished when Ita told her that out of all the women interviewed for this book she was the only mother who professed to have never suffered from guilt. 'The revelation made me examine what I had said to Ita,' Kathryn says. 'Had I given a true and fair recollection? I am satisfied I did.

'The greatest gift you can give your children is independence and the capacity to stand on their own two feet. I wasn't a perfect mother and made my share of mistakes but I had no hang-ups about being a mother. Right from the start, Nick and I told the kids, "This is how it is, team. We have our lives and you have yours but we will always be there when you need us." That's always been my attitude even though it has meant that, occasionally, I've turned somersaults to make things happen. Nick and I went to all the important school functions and although we both worked and he was in politics we gave up things like opera and theatre when the kids were growing up rather than let anything else take us away from the home.

'As a parent you make that kind of accommodation – the accommodating goes both ways – and I have never equated the word "accommodate" with sacrifice. The only thing I have now that I didn't have before is time for me. Looking back I realise how tired I always was but, at the time, I didn't really think about it. You just keep going. It's like hitting your head against a brick wall – when it stops the feeling is wonderful.'

Jan Murray's child-rearing philosophy is similar to Kathryn's but has not been without guilt. 'We can never untie the mother knot and I think women are the natural guilt bearers. We hand it down through the generations. It seems to be in our genes and we recognise it in each other's eyes. But in bringing up my children my guiding principle has been that they came to live with me – I didn't go to live with them – so they needed to fit in. I certainly never felt guilty about thinking this way. We lived spontaneously. If my husband was home early, we would take the kids and go out for dinner or a movie. The next-door neighbour used to say, "They'll grow up as juvenile delinquents." Her children were so regimented. A bell rang and they were called into the bath at 4.30. I just couldn't do that. We lived in creative chaos.

'My kids blame me for their underbite, their overbite, the fact that they don't have a straight row of perfect white teeth; and my daughter blames me for not sending her to a private school. But she would have still been caught smoking behind the toilets, even at a private school. I think the worst thing you can do to a child is to withdraw yourself emotionally from them because then you're a stranger to them and they feel alienated and have no signposts. I'm all for letting kids know when you're angry with them but also letting them know you love them all the while.'

Could it be that the solution to Motherguilt is so simple that women cannot see the wood for the trees? As the Buddhist guru said, children learn from their parents' example. Instead of trying so hard to be perfect with all the guilt that seems to entail, perhaps women should aim to be happy mothers, relaxed enough to have fun with their children so they in turn can enjoy a carefree childhood, which, after all, is their inalienable right.

All mothers want the best for their children and try to do their job as mum the best way they can, but there is no rush and no timetable that must be followed. Motherhood is a journey, not a quick trip down the street. After the dependent stage of development, children's needs and wants may become more demanding but, even so, there is no need to hurry. What children want most is their parents' – and in particular, their mother's – uninterrupted attention. What this means is that mothers not only need to give themselves a chance to smell the roses, but also to leave themselves time to jump and splash in the puddles with their children.

3

Breastfeeding can be a cow of a job!

Not long after giving birth a woman has to confront a major guilt-producing quandary – should she breastfeed or bottle-feed? Either decision can result in a plethora of guilty feelings. A woman who fails to breastfeed satisfactorily is made to feel such a failure that any pleasure she has in being a mother can be completely shattered. 'You won't bond with your baby.' 'That baby will get asthma and eczema.' 'You'll drop the baby's IQ by ten points.' 'Your baby won't develop its immune system.' Many mothers who encounter problems breastfeeding admit to feeling disappointed and angry at what they consider their uselessness; some even confess to thinking of themselves as second-class mothers. Food, it seems, is capable of stirring a range of emotions.

The thing that most worries a breastfeeding mother – and, understandably, this is especially true for first-time mums – is *how* she is supposed to know when her baby has had enough to eat. Even when her baby stops suckling and is clearly not interested in a having a 'second helping', many a mother is often not convinced that her child knows its own mind. She is sure her baby *must* need more.

Many mothers also mistakenly think that feeding is the only way to settle a baby.

It is much easier for the mother who chooses to bottle-feed because she can *see* how much her baby is eating. But, as all mothers know, bottle-feeding is frowned upon. Medically speaking, there is no doubt breast *is* best, but it is also true that sometimes for all sorts of reasons – both physical and psychological – breast-feeding just doesn't work. There is no one-size-fits-all approach with breastfeeding. Every woman's body is different and so is every baby. At the end of the day, it is far better for a mother to be happy and to enjoy her baby, who can, and will, do admirably on a bottle of formula. This is not a case of simple pragmatism but a fact, and one that needs to be repeated regularly to mothers.

Only the foolhardy or the very naïve believe that breast-feeding comes naturally. In her many years editing women's magazines, Ita received hundreds of letters on this subject. Just about every mother has at least one 'disaster' story about breastfeed-ing, even if she ultimately finds the experience rewarding. As usual, like everything to do with having a baby, women are expected to be perfect but it takes time to get used to feeding babies on the breast, not only on the part of the mother but also that of the child.

'What women need to understand is that breastfeeding is a physical and emotional challenge underestimated by the uniniti-ated,' says Penny. 'If all works smoothly, it can be one of the most satisfying of maternal pleasures, but the truth is that it rarely goes smoothly from the outset. You do have to work at it and it can be a downright miserable exercise for a woman, her partner and other family members, not to mention the baby.'

When Susan had her first baby, she expected to be a 'natu-ral' at breastfeeding. No such luck! No milk, cracked nipples, breast shields, and a baby who simply wouldn't attach all contributed to six weeks of sheer misery. She has never forgotten the overwhelming guilt. 'I would go to mother's group – there were about twelve of us – and the clinic sister would make comments about what to do with breastfeeding. Then she would turn to me, in a very loud voice, and say, "*You* don't need to listen to this." Talk about emphasising my already enormous sense of failure! When I finally put him on the bottle at about six weeks, he became a baby whom I could cuddle. We both got some sleep and I started to enjoy being a mum. Up until then, it was pretty horrible.'

Too many women are made to believe they have to get it right from day one and many of them are not well informed about breastfeeding, which is why first-time mothers are assailed with doubts and fears. 'Many mothers have no idea of the importance that basic adequate nutrition plays in satisfactory breastfeeding, and when mothers are leaving hospital, information about this is just about nonexistent,' community nurse Diana Aspinall says. 'Young career women eat differently today to the way their mothers did. For instance, many of them don't eat breakfast. If a woman doesn't eat breakfast at all or doesn't eat it early enough when she is breastfeeding she will have an unsettled baby later in the day.'

Jennifer read as much as possible about breastfeeding and also drank lots of water 'because I found it helped my milk. For me, the most satisfying thing was the bonding experience that breastfeeding offered and knowing my baby was getting the best I could give her.'

Many mothers feel like that about bonding. 'It was so special,' Kristina says. 'Breastfeeding was such a pleasure, although it was hard work in the beginning. But once I got the hang of it I enjoyed it. It is fantastic watching your baby feed, making those contented grunting and slurping noises. My baby and I were so happy together.'

Newborn babies' eyes are still developing, but their clearest focus is exactly the distance between a mother's face and her breast. 'I loved thinking about this when I was breastfeeding,' Penny says. 'My babies could see my face best when they were on my breast.'

Many mothers also like the 'positive' effects breastfeeding has on their bodies, as it helps them get their shape back. 'I could eat anything,' Tricia says, 'and still keep my weight at its usual pre-birth level. I could also feel my uterus contract each time I nursed.' 'Five hundred extra calories a day and still my weight was going down,' Sally says. Some mums do find they keep a bit of extra weight on during lactation but that not long after weaning their babies the weight usually drops off.

⌒

Probably one of the biggest problems a mother faces is that *everyone* feels compelled to give her advice. A first-time mum usually listens to all of it and ultimately becomes more bewildered than ever on what is the right thing to do for her baby.

When the 'breastfeeding Nazis' insist that a mother should never give a baby a bottle, as it will compromise her breast milk, she believes them. If too many bottles are given or if complementing with formula happens on several feeds this can happen, but a mother can safely express breast milk a few times a week so that her husband or some other family member or friend can give the baby a bottle of milk. This gives a mother the chance to have an uninterrupted nap or perhaps get her hair done. Psychologically, having a little time to do their own thing makes mothers happier in themselves and reminds them that motherhood does not mean there will never be time for personal pleasures. Naturally, though, many women admit to guilt because they are actually happy to have some time away from their baby.

A new mother faces pressure from many sources, even her partner – although why any man would consider himself to be an

Breastfeeding can be a cow of a job!

expert on breastfeeding God only knows. 'I was made to feel a terrible person when I told my husband and my friends that I wasn't going to breastfeed,' Mary Anne says. 'My husband took my decision personally. *Why* didn't I want to nurse his child? – that kind of thing.'

Jane's husband told her that if he were breastfeeding he would be better at it than she was. 'I tried so hard to breastfeed our son,' she says, 'but we were both hopeless – although I am sure it was all my fault. He always ended up crying and so did I. We were both much happier when I said enough was enough and switched to bottle-feeding. And I am sure my baby felt loved.'

Midwife Julie McCowage thought she was well prepared for motherhood. 'I thought I was going to be brilliant because I'd just done midwifery. I thought I knew everything but, as I discovered, midwifery only tells you about having a baby, it doesn't tell you about looking after it. I over-mothered my children I think. I breastfed them both until they were fifteen months. I think I gave them colic from feeding them too much. I should have gone to Tresillian [a family care centre] and got some advice from the nursing experts there. They probably would have told me to stop mucking around and stop over-feeding them. I did the same thing twice!'

Then there is the mother who does not want to breastfeed but has been encouraged to do so by the hospital staff. She has great difficulty in coming to terms with her feelings, as does a breastfeeding mother whose milk diminishes and is forced to then complement with formula or give up breastfeeding altogether.

Channel Seven personality and sports presenter Johanna Griggs, who has two boys, Jesse and Joe Buster, watched both her sisters breastfeed without any problem whatsoever, but for her, 'Breastfeeding was such a rotten experience that I would have no hesitation putting the next baby straight on the bottle. It was harder than I thought it would be and I was made to feel so guilty by one nursing sister who told me I'd be a failure as a mother unless I breastfed because it was "the best chance that I could give my baby". I had cracked nipples and mastitis and she just kept saying. "Persevere, persevere, you will get to the other side." It was such an unpleasant experience that I dreaded when Jesse would wake up because I knew what was coming.

'I'd gone six weeks without sleep when one of my friends gave me some good advice. She had brought her baby up on bottles and he was happy and healthy. So I rang my doctor and she said, "Try it and see how you go." Jesse slept eight hours after the first bottle. Before that, he hadn't slept more than a couple of hours because he'd been starving. When I had Joe Buster, I gave him one breastfeed, immediately got one blistered nipple and that was enough, I switched to bottles.

Everyone was fantastic except one nurse. I was admiring some twins who were fast asleep. "They are so gorgeous," I said, and she immediately retorted, "That's because they are breastfed." "Wrong," I replied, and gave her a five-minute lecture. I told her that if I were a first-time mother her remarks would have devastated me. She needed to consider that breastfeeding might be her ideal but not everyone can do it and that if she was serious about the baby's health, which she should be, she should back off the guilt trip that she was trying to give me.'

Sandra breastfed her first baby but not her second. 'I loathed breastfeeding but I couldn't tell a soul how I felt because I'd have been branded a bad mother. My husband didn't like me feeding our first child in front of him so I used to sit in my daughter's bedroom staring at the wall when I fed her. Even in the hospital, the nurses would draw the curtains around those of us who were breastfeeding while the bottle-feeding mothers were allowed to sit on their beds and be seen feeding their babies. Rightly or wrongly I got the impression that breastfeeding was something to be hidden.

'Then there was the sister at the health clinic who kept telling me I was a good cow. How I hated that description because that is exactly what I felt like – an ugly cow, with big udders. My son thrived on bottles and I felt much happier and more relaxed at his mealtimes but I still have the guilts because I worry that in some way I didn't do the right thing by him – and he's almost thirty!'

≈

Many a new mother often feels she does not have a choice – it is simply assumed that she will breastfeed. As Penny says, 'I would have felt guilty if I hadn't breastfed because I would have considered I had failed at one of the first challenges of motherhood. The medical evidence was compelling. What I mistakenly supposed was that breastfeeding is instinctive and that it would all just happen. Then I discovered inverted nipples, cracked nipples, mincemeat nipples and, although I was a doctor, I found that there were at least 1001 different and contradictory pieces of advice on breastfeeding. Needless to say, in the next bed in the post-natal ward was an "Earth Mother" feeding twins with consummate ease.

'Nobody told me that you actually needed to *learn* how to breastfeed, that it wouldn't come automatically and perfectly. I now warn all new mothers that, while breastfeeding is a great option, they shouldn't panic if they can't do it or don't want to, because it is not the only choice. If they are having problems, it can take six weeks or so to get the hang of it.'

Many mothers are not told about mastitis either and yet it occurs in 30 to 40 per cent of all mothers at some stage in their breastfeeding career. 'It is more common during those early difficult weeks when she is trying to settle into her new role, and is caused by milk ducts getting blocked and subsequently infected, resulting in part of the breast becoming hot, red and painful,' says Penny. 'Often the mother develops a fever and feels as if she is getting the flu. If recognised early enough, frequent feeds from that breast will help unblock the ducts and the mastitis will clear but often antibiotics are required as well. In spite of reassurance from their doctors, mothers often feel guilty about their babies getting antibiotics from their breast milk. Many are reluctant to take pain relief (again okay) for the same reason. The experience of mastitis understandably can turn mothers off breastfeeding, and yet weaning at this time can cause recurrent bouts, as the breast is not being drained. Some mothers get caught up in the vicious cycle of dreading the painful feeds, resenting their baby and feeling overwhelming guilt – not a great formula for bonding with their new baby.'

Shunting mothers out of hospital a few days after giving birth – even before their milk has come in – does not help mothers with breastfeeding either. In the past, the ten days a woman usually spent in hospital allowed her to get to know her new responsibility, get some much needed rest, and take her time learning how to breastfeed under the watchful eye of the nursing profession. With the current shortage of nurses and a health system that cannot cope with the demands being made on it, nurses no longer have time to help mothers sufficiently. The health system is letting mothers down but then maybe, over the years, it too fell for the Superwoman myth that women could do anything – even breastfeeding – without assistance.

It is a situation that Diana Aspinall would like to see rectified. 'As a community nurse I frequently see women struggling to breastfeed. There is so much concentration on getting breastfeeding started after delivery but very little being done in encouraging mothers to continue breastfeeding. There is also a lack of realistic information about normal development of the baby and how mothers can clue into their babies' growth spurts and make sure their milk supply can match the extra demand. Often there is no extended family either and new mothers are forced to rely on advice from friends with little expertise in breastfeeding and with their own agendas operating.'

Di Morrissey was living in Hawaii with her former husband Peter and had no family and friends nearby when her first baby was born. 'My paediatrician was adamant about breast being best but Gabrielle, my daughter, didn't want to know. I tried everything my doctor suggested, from laying her on a pillow in my lap to having a small glass of wine to relax and let my milk down before feeding. It took nearly a week and I was starting to feel so guilty I wasn't giving her the best start in life.'

'Susannah fed non-stop and screamed for the first six months of her life as if I was cutting off her leg for most of the time,' Carolyn Hewson says. 'I remember the day I fed her eighteen times and she still screamed. I kept wondering if she was getting anything even though she was getting stronger and stronger – and I was getting smaller.'

Camille remembers with horror the sensation of 'the milk coming in', something that new mothers often are not warned about. 'I'll never get over having rockmelon breasts. I'm not worried about whether I have a natural childbirth or a Caesar next time – it's just those rockmelons!'

Even when mothers breastfeed without a hitch they still cannot escape Motherguilt. Sports columnist and television personality Rebecca Wilson breastfed her first baby for six months but then 'felt guilty it wasn't for twelve months'. Advertising executive Mindi Chisholm breastfed both her children for a couple of weeks and then put them on a bottle. 'Everyone and anyone made me feel guilty,' she says. 'But I wanted to get back to work and I didn't *want* to have every feed coming from me. I wanted sometimes to be able to sleep through the night and occasionally let my husband get up and give the kids their bottle.'

Like most things to do with motherhood, much of the truth about the difficulties women experience with breastfeeding is glossed over. 'There is a lot of hard work in breastfeeding that they don't talk about in the books. When the "experts" go on about four-hourly feeds, we think they're talking about bottle-feeding because breastfeeding takes so long that no sooner have you finished than you have to start all over again. At one stage when we were having problems with feeding and he was constantly crying, I said, "I just can't stand him screaming all the time," and his other mother said, "I'm so glad you said that because I was thinking the same thing." It was a huge relief for both of us.' (Lesbian mothers talking about breastfeeding.)

For the breastfeeding purist not a drop of formula will pass the baby's lips, even in the mother's absence. This explains why an otherwise intelligent woman will subject herself to the weird, and highly inconvenient, process of expressing breast milk. Why is expressed breast milk such a precious commodity? First, it is such a performance to get it out of your breast and into the little plastic bags in the freezer. Archaic tools of torture have nothing on breast pumps – manual or electric they all make you feel like a dairy cow. Secondly, the amount that you can collect and store is directly proportional to the amount of times a mother can "escape" from her baby.

Joy Smithers went back to work full-time when her children were about four months old. 'I would maniacally breast pump away in women's toilets. There was a lot of guilt and separation anxiety on my part but past a certain age I think it's good for mothers – provided they are comfortable with the childcare arrangement – to have something else to do in the day apart from looking after their children, housework and groceries.'

'I was supposed to have several months off after my son

Callan was born,' says Claudia Ketch, who at the time was working for a major advertising agency. 'I gave birth on a Monday and the girl who was going to do my job resigned on the Friday. I got a call while I was still in hospital saying my boss needed me. Within a few weeks, I was back working on Wednesdays. I hired a mothercraft nurse and, after expressing milk, I would go off to a marketing meeting that lasted four or five hours. When everyone took a break, I would go off to the loo to express milk. I squirted it down the toilet. I was in awful pain because I had missed a feed. It would trigger guilt inside me – I should have been at home breastfeeding my son. I took to wearing leather vests so that my leaking breasts wouldn't show.'

Although they ought to understand about the feeding needs of babies, it is women – notably older women – who are quick to condemn a mother who breastfeeds in public. Presumably, their thinking has been conditioned by the narrow-minded community attitudes of the time when they were breastfeeding mothers and more often than not, had to stay 'hidden away' at their baby's mealtimes.

'I was quietly feeding my baby in the corner of a coffee shop when a middle-aged woman and her husband came and sat nearby,' Lorraine says. 'I was so involved in feeding my baby that at first I didn't realise that when the woman said to her husband, "That is *disgusting*," she meant me! Her face was such a mix of anger and disapproval that I was shocked.'

In February 2003, Victorian Labor MP and former world skiing champion Kirstie Marshall was ejected from the chamber of the Victorian State Parliament for breastfeeding her baby. Her 'eviction' attracted world headlines with the *Irish Independent* heading its story, 'MP kicked out for making a meal out of question time'. Kirstie was taken aback by the furore she caused. 'I acted instinctively,' she said. 'I arrived at Parliament just as the bells were ringing and Charlotte was due for a feed, so I whacked her on the breast and walked in and sat down.' The argument used to remove Kirstie was that she had brought 'a stranger' – a hungry eleven-day-old baby – into the Parliament. (The Victorian Government has since amended its rules to allow breastfeeding in Parliament, but only at the Speaker's discretion.)

The Melbourne *Age*'s editorial of 28 February 2003 was encouraging for all breastfeeding mothers, both present and future.

> By choosing to juggle motherhood and parliamentary duties, Ms Marshall, who hitherto has been better known as a champion aerial skier, has taken a difficult path. She should be congratulated for making the attempt, and for giving Parliament the challenge of adapting to the demands she has made on it. If women choose to combine a political career and motherhood, they should be allowed to make whatever transformations are necessary in their immediate working environment. By doing so they can provide an example of how best to combine conflicting responsibilities. It is to be hoped that Charlotte will not be the last baby to appear in the house.

Bravo *The Age*. Mothers everywhere hope the newspaper's wise words did not fall on deaf ears – but it is possible they did, because six months later when comedian Kate Langbroek breastfed her baby on television she sparked the same kind of controversy as Kirstie. Mind you, it is not every day a mother makes television history doing this! Kate was making her first appearance on *The Panel* after the birth of her son Lewis six week earlier. She began nursing him discreetly at the end of the program because the baby was hungry. The watching audience was not able to see a breast, most of them didn't even realise Kate was feeding her baby. But, although Equal Opportunity Commissioner Diana Sisely applauded Kate for claiming her right to breastfeed in her workplace, talkback radio hosts (male, of course) condemned the working mother for doing so. Just as well men are not mothers or many a baby would starve!

It is time society – and male broadcasters – got over their hang-ups about babies being fed in public. No woman should be made to feel guilty about breastfeeding in public. Some women do quietly succumb but others, like a medical colleague of Penny's husband, fight back. She was being chastised at a medical dinner for breastfeeding her new daughter at a Chinese banquet. No sooner had an older male anaesthetist finished saying, 'Geeze, Lizzie, do you have to do that at the table?' than she whipped her baby off the breast and gave the offending appendage a firm squeeze, sending a large jet of breast milk arching over the table and onto his plate. There was more than just soy sauce on his wontons!

It is astonishing in these liberated times, that the sight of a breastfeeding mother causes such negative reactions, yet women can bare their breasts in print and film. Nicole Kidman's breast 'popped out' of the difficult-to-wear gown she wore when presenting an award at the 2004 Golden Globes, but no one batted an eyelid. Why such double standards? It seems that although most men admit to a lifetime of fascination with women's breasts as sexual objects, the idea of those breasts being put to their naturally intended use brings out the worst in some members of the opposite sex.

'I remember the time when my older daughter was a baby and we were entertaining guests for dinner, one of whom was a particularly lecherous psychiatrist,' Penny says. 'All evening, he kept joking about how he would just love to get a bit of my breast milk – he went on and on! After dinner, I was making coffee and as luck would have it, he asked for a flat white. So I expressed about 30 ml of breast milk into his coffee and handed it to him smiling sweetly. When he had almost finished his coffee and yet again made a joke about wanting some breast milk, I said, "Darling, you've just been drinking it." He almost choked – it was a wonderful moment.'

When a mother feels ready to wean – for whatever reason – she should be able to do so without any regrets, but when to wean is another no-win situation that brims with guilt. 'Too soon' or 'too late': either way a woman still cops criticism. Women who wean too early are often accused of depriving their child of 'all those lovely antibodies and the joys of maternal bonding', while those who wean too late are reproached for 'inappropriate' behaviour. The pressures can be subtle or very overt. Jackie was feeding her nine-month-old son when her father-in-law inquired how long she planned to continue breastfeeding. 'I told him I didn't think it would be a good look for my son when he was in his school uniform. The subject was never raised again.'

Gillian, a country GP, had problems with breastfeeding right from the outset but only with one breast. She struggled on trying to feed her baby from both breasts but eventually surrendered to the fact that only one was going to work. 'I didn't feel guilty about that. I just felt lopsided. What I did feel guilt about was hating the fact that I was trapped on the sofa for forty minutes at a time when I needed to be doing so many other things. I enjoyed the feeling that I was doing the right thing by my baby but there was a huge sense of liberation when I weaned him at seven months . . . But oh my, I did feel guilty about that.'

The question about how long to breastfeed usually comes down to an either/or decision. The practical mother knows that there is a third option – some breast, some bottle. This has enabled legions of working mothers to return to work happy in the knowledge that their babies will neither starve nor miss out on the opportunity to breastfeed a couple of times a day and during the night if they wake.

However, in 2003 the National Health and Medical Research Council (NHMRC) released the new Australian Dietary Guidelines advising that babies should receive only breast milk for the first six months. These guidelines also set a target of 50 per cent of mothers 'exclusively' breastfeeding until six months (at the moment it is under 20 per cent). 'Exclusive' breastfeeding, says the Australian Breastfeeding Association, means babies get no other foods, juice, infant formulas or other milks. But unless the NHMRC and the Australian Breastfeeding Association can do something to remove the barriers that prevent women from feeding their babies in the workplace and, at the same time, mount an educational campaign to turn around prejudice about mothers breastfeeding in public places, it is unlikely this admirable objective will be achieved.

Cracked nipples, engorged breasts, starving babies, concerns about bonding, balancing family and work demands . . . All in all, like every aspect of motherhood, breastfeeding does create amazing scope for feeling guilty. There is no evidence that formula-fed babies are less well loved than breastfed babies. Babies can thrive on breast milk; they can also thrive on formula. The 'breastfeeding Nazis' may think they know it all, but in fact, when it comes to how it wants to be fed, a hungry baby knows best!

4

When things go wrong: the not-so-perfect child

The one wish all mothers share is that their babies will be born healthy, but sometimes, in spite of having what appears to be a perfect pregnancy, things do go wrong and a child is born with intellectual or physical disabilities. When this happens it can have a devastating effect on mothers – and fathers – and for some couples, it is such a life-shattering event that it can result in the break-up of the parental partnership.

These days, with sophisticated ultrasound scans to detect major structural abnormalities and the medical profession's ability to check the baby's chromosomes with a variety of tests, some of a mother's fears about the wellbeing of her baby can be allayed. But, regardless of how clever science has become, one in every twenty babies is born with a significant abnormality. Some problems are not immediately evident at birth, only becoming apparent as a baby develops, and occasionally a mother suspects something is wrong with her child long before any medical diagnosis confirms her suspicions.

Thirty-eight-year-old Megan had a normal pregnancy

and vaginal delivery. 'I became concerned when Max was eighteen months. He didn't seem to be reaching his milestones – it was just little things like not pointing. I discussed it with the clinic sister but she didn't seem overly concerned. The thing I really noticed was his language. At twelve months, he started saying, "Mum, Mum, Mum," and then he stopped. He didn't say Mum again until he was four-and-a-half years old.

'At first, I thought he was deaf so I took him to my GP who arranged to have his hearing tested. The test was normal but I still thought something was wrong. After that, it was really just a matter of eliminating things. Eventually I took Max to a "special playgroup" where various different health professionals – physiotherapists, speech and occupational therapists – observed him and suggested I have him properly assessed. At the time, Max's behaviour was such that he couldn't be in a group – he was distressed at being with anyone else but me. When I look back I realise he was frightened.

'At the Assessment Centre he had a thorough check-up – psychologists, paediatricians, everyone poked and prodded at him. This was twelve months after I'd initially mentioned my concern to the clinic sister. It was the most difficult day because my husband and I sat behind a glass wall watching it all happen and weren't able to help Max who was so upset.

'When we were told our son was autistic, we were in shock. In the early days, the thought of autism had crossed my mind, but because he is so loving, I dismissed it. I had the mistaken belief that autistic kids weren't affectionate. We were dumbstruck. It was as if they were talking about somebody else. Max was with us, playing in the corner. I really grieved and I think my husband grieved equally, but in a different way.

'As my husband had to get back to work, I took Max back to where I'd parked the car and sat in it crying. I thought of all the other mothers in similar situations who must have sat in other car parks crying over their sense of loss, contemplating the fact that their child wasn't normal. I felt guilty and concerned that I might have done something that caused his autism. I wondered about a big night I'd had out with the girls before I knew I was pregnant. A friend had told me that there were reports that autism had been linked with measles, mumps and the rubella vaccination.' (This has subsequently been disproved.)

'The grief involved with a child with a disability is chronic grief,' bereavement counsellor and sociologist Dianne McKissock says. 'There is not much acceptance in our society to grieve over "what you don't have" and these mothers don't have the perfect child that we all dream about. Mothers of disabled children have to grieve the "loss of the perfect" in order to attach to and love the imperfect.'

Megan found the process of her acceptance of Max to be 'long, slow and painful at times and very challenging. I worry about my daughter Katie, who is now ten, because of the responsibilities there will be for her when we're older or not here. She is an amazing, compassionate girl but sometimes when there are children around that she doesn't know well and they don't understand Max's bizarre behaviour, it is embarrassing for her. There are times she feels that Max gets most of our time and attention. We recently left him with my family and took Katie to Disneyland. It was wonderful for her to walk along holding Mummy and Daddy's hands and have our undivided attention.

'I try not to look too far into the future, it's safer just one day at a time but realistically, he will probably live with us forever or, if not, then somewhere very close by. The likelihood of Max ever marrying is slim. He will never be able to drive. There are some days when I feel I don't have enough energy – taxing days, when he'll do things like bend a pair of sunglasses until they snap, or cut up some of his clothes with scissors. If I yell at him, I feel very guilty. Sometimes if I reprimand him, he becomes so anxious that his behaviour is worse than what caused the scolding in the first place. There are also some days when I could walk out that front door and never come back.

'It does help to talk to other mothers of autistic children. In fact, it's vital. I have a friend who has become very close – her son is autistic and is six months younger than Max, who is now eight. She and I have laughed and cried together for the last seven years. We share a special bond of understanding and friendship. Mothers of "normal" kids don't really understand – how can they? Mothers of autistic children have to live with it day to day. Max is such a good-looking little boy and he looks "normal" but his behaviour doesn't match. Many times in public places, other mothers have given me "the look" – like he's a very naughty boy or I'm a hopeless parent. So I always tell people that he is autistic because I want to make people more aware. Max really is a gorgeous boy because he is just him. I have a strong belief in God and I know he sent Max for a reason. It is difficult and I do get tired but I have learned so much from this magic little boy.'

Both Ita and Penny have first-hand experience of the anguish a mother endures when told all is not right with their baby. 'I knew that childbirth had risks attached to it but you never think these things are going to happen to you,' Ita says. 'When it does it is awful – my heart ached with pain. Not long after Ben's birth, I could tell from my doctor's manner that something was wrong but he didn't say anything. Later, when I was back in my room and after having a sleep, I asked to see my baby and was told he was in intensive care but the nurse wouldn't tell me why. This hadn't happened when Kate was born. My alarm bells instantly went off. They took me in a wheelchair to see Ben through the glass of the intensive care unit. I did so want to cuddle him but of course this was not possible.

'The following morning my doctor came to inform me that he was concerned about the size of Ben's head, which was bigger than normal, and the fact that his birth had been very rapid had rung all kinds of medical bells. When we left the maternity hospital I would have to take Ben to the Children's Hospital to consult a paediatrician who would examine his head and carry out some tests. I was frightened. Was there something seriously wrong with my baby? My husband and I told no one, except my Aunty Billy with whom I've always been close and who was a tower of strength.

'Two days after I returned home with Ben I took him to the Children's Hospital. His head was measured. Even in the short time he had been in this world it had grown perceptibly. As the doctor told me, heads grow at a certain rate and follow a set curve. Ben's head was growing faster than the normal rate and was not following the curve. I was sent to see a neurosurgeon who told me Ben might have hydrocephalus – a condition resulting in an abnormal enlargement of the head and pressure on the brain tissues, caused, so they said, by an excessive accumulation of cerebro-spinal fluid in the cavities of the brain. The doctors told me that some children die from the condition but others had been helped by an operation known as the shunt technique in which a small tube is placed under the skin behind the ear that drains off excess fluid into the jugular vein.

'This was one of the most terrible periods of my life. I was worried sick. What if Ben did have hydrocephalus? What would I do? I decided that I would stop working and look after him full-time. Whatever might be wrong with my son I was going to give him the best mothering possible. In the meantime life went on more or less as usual. I was editing *Cleo*, looking after Kate and my husband, and once a month I'd take Ben for a brain scan. I would leave him at the hospital, he would be sedated and the scan would be taken. I would go back and pick him up and take him home. Then I would have to go to the neurosurgeon for a report on the scan and another head measurement.

'Ben's head was still growing but so was the rest of him. He was a bright baby and seemed normal to me and in my heart of hearts I was sure that there was nothing wrong with him. But, in the middle of these visits to hospitals and doctors, Ben contracted a virus. I called our local GP who specialised in child health. After one look at Ben, his first question was, "Has this baby been examined for hydrocephalus?" My heart sank.

'I had been taking Ben to the neurosurgeon for nine months, by which time his head seemed very large. The doctor showed me the pattern of growth for Ben's head on a chart and compared it against the "normal" pattern his head should have been following. All too obviously Ben's head did not confirm to the chart. My heart sank again. But then, the doctor smiled. "I've got good news. You've just got a big baby with a big head. He is absolutely fine." If the previous nine months had been the most horrible time of my life that day was one of my happiest ever. I've kept all the charts and details of Ben's head in case his own children (when they eventually arrive) have similar big heads. I wouldn't want him to go through the agony I did.'

'The possibility of having a baby that might not be 100 per cent is one that crossed my mind several times during all three of my pregnancies,' Penny says. 'In my clinical experience, it is something that all pregnant mothers worry about at some stage. It isn't necessarily rational, but I clearly remember episodes that usually lasted for a few days where I'd torture myself with the "what if" questions.'

When it comes to having babies, female doctors are no different from other women. 'There are times when being a doctor is a double-edged sword,' Penny says. 'We know a lot but when it comes to childbirth we are the same as any other mother – wanting a perfect baby and heartbroken when something goes wrong. When Olivia, my third child was born, they put her on my tummy and I looked at her beautiful face with such joy. She looked like a little possum with her wonderful big eyes but, when I reached down to pick her up and pass her to the nurse, I suddenly saw that her right leg was bent – a hideous deformed leg, bent back on itself from the knee in some sort of dislocated mess. I then realised that everyone else in the room looking on had already seen the leg, but had said nothing, waiting for me to notice. I cried out, "What's wrong with her leg?" The response makes me laugh – now. Chris, my wonderful obstetrician said, "Someone get a paediatrician," and my husband said, "And someone get a psychiatrist." (He knows me well.)

'Fortunately, a paediatrician did turn up promptly, with the diagnosis of a rare abnormality called "congenital dislocated knee", which occurs in only one in every 200 000 births. I was devastated. What did this mean? Would Olivia ever walk? Would she look normal? What else was wrong with her? I was reassured about the last of these questions by the paediatrician, who confirmed there and then that Olivia's leg was an isolated deformity. None the less, I was miserable. I didn't want to see anyone except my mother and my children. By the time they arrived I was sitting in a chair in the corner of the room, a pathetic sight, miserably holding my "deformed" baby.

'If I love my mother for anything, I love her most for how she was on that night. She barrelled into the room and said, "Show me this baby." I passed over the swaddled bundle. "Show me her leg," she commanded. I unwrapped Olivia. Mum looked for a moment, then turned to me with a bright face and said, "It's just bent! They can straighten it just like they do teeth. Now I could understand your being upset if she didn't have a leg but she does. It's just bent and they'll fix it. The problem with you is that you need a gin and tonic – it's been far too long since you've had one." With that she produced a large bottle of Gordon's gin, some Schweppes tonic and a couple of glasses.

'The physiotherapists did fix Olivia's leg – although it involved trekking out to the Children's Hospital every three days for fifteen months for repeat plastering – but they straightened it as my mother had said they would, and at age twelve Olivia now plays a great game of netball. I learnt some valuable lessons. I experienced first-hand just what it feels like when there is something wrong with your baby and that in a crisis, my mother, with her insight and her humour, is amazing.'

⌐

Before she had Sally, Carole always told people that if there were something major wrong with her baby she did not want to know about it and that they should just 'take it away'. Her attitude changed forever after her second daughter was born.

'After my experience with Sally, I'd take any baby, even one with no arms. Babies like mine are special people and they change your attitudes. I'm not a religious person but I thank God that she was given to me. Sally has an "old soul" as if she has been here before. Sally almost mothers me now. She says she knows best and she usually does.'

Carole had a normal pregnancy and birth and Sally, her second daughter, was a perfect-looking baby. She cuddled her briefly before the baby was taken away to be examined, a routine procedure. 'But they didn't bring her back because she had started to go blue. The next time I saw her, about an hour later, she was in a humidicrib and wrapped in foil. A nurse wheeled her in for me to quickly see her while an ambulance stood by ready to take her to the Children's Hospital. I was still dazed from the birth but I was told there was a problem with her heart.

'All I could think about was that she needed that first special breast milk – the colostrum. So six hours later, my husband drove me from the maternity hospital to the Children's Hospital so I could express milk. Sally was in Intensive Care – "plugged in" to a million lines and tubes. A paediatrician tried to explain the problem. She had "transposition of the great vessels", a life-threatening "plumbing problem" affecting the way blood enters and leaves the heart. I couldn't really take in what he was saying.

'I went back to my maternity hospital and it started to hit me. I was in a room on my own and my baby was in neonatal intensive care in another hospital. I kept pacing the corridors and asking for sleeping tablets. I said to the nurses, "I'm at risk here . . . I have a precious baby, with a serious medical problem. I'm distraught. I don't want to go on. I need someone to help *me* too."'

Our overstretched health system badly neglects the mothers in these situations. While the high-tech care of baby Sally was first-class, her mother was crying out for treatment of a different nature. Carole even used the words, 'I'm at risk'. 'Those words always ring alarm bells for me as a GP,' Penny says. 'Mothers in these situations are at great danger of developing post-natal depression. They need counselling and de-briefing, and support with their shock and grieving, but all too often their needs are overlooked.'

'The doctors did a stop-gap procedure to stabilise Sally and said that we would have to wait until she was nine months old when her heart would be big enough to allow them to operate. We took her home but those nine months were hell. She took only breast milk, looked unwell because she was bloated and a bad colour, and she didn't smile. It seemed to me as if my baby was slowly dying before my very eyes.

'I felt incredibly guilty. I thought it was my fault. I'd taken some tablets for nausea early in my pregnancy and I was sure they must have caused the problem. I wanted it to be my fault. A university researcher who was doing a study on babies with serious heart problems and how their mothers dealt with them came to interview me, and I kept telling her, "It has to be my fault – something I ate – something I did." She kept trying to reassure me that Sally's condition had nothing to do with me. I remember her saying it was a miracle that so many babies are born normally.

'Sally had her operation at nine months. I looked after her so carefully, I did everything by the book and when I took her for her check-up six months later I thought I'd get a gold star, but the news wasn't good. The doctor said that her blood wasn't flowing properly and that Sally would need another operation. This was even worse than the first time and much more stressful because I really knew my baby now. She and I had bonded. Thankfully, this time the operation was successful. The relief was simply overwhelming. I cried. I laughed. I think I experienced just about every emotion but most of all an exhilarating feeling of relief!

'When Sally was growing up, I was over-the-top protective of her but I couldn't help myself. If she caught a cold, I was terrified. I always worried about her playing sport. I felt guilty that I was holding her back and turning her into a non-sporting person and although she is now twenty, I'm still overprotective of her. She started going to the gym recently and I worry about that despite the fact that she has come through all her check-ups with flying colours – but whenever I think about Sally's first eighteen months, I still cry.'

When things go wrong, most women have a terrible time struggling with conflicting feelings. On the one hand, a mother is looking forward to getting to know and love her new baby. On the other hand, there is a sense of confusion as those feelings become mixed up with ones of disappointment and hopelessness as the mother comes to terms with the fact that there is nothing she can do to change things. No mother likes to feel that powerless.

Jane knew her baby was different from the moment she was born. She was living with her husband, who was in the army, and two older children in a remote settlement at Beswick, 80 kilometres south-east of Katherine in the Northern Territory. A 'very rough midwife' delivered Sarah at the local hospital in Beswick. 'Although she suckled well right from the beginning I just knew she was different. Eventually I asked the doctors and nurses if she was a Down's baby but they all assured me there was nothing wrong with her.

'It wasn't until she was nine months old that I could get anyone to take my concerns seriously. A friend of mine who was a doctor was visiting and I asked her to examine Sarah saying, "If there is definitely something wrong with my baby I'll probably want to jump off a cliff with her." My friend confirmed my fears – Sarah did have Down syndrome but she told me that "some of these babies do very well" and so I didn't panic. In some ways, it was a relief to have someone agree with me, to know that I wasn't imagining it. I was never repulsed by Sarah – that was probably mother love – I just knew she wasn't like my other children had been as babies.'

Jane wanted to be 100 per cent sure, however, and so the family flew to Sydney to see a paediatrician. 'It was around the time when they were making a lot of discoveries about chromosomes. The doctor confirmed that Sarah had Down syndrome but said she was a mild case – a "mosaic", which meant not all the cells in her body were affected. The doctor then asked if he could show Sarah to his medical students. He took her from me and as the door to the lecture theatre was closing, I heard him say, "Now here's a lovely baby. I want you to tell me what's wrong with her."' Even though it took place so long ago, Jane sobbed as she remembered the events of that particular day.

'Bad news travels fast. I was staying with my mother in Sydney and all the family wanted to come and see us but I didn't want them to because I had this terrible protectiveness about her.' Jane was forty when she had Sarah and says, 'I did wonder if I'd been too old but I didn't feel guilty. When I later became pregnant again, I begged my doctor for an abortion but she wouldn't do it and I had the most hellishly worrying pregnancy, but my fourth child was normal.

'Although I was often anxious about Sarah she was a wonderful little baby. As she grew older, I used to get very angry with people who would stare at her and nudge each other. Schoolgirls would sometimes look at her and giggle and I'd feel like giving them a damn good kick in the behind. Once, outside a department store, a woman nudged her daughter to look at Sarah. I walked right over to her, stood in front of her and said, "You are so cruel."'

When Sarah was five, the family moved to Sydney permanently. 'We sent her to a special school that had only twelve pupils and she loved it. They taught her to read and write and when they tested her IQ told me she was in the high level for Down's children. She was such a happy child and gave us all great pleasure. My other children were always great with her. They loved Sarah and were never embarrassed. I explained to them right from the beginning what was wrong and treated her just as I did my other children. She had to toe the line and mind her manners.

'After she left her first special school, Sarah was home for about a year. I kept trying to get her into Inala, a day and residential special school for people like her, and eventually she was accepted as a day pupil. Some time later, my husband pressured me to see if Inala would accept her as a residential pupil. I felt guilty about doing this because my mother had always told me, "Never part with your children. You can't trust anyone else with them." However, I had become unwell and needed to have surgery and it became imperative that Sarah live-in. She loved it and was always so happy to go back to Inala after her weekend with us that I stopped feeling so guilty.'

Making difficult decisions is part and parcel of being a mother of a child with special needs. For instance, when Sarah started her periods they were heavy, painful and frequent. 'After a lot of soul-searching, we decided she should have a hysterectomy but the doctor only took her uterus and left her ovaries so her hormones would be normal.'

However, just like normal kids, children with Down syndrome not only have distinct personalities, they can also excel at various things, like sport. 'Sarah loves cricket and she used to surprise everyone when we played in the backyard – she was always hitting them for six. She wrote a letter to Steve Waugh when he captained the Australian Test Cricket team, and I included a note explaining Sarah had Down syndrome. Steve wrote her a note that said, "Sarah, we always need your support," and he included some photographs. It was the loveliest letter and she treasures it.'

There is an air of sadness about Jane – a gentle, kind woman – that is impossible not to notice. When she tells Sarah's story the tears are never far away. Now eighty-two, Jane's big fear concerns what will happen to Sarah when she is no longer here. Although only forty-two, it seems Sarah may be developing Alzheimer's. It is common for the condition to develop in Down's people when they are relatively young. 'Even though my other children always include her in family functions, I can't expect them to look after her when I am gone. I often cry about Sarah and worry desperately about her future.'

More than 300 babies are born annually in Australia with Down syndrome but statistics also show that 98 per cent of expectant mothers who receive a positive diagnosis for the syndrome terminate their pregnancies. The 'benefits' of pre-natal diagnosis have opened up a whole new Pandora's box of choices for mothers and while choice is a good thing, it doesn't necessarily make life any easier for a mother.

A woman's chance of giving birth to a child with Down syndrome increases with age. At thirty-five the risk is one in 400, but by forty it is one in 105. Other syndromes caused by similar chromosome abnormalities also increase with maternal age. With more women delaying child bearing – more than 12 per cent of Australian mothers are thirty-five or older when they have their first baby – and most electing to check for any chromosome abnormalities during their pregnancy, an increasing percentage of mothers-to-be will face the agonising decision of whether to continue or terminate an affected pregnancy.

Pregnant at thirty-seven, Rachel chose to have an amniocentesis. 'I didn't really think too much about the decision-making process I would have to go through if there was anything wrong. It was sort of like an automatic thing a mother has to do if she is a certain age and becomes pregnant. I assumed everything would be okay. I was far more interested in finding out what sex the baby was. When I got a phone call to come back in, I knew there was something seriously wrong. I rang my husband and he came with me. The news that I was carrying a baby who had Down syndrome was almost unbelievable. I already had two beautiful healthy children and there was no family history of the problem.

'It was such a difficult decision. I knew that some Down syndrome babies had happy productive lives but I was also aware that others have multiple associated problems, including intellectual impairment. As a health professional, I had seen these children. The decision was not immediate but eventually I decided not to continue with my pregnancy. My husband said he would support me either way but in my heart I felt that he wanted me to have a termination.

'Did I feel guilty? Yes – but it was so much more than that. It was the overwhelming sadness I felt. I'm glad now that I made the decision I did and perhaps I've rationalised away the guilt, but there will always be some sadness and some pain.'

Barbara's two sons are aged sixteen and fourteen. Her first son has been diagnosed with neurofibromatosis, a genetic disorder of the nervous system that causes tumours to form on the nerves anywhere in the body at any time. Her second son, who Barbara says causes her acute guilt, suffers from cerebral palsy. She remembers feeling 'fretful' all through her pregnancy with her second son. 'I don't know why. There was no good reason. I just had this constant feeling he was going to be a child about whom I would worry all my life.

'The doctors seemed to struggle to work out what was wrong with my baby. The eventual consensus was that if he did have anything wrong with him, he probably would have a hemiplegia – a weakness or paralysis on one side of the body that occurs when there is a disruption of blood flow to the brain, causing part of the brain to die. Once I got him home, I kept looking at him to see if he was moving both sides – all that sort of stuff – and he was. The doctors said, "We'll get him a bit of physio."

'Finally, two days before Christmas, I went and saw the paediatrician, and he told me my son had cerebral palsy. I knew he had been developing very slowly but premature babies are slower in development and because everything was moving equally on both sides, it hadn't occurred to me that he might have cerebral palsy. I can remember walking out of there thinking, "I have to work out a way that I can kill this child so that he doesn't have to live this life." I walked back to the car in tears, carrying him in his little capsule, trying to figure out how I could do it without being caught.

'The doctors had told me if I needed to speak to a social worker there would be someone at the hospital to talk to me. I rang the next morning, but because it was Christmas Eve, there was no one there.' (Once again, here was a mother in desperate need of professional counselling. At least in this case the need was recognised, but our health system still failed to provide an essential service for her.) 'Then my husband's parents arrived for Christmas. We decided we wouldn't tell them so that we didn't trash Christmas and waited until the day before they went home to break the news. They were in such shock they couldn't say anything.

'Thinking back now, finding out about my son was probably the worst moment of my life. I did it on my own, my husband wasn't there – bloody husbands are never there when you want them. I mean shit happens and they are *never* there. It had never occurred to me that I would have children with anything wrong with them. When we were getting our heads around our second baby having cerebral palsy we had no idea that our first would end up having neurofibromatosis. I feel guilty, we both feel guilty that this has happened to him. There is no family history of it. We all have so many expectations for our children. We expect them to grow up, to be successful, to be healthy and well, and then when it doesn't happen it's a real kick in the groin.

'And even if you manage to drag yourself out of the guilt quagmire, there are plenty of people who would like to push you back into it. My mother-in-law always makes me feel guilty. In the beginning, she wouldn't tell her friends that her grandson had cerebral palsy because he was the less-than-perfect grandchild. She used to be embarrassed to walk along the street with us if we were letting him try to walk, because his little legs would go everywhere and he looked a bit odd. She still calls him a spastic.

'There have been many times when we've come home after being out in the evening and we've known that a babysitter hasn't looked after our younger son properly; that he hasn't been given anything to eat or drink or that he has just been left with the same video running for three or four hours. It makes me feel dreadful and so guilty for having gone out. After I'd had my first son, the aim of having a second child was so that he would have a sibling with whom to enjoy all those things children do together when growing up. I haven't quite given him that and I agonise over that too. I suppose guilt and agonising are the same.

'But you know, my kids are still the best things that have happened to me! My little guys are my buddies and they have added the most extraordinary perspective to my life.'

5

When mothers go out to work

Most epidemics begin when something disturbs the status quo. A virus can lie dormant for many years until, without warning, some outside factor sets off a reaction, causing it to spread. Similarly, women might have gone on quietly living with guilt – accepting that it was caused primarily by a lack of confidence in their mothering skills – had it not been for the impact of Women's Liberation. Nothing, including guilt, has been the same ever since. Motherguilt has grown to plague proportions and many women believe the condition is incurable.

They are wrong! Motherguilt can be treated but first it is necessary to understand what causes it to happen. Being a mother is, and always will be, a full-time job, but when women enthusiastically heeded liberation's clarion call they embraced the idea of taking on a second full-time job without thinking through the consequences. Working was fun and stimulating and seen as an adventure. Earning money and being financially independent gave women a sense of freedom. Even though their husbands may have been good providers, many women had worked before marriage and motherhood and missed having money of their own.

Being a pioneer was not without its challenges however, and working mothers had their fair share of critics, many of them other women. Their presence in the workforce was often resented, especially in areas considered 'the preserve of men' – like the board-room for instance. But women persevered and, unlike men, did not just pay lip service to the idea of equality; they believed in it passion-ately. They liked using their brains, learning new skills, making a contribution and being seen as a person, not just someone's mum.

That is not to say they did not enjoy or did not want to be mothers. Perish the thought! These revolutionary women never thought of *not* having children – although it could be argued they did not think through well enough how having a mother in the workforce might affect children. They never would have envisaged an Australia where childlessness was becoming normal for many working women. Yet in 2004 almost one in four women is childless, and figures released by the Australian Bureau of Statistics predict that within seventeen years childless couples will become the aver-age Australian family. The nation's fertility rate looks doomed. Would this sorry state of affairs have occurred if the workplace had been a more family-friendly place? Possibly not.

If only those early pioneers had asked for help things might have turned out very differently for mothers in today's workforce. But when it did finally dawn on them that their workload was too heavy, what did the libbers do? They took on yet another role – that of Superwoman! How could they hope to be considered as equals to men in the workplace if they asked for any kind of special consid-eration to accommodate their family obligations? So, rather than be honest about the stresses and guilt their multiple roles were causing them, women hid behind the façade of being seen to be in control. They were models of perfection!

The subterfuge still persists today as women continue to

struggle to find the best way to balance work and family commitments while still not admitting the truth, fearing it might work against them as they will be seen as not being able to manage. Women rarely talk about the one issue that relentlessly eats away at them: the lack of time and energy that makes it so hard for them to simultaneously juggle work and motherhood. How can they be expected to cope with work as well as cook, clean, find daycare, stay home when a child is sick, help with the homework, get involved in school activities, teach their children right from wrong, play with them and enjoy their company?

Just about all working mothers are short on time and the demands of today's global world mean that many women are working even longer hours then their mothers did. Modern forms of communication, like mobile phones and email, mean that work is a constant companion. Working mothers lead busy, busy lives and in order to get everything done they have to keep to a tight schedule – well, they try but life is never that predictable and neither are children! When things do not go to plan, there is occasionally chaos, often stress and always guilt.

'Sometimes I think I am going nuts but I just can't stop,' says Catherine Rodgers, who has a senior management position with a large multinational food company. 'My work gives me a real buzz – but my kids give me a buzz too and I wouldn't want to be without them. However, I often wish there were more hours in the day because there is so much to do.

'Some stay-at-home mothers at my kids' school have accused me of sacrificing the welfare of my kids for my ambitions. They didn't say this to my face but to a couple of my friends who of course told me. I think this is unfair and judgemental. How the hell would they know the kind of mother I am? I think I'm a good one and I take parenting seriously. I do feel constantly tired, something I feel a bit guilty about because I worry that I'm too tired to really enjoy my children but I do my best to give them quality time.

'On those rare nights when I watch TV I fall asleep within seconds of sitting down but as a rule, once the kids are in bed, I pull out my laptop and start talking to my overseas colleagues by email. I often don't go to bed until late and, most nights, get by with about five or six hours' sleep. My husband is the same but we're happy and neither of us wants to change the way we live. My husband says the kids benefit from my working because I'm a positive role model for them!'

'I've never felt I couldn't have it all because having grown up in the Superwoman era I have been conditioned not to feel guilty, but, even so, I do think about work versus baby all the time,' publicist Sally Burleigh says. 'When I was home on maternity leave, I told myself I had to go back to work, that I couldn't be a stay-at-home mum full-time. Although I love my job and my success, there are times when I sit in my office and wonder what I'd be doing if I were at home with Scarlett . . . Probably laughing and giggling. But I really do enjoy my work and sometimes I just can't stop . . . My guilt is not about working but about not being with her every day. No matter what you do, it's simply that.

'My husband Steve was very supportive about me returning to work. Mind you, I only went back three days to begin with and I'd go home to breastfeed and express milk when I couldn't be there. I worked my butt off to make sure Scarlett wasn't deprived (except of me). He says I'm a wonderful mother and he is proud of what I've achieved as a mum and a businesswoman.'

How times have changed. June Dally Watkins had just started her well-known school of deportment and modelling agency when she married John Clifford in 1952. When she fell pregnant, she kept working. 'Going to meetings pregnant back in the mid-1950s was considered not "quite" polite. It wasn't *decent* to be a working mother.' After the birth of her children (she has four) June used to receive anonymous phone calls saying, 'Go home to your children. You are neglecting them. They are deprived. You are a bad mother.' How did a 1950s husband cope with a working wife? 'My husband felt he was badly done by. He was the only man whose wife was working and I think he felt very sorry for himself. His male friends gave him a hard time as well. "Why do you stand for it?" "Why don't you make her stay at home?"'

The working mother of 2004 would treat such a suggestion with the disdain it deserves. Mindi Chisholm, a 31-year-old advertising executive in Sydney's western suburbs, says that being a successful businessperson makes her a successful mother. 'I'd go stir-crazy if I was at home all the time. Three weeks at home with the kids over Christmas was enough for me. I am a driven, career-focused person and I enjoy what I do. Sometimes I do think it would be nice to have a coffee with my friends, most of whom are stay-at-home mums, and chat with them with no time restraints but the urge is not strong enough. If I thought my kids were suffering anxiety problems because I worked I would probably reconsider.'

Lately, three-year-old Zara has begun telling her mother, 'I don't want you to go to work.' Mindi has handled this by teaching her daughter the following question and answer routine:

'Why does Mummy go to work?'

'To make money.'

'Why does Mummy have to make money?'

'So we can shop.'

Other working mothers use similar tactics. When Veronica Wheeler's youngsters, aged eight and six, tell her they don't want her to go to work, 'I explain to them that if Mummy didn't work we wouldn't have the money to do the things we like, such as going on holidays and to the movies.' No amount of justification, however, can stop the guilt Veronica feels when her kids tug at her emotions this way. 'It's as if someone has put their hand inside my chest and ripped out my heart. I often drive down the street with tears in my eyes. I worry that when they grow up the kids will say, "Oh Mum, she just got into the car every day and drove off."'

≈

One of the big differences between today's working mums and the early women's libbers is that although many of the latter had a job before they married, they did not have a career plan. Their 'career' was going to be motherhood. When they did exercise their choices, their children were older or at least at school and mothers were happy to have any kind of job to earn a bit of money they could spend any way they chose. But these days work is more demanding, women determine their career paths when they are at school and then apply themselves diligently to achieve their goals – whatever it takes. Finding a partner and having a baby is part of their plan, although as their career progresses, many women are secretly wondering how they will ever find the time to cram kids into their jam-packed timetable.

But somehow they do and most of them make the decision about returning to work before their baby is born. After giving birth however, the depth of their maternal feelings stirs their emotions in a way they never thought possible. The joy and wonderment of mother love, the smell of a baby after bathtime, the softness of its skin, the captivating first smiles – these are things a woman never forgets, and most mothers suffer immense guilt at the thought of not being there for their child. They have to wrench themselves from the nursery and put themselves back into their work role while all the time their instincts are pulling them in the other direction.

When her son was six weeks old, Carla Zampatti realised she didn't want to go back to work. 'I think it was a biological reaction – nature says to a mother this is a new human being and you have to look after it – but my career was important to me.' So Carla fought against her natural instincts and her guilt, and hired a nanny.

'When I started work again I felt terrible,' Sally Burleigh says. 'While I was on maternity leave there was a part of me that missed work but when I got back to the office, all I could think was, "Oh my God, I'm not at home with my baby."'

Women bury these feelings and Motherguilt just nibbles away. Stay-at-home mums rub the guilt in further by saying things like, 'If I wanted other people to raise my kids I would not have had them.' They often condemn women who work, labelling them as 'bad' mothers. Who needs this? A working mother has enough on her plate but never too much to divert her from her objective of being a good mother.

However, working mothers in turn are equally critical of stay-at-home mums, claiming that such women have no idea of what being busy is really like and wondering how they can justify doing so 'little' with their lives. Sally Burleigh admits to often feeling guilty about the negative thoughts she has about women who stay at home. *Why* are women so judgemental about each other? What ever happened to the belief that women were entitled to make choices and exercise them? Why would any woman want to inflict guilt on other women?

Rebecca Wilson says women need to be more like men, who 'do not pass judgement on each other the way we do. I found being home all day with a baby shockingly tedious. I'll never forget my husband getting home from work one day and I was in my flannelette pyjamas in the bathtub scrubbing between the tiles with a toothbrush and I said, "I need to go back to work!"'

Even when their job gives them enormous satisfaction some women feel the need to almost apologise for liking what they do. Susan, a mother of four girls, has returned to midwifery one day a week but many of her female friends want to know why, telling her, 'You don't need the money and the pay is lousy.'

But why wouldn't a woman enjoy the stimulation that a job can bring? Today's woman is better educated then any generation before her and women outnumber men at just about all of Australia's major universities. They want to use their education. 'The career factor is an important issue for young women,' Carla Zampatti says. 'They are well educated and have skills that they want to use so they can be in control of their lives. The certainty of being able to look after yourself gives you a sense of independence. I always had that and it helped me deal with my guilt. If you are strongly independent you can control guilt because you can rationalise it.'

So why do some women feel they need to be apologetic about working? Could it be they worry they will be considered selfish and that they are just doing something for themselves? That cannot be the whole answer. Many women simply cannot afford not to work. They work for money, not satisfaction, because the cost of living, in particular housing, is so high in Australia. Families need the income that women earn. So does the Australian economy. If all mothers in Australia's workforce gave up their jobs tomorrow the economy would crumble.

But the strain and responsibility of caring for children plus holding down a job does not allow mothers much time for the joy of parenting. There are times when her life becomes so unbearable that a working mother is forced to take stock of her situation. In March 2002 Federal MP Jackie Kelly gave birth to her second child. Towards the end of her pregnancy, she decided to stand down as

Federal Minister for Sport and Tourism to spend more time with her family, although she remained in Parliament as Parliamentary Secretary to the Prime Minister. Incredibly, some women accused her of letting down the side. Jackie, they said, should have kept on being Superwoman.

'Those women have no idea what they're talking about,' Jackie says. 'My life might have looked good from the outside but the workload, the travel, early morning media interviews, the weeks being away from the family when I had to be Canberra – quite frankly my life was a mess. Just about everything I did made me feel guilty. I was always getting upset about trying to do everything perfectly. I was permanently tired too. Giving up being Tourism Minister was probably one of the best decisions I ever made and if I hadn't I'd probably be divorced by now.

'When you're a politician there's always something to take up your time. You can jam your diary full and always be seen to be doing something. Your personal life is just so tragic. My husband and I skied every year before we got married but we haven't been skiing since I entered Parliament.

'Gary and I have had some tense moments. One time he said to me, "I really don't mind coming behind the Prime Minister and the national netball finals but when I am actually second to a boy scouts meeting or the girl guides I have a problem here. Where do I fit into your priorities?" He has never asked me to give up my career but he has put alternatives to me. "You can do A, and these will be the consequences, or you can do B and here are the options, but I am certainly not putting up with this."

'Motherhood is just another name for guilt,' Jackie says. 'You saddle on this big load of guilt and walk around with it for the rest of your life. There have been plenty of times when I have been at the end of a phone line distressed about missing something that Gary and the kids were doing. Each time I come back from

Canberra my son has grown and changed in some way and I missed it. Everything makes me feel guilty, leaving in the morning, the way my kids can howl . . . Having been through this with my daughter, I thought I'd be fine with my son. But even though you are an experienced mother, kids get quite smart at twisting the knife and you do have a weep as you drive down the street.'

Occasionally Jackie thinks her behaviour might qualify her for a bad mother award. 'When the kids wake in the middle of the night they never ask for Dad, it's always Mum. Usually I drive to Canberra on Monday morning, but sometimes I just *have* to get a good night's sleep. I don't want to be woken at 2 a.m. So I say to Gary, "I'm going to Canberra Sunday night, darling, I have something on."'

It is not uncommon to hear a working mother wistfully say she wished she had a wife to help her cope. The authors believe that one of the reasons men do not suffer from guilt is because they have partners who make their lives easier for them. Men are not required to learn how to juggle because women do it for them. Some women pay a high price psychologically because of their timetable lives. Others, like Jean Kittson, get tired of bearing the load and are brave enough to do something about it.

When she was working full-time, comedian Jean found 'motherhood really difficult. All the other mothers seemed to be able to do it so I told myself that if I was finding it hard to cope, it was only because I hadn't organised myself properly.' Jean was back at work within a month of the birth of her first daughter, Victoria. 'I was writing and working extremely long hours. By the time, she was six months I was performing on stage. I also felt guilty because Victoria wouldn't sleep. She had colic, which made me anxious. I was in Brisbane for some gala performance when she was about seven months. I had her with me in my dressing room. Ita was on the same bill and asked me now much Victoria weighed and I didn't know! I thought Ita looked horrified. Her reaction added to my guilt, layer upon layer.

'My mother's disapproval didn't help things. She didn't like me working, "dragging Victoria into film studios, television studios, on and off planes to strange hotels". When I was at home I'd come in from work and Victoria wouldn't have settled so I would play with her and then put her to bed but she still wouldn't go to sleep. My anxiety levels would start to rise because I had deadlines, things I had to write for the next day and I had to learn my lines. Then I'd start worrying about Victoria not sleeping and she would get more and more worked up. I would lie in bed with her, hugging her, almost begging her, "Go to sleep, please . . ."'

Jean soldiered on but all the while 'this whole guilt thing was building up'. By the time Victoria started school Jean was doing breakfast radio. 'I wasn't able to see her off to school on her first day. Patrick took her. He was always good at helping and never made me feel guilty. I did it to myself. I was doing all right at work but I was slowly realising that I was not doing a very good job as a mother.'

Everything came to a head when Jean had a miscarriage, a tragedy that also put her life at risk. 'Getting over that and still wanting to have another child, I looked at the work I was doing and told myself I wasn't exactly finding a cure for cancer! I was putting all this effort into having children but not putting the effort into bringing them up. I was finding it impossible to live with the guilt of thinking that I didn't know what was going on with my child all the time and that perhaps in some way I was disadvantaging my daughter.

'Life changed a lot after I had Charlie. It took me six and a half years to get pregnant with her. I gave up breakfast radio – a decision that gave me enormous relief. It might make me feel fantastic about myself to give people a few laughs, but the real value I can contribute as a person and as a woman is helping my children achieve their potential. I work part-time now. I feel I do that well and that I'm being a really good mother. I do reading at school. I've done a few canteen jobs – the kids love me doing the canteen. I have time to look at the school newsletter so they hardly ever miss major happenings and they usually have the right gear for PE. I am getting to know the other mothers and we have a good support network. I rarely talk to the mothers who have jobs because they are all so busy and simply rush in and out.'

Part-time work suits a lot of mothers. *Sydney Morning Herald* journalist Adele Horin finds it allows her to get the balance right. She works four days a week. 'Mondays off started as a day for the children but when they started school I turned it into a day for me. It's the only way I can have some time for me because with two sports mad boys who are also keen on music, weekends are totally taken up with soccer, music lessons, shopping, cooking and so on.'

Company director Carolyn Hewson prefers part-time work because it gives her the opportunity to sometimes pick her daughter up from school or perhaps sit on the beach with her. But that doesn't stop her from worrying about the effect her working might have on her daughter. 'Every six months or so I ask her, "Darling, when you are older do you think you will work?" She always says yes. Then I ask, "Full-time or part-time?" Her reply never changes. "Part-time, just like you do." I think to myself, okay it can't be too bad for her. I work because I love it, because it gives me those senses of satisfaction, fulfilment and self-esteem. If I were in a job I hated she might react in a different way but Susannah sees me happily going off to work so she wants to do the same.'

She hates seeing her mum in work clothes though. 'Susannah prefers me to wear jeans and T-shirts because she thinks that is young and dynamic rather than old and tired.' Carolyn was forty when her daughter was born after eight years of trying to conceive and one miscarriage. 'I'm conscious of the fact that Susannah would prefer to have a younger mother. She often asks me, "How old will you be when I am twenty . . . When I am thirty?" and "How long are you going to live, Mum?"'

⁓

Sometimes in their haste to get through all of the things they have to do, working mothers forget some of the most important things in life – like living, for instance. Society not only puts a lot of pressures on working mums, but women put unrealistic pressures on themselves as well. Mothers do not have to be perfect, good enough will do – but that is so much easier to say than to remember.

Johanna Griggs often castigates herself for not feeling guilty about being away from her two boys when she is working. 'I love what I do and when I covered the Melbourne Cup for the Seven Network I had the time of my life, but then I thought this is *not* how a responsible mother should be feeling when she is away from her children for seven days. Even though I spoke to them every day, knew exactly what was going on in their lives and had organised care, food and all those sorts of things I still ticked myself off.' Why? Motherguilt is never rational.

As Editor-in-Chief of *The Australian Women's Weekly* Deborah Thomas has a job that she loves. Now forty-eight, she says two-year-old Oscar changed her life completely. 'I used to be very career obsessed and I would obsess about things when there was probably no need to do so. I now have a much clearer view of what life is and what it should be. Oscar has brought such joy into my life . . . It's extraordinary. The most positive aspect of having a baby later in life is that obviously you're more secure in your job and more financially secure. I do feel guilty that I work five days a week, so I make sure that weekends are totally devoted to Oscar. I tell myself it's quality rather than quantity but as time goes by it gets more difficult to say goodbye every morning.'

Sometimes women get so preoccupied with the job at hand they forget everything else. Amanda's job at one of Australia's major teaching hospitals gave her so much pleasure that she was often late picking up her daughter from kindergarten. 'I would become so engrossed in projects or meetings with people that I found it difficult to just drop everything ... Then I'd look at the time, panic, rush out of the hospital and not be able to remember where I'd parked the car! My major guilt is not being on time to collect my daughter. We adopted her and she has always been insecure and I worry that I might have contributed to this, that when I was late she might have thought I wasn't coming at all, as if in some way I'd abandoned her.'

Carla Zampatti remembers being late for parents' day. 'On one occasion I forgot altogether and received a call from the school and I did feel terribly guilty at missing out.' But what about her husband John Spender, who was in Federal politics? He must have failed to attend many a school function? Did he ever feel guilty? 'I don't think any men feel guilty,' Carla says. 'Women are programmed to believe that they are the responsible people for children and men believe that it is the mother's role to look after children. The male is the breadwinner; the woman is the nurturer. It is an evolutionary thing but I think this is changing. For instance, my son took time off when his first child was born.'

Occasionally exhaustion can land a woman in a terrible predicament. After one arduous shift at SBS television, journalist Rebecca Le

Tourneau fell asleep and forgot to pick up her kids. 'The childcare people threatened to take the children to the police if it happened again. I was devastated.'

'When both my kids were little and I was running *The Australian Women's Weekly* and also responsible for several other magazine titles, I sometimes got up in the morning feeling anything but bright-eyed and bushy-tailed,' Ita says. 'As I made the bed, I would count the hours before I would be home and able to get back into it again. Occasionally, if I had an evening function with lots of speeches to attend, or a first night at the theatre, I would take No Doze tablets to make sure I stayed awake. It never crossed my mind to tell anyone how tired I was. I used to hum that damn Helen Reddy song . . . "I am woman, I can do anything" . . . I was in full Superwoman mode!'

Weariness often means that working mums have a short fuse. Federal Sex Discrimination Commissioner Pru Goward, mother of three daughters, says, 'I had a terrible temper, which used to explode quite often because work-wise I was so professionally stretched. There is only two years between the two older girls and they fought like you wouldn't believe. I always had ten things going on in my mind. I might have had a press secretary blow up at me, that kind of thing, I'd get home, one of the children would ask for something, and I'd snap. I was always impatient. "Get out of the car now. Do it now. Why haven't you made your bed?" I still do feel guilty about the way I was.'

Working mums usually yell because they are scared all is not well with their children. 'My housekeeper rang me at the office one afternoon to say that when she went to my son's school to pick him up, he was not in his usual spot and that an hour later Ben had still not arrived home,' Ita says. 'All sorts of terrible things flashed through my mind, even that he might have been kidnapped. I dropped everything and tore home only to find that he had walked in a few minutes ahead of me. "Where the hell have you been?" I said angrily. He muttered something about going to one of the other boy's home – something that was forbidden without my permission. I was furious but only because I was petrified something had happened to him. I yelled at Ben, "You know the rules, don't ever do that again." I went on and on and then ordered him to go to his room. As Ben left the dog got up and slunk out of the kitchen with its tail between its legs. It was such an abject sight that I wanted to laugh but I couldn't – I was still worried about all the possibilities of what might have happened to Ben and the knowledge that it would have been my fault because I was at work.'

Geraldine Doogue's nineteen-year-old daughter unexpectedly pushed her mother's guilt button in 2003 when she was studying for her university exams and Geraldine was busy preparing material for ABC-TV's religious program *Compass*, which she hosts. 'I went overseas to do some filming, something I hadn't had to do before. I was away for three weeks and although I came back in the middle of filming to make sure everything was okay on the home front my daughter found my absence tough going and confronted me. When she said, "I've always had to slot in, Mum!" I was shocked. The idea of my slotting my child into my timetable horrified me. Then she challenged me further by asking, "Do you like living like this, Mum? Is this what I am in apprenticeship for?"

'I was in a bit of a mess for the next two weeks until we had a big conversation about it. All sorts of doubts went through my mind. Had I achieved at her expense? Had I sold her short? I wouldn't intentionally let her down for anything. Yes, I have asked a lot of her and in some ways, she has been my rock. I think I've given back but *have* I sufficiently? I went through an entire self-conversation. Intellectually, I understood what she was doing – she had been through a break-up with her boyfriend and was in the process of re-positioning herself. I know she didn't want to make

me feel guilty but she was saying, "I want more from you, Mum."
It was really confronting.

'Would I do some things differently if I had my chance
over again? In some ways, yes, but I know I've contributed to the
family through my career. I am too busy. I don't live a life of balance. I try. I do the best I can. Some people might think that's not
a good enough answer. Maybe it isn't, but my career has been very
good for me and I hope it has been a reasonable trade off for my
family.'

'I've found that when women give men the opportunity to look after kids
without us being around, men do it well,' says swimming champion
Lisa Curry Kenny. 'I was wracked with guilt when I was training when my three children were younger because I felt like I was
neglecting them. Then I realised that between 4.30 a.m. and 7 a.m.
when I was training, the kids didn't even know I was gone – they
weren't awake!'

Lisa talked things through with her husband. 'I told him,
"I'm not only a mother, not just a wife, I am a person as well. I like
to go out and do what I want to do. I want to see my friends. I don't
want to be caught in the mother-who-stays-at-home-and-does-
everything routine." Being a mother and wife is just half the story;
the husband is the other half. Grant picks up the kids from school,
cooks, does his own ironing – I have never done his ironing. I take
out the garbage, he does the cooking; we share things.'

Mindi Chisholm agrees. 'I hear so many women, especially
stay-at-home mums, say how little their husbands do. We have a
good marriage because my husband is so willing. Zack appreciates
that I work full-time and shares the load. He puts on the washing
and does the cooking.'

'Being a working mother is a positive in that it makes your children independent and able to cope with other people,' Mindi says. 'My children have seen that if they want to achieve, it is necessary to work hard and apply themselves. What children learn from their working mothers is a discipline of application. Guilt often works against a woman's best interests. I never thought that just being a mother was enough for me. I made the choice to work and sometimes I had to compromise, but I didn't want to be a martyr and feel that I had wasted my life. Even though a woman is a mother she is still an individual and she should never be made to feel guilty about wanting to keep that individuality.'

Sally Burleigh accepts that she might always battle her guilt feelings, 'but if I didn't work I'd feel guilt-ridden about not contributing financially to Scarlett's future and perhaps even worse that I wasn't doing the right thing by myself and the goals I want to achieve in life. I hope the example I've set will encourage Scarlett when she grows up to explore every opportunity, to follow the directions in life that suit her – and only her. And that she has a partner who treats her with respect and true love, happy to share the load without the added backpack of guilt.' Go Scarlett!

6

The agony and ecstasy of childcare

Whenever mothers are asked to talk about the things that most concern them, childcare almost always comes out on top. This is particularly true for full-time working mums, who complain that the demands on them are much greater than for men who work full-time. Many of these working mothers are wondering if this is as good as it gets, with 20 per cent of them claiming that parenting is more work than pleasure – compared with 15 per cent of fathers. The situation is so grim that many working women, who once happily would have said they were going to have children, are now saying they no longer intend to do so because it is just too damned hard.

A working mother is often dead on her feet from exhaustion from trying to 'do it all'. The family demands a great deal from her and so does her boss. No matter how competent and organised they may be, few women can hope to please two masters on a never-ending basis while trying to snatch some kind of a life of their own. It is an impossible dream. Wherever mothers are – whether in the paid workforce or in the home – they all need to be able to use childcare at some time or another; but for the working woman easily accessible and affordable childcare is imperative.

'It is devastating for a woman with children to admit that she finds no joy in being a mother,' says Federal Sex Discrimination Commissioner Pru Goward. 'It is not all that unexpected though because not only is there no infrastructure to support working mothers, but childcare provisions have lagged behind women's gains in the workplace.'

ACTU President Sharan Burrow believes, 'Childcare is the issue set to explode across Australia as families become increasingly anxious about balancing work and family and making ends meet. With 57 per cent of women returning to the workforce by the time a child is in its second year and 68 per cent by the time their child turns three, up to one million children will require childcare for some period of time before they go to primary school.' Conservative estimates put the national shortfall of childcare places at about 300 000.

Childcare is also expensive. In her book *The End of Equality: Work, Babies and Women's Choices in 21st Century Australia*, published in 2003, Anne Summers says, 'The cost of care is out of the reach of most families. Formal childcare, which costs an average of $50 a day, has become something only well-off families can afford. Most parents don't have that kind of money and consequently they have to rely on their families to help them look after their kids or arrange their working lives so that one parent is always at home. As a result couples rarely see each other and their relationships are under stress.'

Mindi Chisholm's long daycare in Sydney's western suburbs costs her $120 a day in 2004. Paula pays $58 a day with meals provided at the daycare centre her four-year-old attends. A professional mother, who prefers to remain anonymous and lives in Sydney with her three children under the age of four, estimates she pays $38 000 a year for a variety of care for her children that includes a part-time nanny, family daycare and pre-school.

'I know I wouldn't be able to work like I do,' says Leanne, who works in banking administration, 'if I didn't have support systems in place – friends, families, pre-school, daycare – and it costs a lot of money. For a professional woman on my salary my care arrangements cost me one week out of a month's salary, so the financial gain for me is greater than the cost. If a woman isn't well paid I don't think it's worth her while to work when her children are little.'

'You'll either forfeit the years of your working life to bring up your children – because you want to do that or you can afford to – or if you go out into the workforce, you'll sacrifice your children because somebody else will be bringing them up, requiring you to shell out a great deal of money from your salary because you will be paying somebody else to look after them,' says Sally Loane. 'I've paid for a nanny for the last eleven years because that's the way we've decided to do it as a family.'

However, the decreased time working mothers spend with their children could be having unwelcome consequences. The proportion of children who are overweight in Australia has increased noticeably in the last thirty years and could be linked to maternal employment. It might be coincidental but, on the other hand, there is plenty of evidence showing Australia's eating habits have changed since mothers joined the workforce. These women are strapped for time and their jam-packed schedules allow little time to shop for food let alone cook nutritious meals. Instead, they rely on prepared and fast foods that are often high in calories.

Even traditional family mealtimes have changed for the worse. In most Australian households a family meal is served only three nights a week. One in ten families never eats an evening meal with all household members present, while one in five families eats their dinner in front of the television every night. A couple of years ago Jennifer, a friend of Ita's, was working as a waitress in rural Victoria at an accommodation house that specialised in catering to bus groups. 'One winter we had a bus load of youngsters from one of the inner suburbs of Melbourne come in. They all found it difficult to actually sit at a table for their meals as they were used to eating off their laps in front of the TV. One girl aged about ten stopped me as I walked behind her chair. She had her knife and fork grasped in a fist in both hands and asked me how to use them.'

This kind of eating has produced a generation of kids who seem unable to go to the movies or watch a sporting match without at the same time eating some kind of junk food washed down by huge cardboard cups of fizzy soft drinks. Children who are in childcare centres follow an eating routine dictated by the centre's timetable, which means they no longer rely on natural indications of hunger. Because their mothers are at work many older children are at home on their own after school and, as all parents know, unsupervised children usually make poor nutritional choices for snacks and meals.

What all this means is that mothers need help. If they have to work – and many do for economic reasons discussed elsewhere in this book – a realistic assessment of the needs of children of working mothers, and fathers, must be undertaken. Perhaps consideration needs to be given to the introduction of daily free milk (this was once the norm) and hot main meals in the middle of the day for all school children. Such a course of action would not be without a cost, but the long-term savings to Australia's future health bill would justify the expense.

'The signs of children not being cared for well enough are evident,' Pru Goward says. 'High obesity rates in Australia's children have resulted in an increase in the incidence of diabetes and also heart disease in children, some as young as six. These are all diet-related problems.' In 2004, doctors at Sydney's Royal Prince Alfred Hospital reported they were seeing children who by the age of ten have damaged blood vessels normally seen in heavy smokers or people with really high cholesterol levels. Failure to take positive action to correct and curb the appetites of Australia's overweight and obese boys and girls means that ultimately these children will eat themselves to death – and that would give everyone, not just mothers, something to feel guilty about.

'Governments have been promising women affordable, quality childcare since my children were born and my daughter is now thirty-five,' Ita says. 'We are still waiting! Nothing will change until childcare stops being seen as "just a women's issue". Urgent action is required, otherwise not only will children continue to suffer but Australia's fertility rate will go on dropping. The nation needs women to have more children not just because their efforts are necessary for the efficient functioning of the workplace but because the money they pay in taxes contributes to the effective functioning of governments. Unless there is an increase in our population the viability of our workforce in the future will be under threat. It's already being affected by the ageing of our population, which in turn is putting economic pressure on governments to deliver the kinds of services that older Australians need.

'Governments have no money of their own. We taxpayers foot the bill for everything they do so "affordable" universal childcare would have to be paid for out of our taxes. But we need to find a solution rather than look for excuses not to find one. Governments might have to raise taxes to subsidise childcare or cut their spending elsewhere. Maybe even the sacred cow of sport would have to make do with a little less!

'I think big business needs to be involved in finding the solution too. The workplace has not kept up with the changes that have taken place in women's lives and, for the most part, still operates as though there was someone at home to look after the children. It is not in a company's best interests to have employees who feel constantly stretched to the limits as working mothers do. No employee is as productive as she could be under such circumstances and everyone gets sold short – the woman, her children and the company. I know some companies do provide childcare but there is still a long way to go and there needs to be a far greater national commitment.'

There is growing evidence that politicians are at last becoming aware of the need for action. With its return to power in the 2004 federal election, the Howard Government has comitted itself to spending $1 billion on providing a 30 per cent rebate for out-of-pocket childcare expenses. But even so, Anne Summers would like to see more leadership from Government. 'When Bob Hawke was Prime Minister he told corporate Australia that he wanted to find a way to improve women's equality in the workforce. They didn't like it but they fell into line and more opportunities became available for women. The same approach needs to be taken for women's employment today, and that includes childcare.'

'I never would have been able to carry out my high-powered job without the enlightened thinking of Kerry Packer, the boss of Australian Consolidated Press, the company that publishes *The Australian Women's Weekly*,' Ita says. 'He was way ahead of his time. Although when I first went back to work after having Kate I paid for her childcare, as I began to climb the corporate ladder Kerry adjusted my package to include firstly a live-in mothercraft nurse when Ben was born, and then, as he grew older, a live-in housekeeper. When women are negotiating their packages they should forget about the car and ask for a nanny.'

Australia remains among the few industrialised nations without any guaranteed paid leave from work at the time of childbirth. In 2003, the Federal Government rejected a proposal for paid maternity leave for all women put forward by Pru Goward as Federal Sex Discrimination Commissioner. Predictably, one of the reasons Prime Minister John Howard offered for its rejection was 'the cost to taxpayers'.

Pru Goward believes working women are 'Aussie battlers of a different sort', shouldering both immense responsibility and constant guilt. 'In some ways, the clash of work and family seems impossible to reconcile, the demands of each insatiable. Seventy per cent of Australian mothers work and many of them feel "blamed" for not spending enough time mothering and then guilty for leaving work early or requesting flexible work arrangements.'

Anne Summers believes childcare is more important than maternity leave. 'It is not just a feminist issue but a community one, just like education. We need to take responsibility for children the moment they are born. It's much harder for women in employment these days because work is more demanding and employment is tougher. Things used to be more casual. Now people are expected to work longer hours, too. Australians used to work a forty-hour week, now it's commonly fifty hours and for some even sixty.'

The majority of Australian workers are finding the increased pressure of longer working hours stressful because they have little time for other pursuits, but for a woman with children the hours are intolerable. Longer working hours are widespread in corporations, where workers are more or less expected to clock up long hours as 'proof' they are committed to their jobs and where meetings can be held at any time. 'A woman with a two-year-old finds it hard to get to an

8 a.m. meeting or stay back for one at 6 p.m. because she'll be late home to make dinner,' Anne says.

There are plenty of examples of unreasonable hours – in nursing and policing, for instance, women are expected to work twelve-hour shifts. Even supermarkets, where being a checkout operator was once a pleasant occupation, 'civilised' working hours are a thing of the past. Starting times can be as early as seven in the morning (when mums are usually yelling at the kids to get out of bed and get ready for school) and, because many supermarkets are open until late at night, knock-off time can be eleven or even midnight. There is a lot of rhetoric about family-friendly workplaces but as mothers (and fathers) know first-hand it often does not amount to much more than talk, which is why so many women opt for part-time work

'Family-friendly policies are a joke,' Helena says. In 2002 she worked as an area manager for one of the major banks. Her children were then five and two. She rarely finished work before seven at night and often got calls from the office at home as late as 9 p.m. 'When my kids were sick I was told, "Can't you organise something? Why don't you ring your mother? We pay you good money, you should be able to manage."'

Finding it impossible to handle the many demands on her, Helena asked her (female) boss if she could switch to part-time work until her children were older. 'I was told I could kiss my career goodbye and offered work as a part-time teller. When I pointed out that I was somewhat overqualified to be a teller my boss told me if I couldn't cope with my job I should leave. So I did.' Helena now works for a company that accepts that, while she loves her job, there are times when she will have to put her family first.

Much is made of the financial independence of a working mother, but more often than not, the financial benefits of working are gobbled

up by the expense of childcare and the fact that it is not tax deductible. Joy Smithers believes, 'Care should be free or at least tax deductible and everyone should have access to it.' However, despite the expense of childcare, many women are reluctant to reduce their working hours because there is a need to keep pace financially and, even if flexible options are available, many ambitious women fear they might harm their future prospects. In these days of redundancies and downsizing, job stability is a huge factor.

'A couple of years ago my husband was made redundant,' says Cathy, who has two children. 'It was twelve months before he got back into the workforce and we had to live meanly and leanly on what I earned, in order to pay the mortgage and the kids' school fees. If I hadn't been in full-time employment we never would have survived. I'd prefer to work part time but what if my husband lost his job again? I'm not prepared to risk our future by changing my employment conditions.'

Emma Macgregor works in the sales area of a major multinational company. 'Much as I love my son I like being "me" too. I'm expected to work until 7 p.m. most days and go in on Saturdays if the boss wants to see me, which happens quite often because she says it's the only time she has available. Paying someone else to care for my son does take a great slice of my salary but long term I am securing my future and helping my family. One stressful day, when my son was almost twelve months old, I did suggest to my husband that perhaps I should give up work and become a full-time mother. He immediately told me I'd be bored but I know he was really thinking of the money I bring home and how he'd miss it. To be honest, so would I.'

In her book, Anne Summers quotes 2002 figures showing that women held 70.5 per cent of all part-time jobs. Only 15 per cent of employed men are in part-time jobs, compared with 45 per cent of employed women. 'This is one of the highest rates of part-time employment in the world, and is double that of the United States. In other words, despite Australia priding itself on being an advanced modern country with great opportunities for women, when it comes to employment we are selling women short. Not all of these women are working part-time by choice. Around 22 per cent of women working part-time said they would prefer to work more hours with one-fifth wanting full-time work.'

When their children are small many mothers like working part-time because of the flexibility it provides. Thirty-six-year-old lawyer, Sharon Freund works three days full-time and spends two days at home with her three children under six. 'I love my job, I'm passionate about it. Every day is a challenge with the stress, the adrenaline and the brain drain but when I accomplish something (often it is simply crossing something off my "to do" list) there is that great sense of achievement. It doesn't mean I love my children any less. On my good and confident days I believe they get the best of me. I'm happy to have my quality time with them and then I am giving them my all without regrets with respect to my career. I have time to kick a ball in the park, tend to kids when they graze a knee, go to mothers' group, and the next day attend corporate meetings and help my clients when they have difficulties. I love both roles and despite the hectic pace and stress that goes with attempting to prioritise everything (which is sometimes like running two full-time jobs) I wouldn't change a thing.'

As a young intern, Penny worked 'appalling hours – all week, plus one night a week until midnight, and one weekend in three, all weekend continuously from Friday morning until Monday night! Trying to juggle the rostered hours was hard enough, but the added burden of actually having to try to leave on time because you had a babysitter who was expecting you – and feeling the resentment of colleagues because of it – eventually became just too much. I finally left for some sanity in part-time work in general practice, only to be described by one of my (male) specialist colleagues as a "shit-kicker GP playing at being a doctor".'

≈

Interestingly, Australian Bureau of Statistics figures show that Australia's low fertility rates tend to be associated with higher levels of education and involvement in the workforce. The 2002 HILDA (Household, Income and Labour Dynamics in Australia) survey reinforced this, finding that women who are less inclined to have children tend to be more career oriented and are more likely to be highly educated and employed full-time. They are also less likely to be in lower income brackets, are somewhat more satisfied with employment opportunities and place greater importance on employment and work. Between the ages of eighteen and fifty-five, 23 per cent of women who have postgraduate qualifications expect to remain childless compared with 9.5 per cent of women with Year Eleven education or less.

'Australia has a birth-rate crisis yet we are making it so difficult for women, particularly educated women, to have babies,' Anne Summers says. 'It is completely illogical. We should be doing everything in our power to encourage these educated, pay-earning women to have babies and to support them with special payments. It is much cheaper than bringing in people through immigration.'

Immigration is often mooted as the answer to Australia's need for more people, but most industrialised countries have ageing populations and lower fertility rates and they too are looking at immigration as the solution to their problems. How can we be sure people will want to migrate to Australia? They might prefer to immigrate to England, Japan or Germany.

≈

In the meantime the working mother does her best but childcare is fraught with emotional conflict that few mothers are able to escape.

Jean Kittson thought the nanny who looked after her daughter was terrific. 'She was with us for two years but when she left one of our elderly neighbours said to me, "I am so glad she is gone; she was horrible. Your daughter was always crying." "Oh my God," I said to her, "don't tell me that! Why didn't you tell me when she was here?" I felt sick, absolutely sick. Did I have one of those nannies who abused my daughter when I wasn't looking?'

The possibility that the person she has entrusted with the care of her child might turn out to be a disaster is never far from a working mother's mind. No matter how thoroughly she has checked out the carer or the care centre a mother knows that the best-laid plans can go wrong, and when they do, it is her fault. Nothing and no one can convince her otherwise. She has *failed* in her primary responsibility of making sure her child is well cared for – Motherguilt strikes again!

When Jean finally did manage to clamber out of her mountain of guilt, she sat quietly and thought things through. 'Most of the time I was at home when the nanny was there, working in another part of the house, on the computer. She was there to help with some of the everyday chores, make Victoria's meals, keep her company, that kind of thing. I would have noticed if something was wrong . . . *Surely* I would have . . .'

Paula's experience had a frightening twist to it. 'I had hired a woman through one of those mothers' help places that advertise all the time; she seemed charming and the children liked her. I presumed the agency had checked her references – a big mistake on my part. They assured me only the very best kind of women was on their books. I went off to my conference satisfied that the kids were in good hands. I had left my contact details and, on the second day, I got a call from a woman who introduced herself as my carer's daughter. Her mother, she said, was unfit to look after anybody's children, as she was an alcoholic. You can imagine how

I felt. Thank God the daughter was responsible – the poor thing was mortified about her mother. She arranged for her brother to take their mother home, rang the agency and ticked them off for hiring people without references while she waited until I had organised for my sister to come over. My husband was furious with me, I was angry with myself. I couldn't sleep for weeks. What if something had happened to the kids? It would have been *my* fault.'

In its 2002 Childcare Australia report, the Australian Bureau of Statistics noted that 1510500 children under the age of twelve (49 per cent) used some type of childcare. The numbers of children in care are high, but as Claudia Keech says, 'A lot of women have no choice but to hire a nanny, or put their children into a creche or childcare centre because they have to work and don't have a strong family support network, but it isn't easy.' After much agonising and indecision Bronwyn could not make up her mind which nanny to choose to look after her baby daughter four days a week. When her husband said, 'For Christ's sake darling, we're not hiring the CEO of BHP,' she burst into tears and said, 'I know, this job is much more important!'

Hiring a carer is often the first time a mother has ever employed anyone. 'I didn't know the first thing about employing people, especially a nanny,' Jean Kittson says. 'My first nanny let me do everything. While I did the chores, she would sit in the lounge room with Victoria. I was "allowed" to make the tea and after taking it in to her would withdraw. In the beginning, I had quite a turnover of help and minders because some of them just weren't suitable. It took me a while to get it right.'

Although Sally Burleigh is used to hiring people she still found employing the nanny the hardest day of her life. 'It took me all day Saturday to interview some twenty prospects and I spent the whole of Sunday in bed sobbing my eyes out. I felt awful. I had this fear of putting my baby in the hands of a complete stranger even though I was at home for the nanny's first week and so was Steve. I kept thinking, "I can't believe I am doing this."'

Now that Scarlett is older, Sally finds leaving her even harder. 'When I first went back to work she was sleeping most of the time. Now she is a real person and I've just had two weeks' holiday and spent every day with her. It tears me apart to walk out the door especially as she goes crazy when the nanny walks in the door. I know she is missing me. I want her to like the nanny but a little voice in me niggles, "But hang on, you don't have to like her *that* much."' Many other working mums know all about those particular pangs of jealousy . . .

Joy Smithers had a nanny twelve hours a day for her first child and hated it. 'I felt disconnected from my baby because all the decisions as to what she ate, when she slept, and what she wore were made by someone else. When she was three, I put her in full-time day care feeling very guilty – I don't know why I equate childcare centres with jail, but I do – but she loved it. My second daughter was in full-time day care from six months. It was always a wrench leaving her and if I picked her up after 4 p.m. I would have a mild form of separation anxiety. She is almost three now and it's a big comfort for me to know she has had a good sleep and a solid meal there, so if she is picky at dinnertime I don't have to worry. When I get very busy and the kids are the first ones in and the last ones out with my husband having to pick them up I always feel kind of emotionally bankrupt.'

Not all working mothers are as honest as Joy, probably because there are times when mothers have to accept less than the best kind of care for their children – a decision that naturally makes them feel guilty. There could be any number of reasons, such as budget restrictions or the scarcity of childcare places (all mothers know that the demand exceeds the supply in Australia). As Jean Kittson points out, 'No woman on earth will tell you that the childcare centre she puts her child into has anything wrong with it. I've never heard a mother say, "Well yes, I think there are too many kids and not enough carers," for instance. There is such a turnover of carers too. I think childcare centres are so hard on little kids . . .'

All mothers agree that putting a child in care is not without heartache. Each time Melbourne businesswoman Nanette Moulton went to put one of her sons (she has three) into creches, 'I cried and cried. I lasted one hour with both the first and the second one before going back to get them and taking them home. When my third son was born, I thought I'd have toughened up a bit. I lasted one day. He and I were both so upset I never bothered again. Really, if I was away from any of them for more than two hours I used to feel sick.'

'The first time you put your child into care is dreadful and it is impossible not to cry,' Mindi Chisholm says. 'There is so much anxiety, so much guilt. Although my mother is my best friend and the best carer – apart from me – she is a major cause of my guilt. She can't help herself. She tells me work isn't everything; spend more time with your girls. I tell her it's different now and that she didn't have to work because Dad was able to provide for her but to do that he had two jobs. Today, if you want a high standard of living, both partners have to work. My children spend most of the week in long daycare from 7 a.m. to 6 p.m. and one day with my mother.

'I know that kids can turn out all right with a full-time working mother even if they have a variety of care. My kids are socially well adjusted; everyone tells me what a pleasure they are to take anywhere. I know I'm waving the flag and justifying myself, but I can go to church on Sunday and leave them in creche with carers they don't know and they will be happy and well behaved, because they know I will be back to get them.'

There is no one-size-fits-all solution to childcare. Every child's needs are different. What suits one person's family will not necessarily suit another, and it can take just one thing to make a woman's care arrangements unworkable – like the dreaded words, 'Mummy, I don't feel well.' It is the last thing a woman wants to hear as she is rushing around her home in the morning trying to do the million and one things that must be done before she leaves for work. 'Our *motherInc* surveys show that only one in five mothers has anyone they can rely on to help out when the children get sick, and that an ill child is the most stressful thing that can happen to them,' Claudia Keech says.

Penny sees many sick children in her surgery. 'Invariably, during the consultation, particularly if they are working, mothers ask, "When can they go back to daycare or school?" I feel for these mothers,' says Penny. 'Not only are they worried about their little ones being sick, but I know as I'm talking to them that they are scrolling through the list of possible alternative childminding arrangements, so they can get back to work.'

'My son told me he was feeling sick one morning but I still sent him off to school saying something like, "Oh, come on, you're all right," while I was probably thinking, "Oh, my God, how can he stay home; I've got to go to work!"' Adele Horin says. 'I should have known better – he isn't a whinger or a malingerer. He didn't even make it through first period and he pretended to the school nurse that he hadn't felt so sick when he got up just to protect me. They had to send him home in a taxi. That story has gone down in the annals of my children as one of the classic examples of my bad mothering!'

Co-workers' attitudes to working mothers can be downright unfriendly. 'I have excellent childcare arrangements in place and usually everything runs smoothly. But there are occasions when one of the children is sick – or the carer is – or certain times of the year, like the week prior to Christmas when most childcare places are closed, that I find it necessary to leave work early,' Kylie Douglas says. Some of my work colleagues – particularly the men, who for some reason think they must work 7 a.m. to 7 p.m. to impress the boss, mutter things like, "Gosh I'd like to have her job," loudly enough for me to hear. What they never take into consideration is the number of hours I work at night or on the weekends to make up for my early leave pass!'

When her children aren't well Katharine yearns for grandparents. 'My life would be so much easier if Nana and Pop were on call when I needed them but they died in a car accident a couple of years ago. If your kids are sick you're not supposed to take them to daycare in case their germs get passed on to the other kids and start an epidemic, but I wouldn't be the first mum to dose her kids up to dry up their noses for the first hour after I've dropped them off! I've had calls in the middle of the day at the office to come and pick them up when they are off-colour or suddenly start running a temperature, and my whole day is turned upside down while my guilt levels go through the roof.'

'When my kid was sick I still went to work,' says Sally Cocks, who was managing a restaurant in the Victorian Alpine town of Bright when her son Tassie was born. 'If he was really ill I'd get my mother to come around; otherwise if he was just unwell I'd still send him to childcare. I always chose work first because the guilt of not going to work and not being productive outweighed any guilt I might feel about Tassie. I'd think, "I'll make it up to him," and I'd come home with a chocolate frog.'

Mothers are prepared to go to any lengths to find the best ways to look after their children. Initially, Carla Zampatti took her son to work, 'But it was impossible, I couldn't mother him properly and I couldn't do my job well either. I had him in the same room where I was working and it was just too distracting.'

Jenny, a divorcee with two children, prided herself on being well organised. She had an executive position with a major Australian company and employed live-in help. When she went interstate or overseas on business, her father, a widower, would come and stay. The kids adored their grandfather, he loved spending time with them, and the arrangement worked well until one unforgettable trip.

'I was in New York when my daughter – she was ten at the time – phoned. "Mum, I feel sick." Sniffle, sniffle. "I have headache and my tummy hurts." I comforted her, said I'd bring home a special surprise present, spoke to Dad who reassured me that he thought it was just a cold and went back to work.' But Jenny had overlooked one possible hazard in her well-planned system. After hanging up, the little girl rang her father and went through the same routine as she had with her mother. Knowing his former wife was away, the father asked his daughter if she would like him to come around. Of course she would. He was sitting on his daughter's bed, having a cup of coffee that the housekeeper had made, when, as Jenny recounts, 'Dad came in from walking the dog. He had never approved of my husband. "What are you doing here?" he demanded to know. "We don't need you."

'My daughter rang me again and wailed, "Mummy, Mummy. Daddy and Grandpa had a big fight and Grandpa told Daddy never to come to our house again. Mummy I want to see Daddy."' Jenny knew what she had to do. 'Most of the flights to Australia were booked out. I managed to get a seat on a flight that went via Chicago and Tahiti and arrived home forty hours later dead on my feet. As I walked through the door, Dad said, "What are you doing here?" I love my father very much but, at that moment, I cheerfully could have strangled him!'

The agony and ecstasy of childcare

Some mothers like Kelly prefer au pairs who live in. 'These girls, in their twenties, usually come from overseas – Japan, Sweden, Korea. They fit into our family routine and I like the multi-cultural dimension they bring to my kids as they share stories about their countries. And, because they live with us, I don't have those rushed drop-offs and pick-ups – they just take over when I have to leave for work, or if I need to duck out to the shops. That's not to say we haven't had our problems though. One day I came home to find that Kristine, a rather buxom Swedish girl, had broken her bed. It turned out that she had a penchant for entertaining big Maori boys in her bedroom when I was at work and the kids were at school. That was just a bit *too* multicultural for me.'

Of all the services easily available the most popular is family day care where mothers look after other children in their homes with their own family. These care-mothers are permitted to take only five children at any one time, which means kids get plenty of attention while learning to play and interact with other little ones. Sharon Freund's two-year-old twins 'love their daycare family. There are lots of kisses and cuddles.' Tanya's daughter was ten months old when she went to a local family day care centre, and as 'her care-mother originally came from Greece my daugh-ter's first words were Greek!'

Many working mothers would never get by without their mums. 'Mine has been wonderful,' says Lisa, a hairdresser from an Italian background. 'However I do feel guilty about "using" my mother who looks after my two-year-old son while I work. When I go and pick him up and see how tired she is, I feel guilty.'

'My children tell me that *all* their friends' mothers are looking after their babies,' says former Brisbane Lord Mayor Sally Anne Atkinson, who says she now suffers from Grandmother Guilt. 'My friends fall into two categories – there are the ones like me who go out to work and there are the others who mind kids on a regular basis. Grandmothers have certain days on which they mind their grandchildren. Some days the apartments in my neighbourhood look like childcare centres because there are kids coming and going all day.'

When their mum approves of the way they are raising their children it does make a big difference to a working mother's self esteem. Johanna Griggs' mother makes her feel good about herself because, 'She regularly tells me that I am doing a great job with the boys. They have three points of stability – me as their main carer; my mum, who is a big part of the boys' routine; and our nanny, who is extraordinary. I look at my sons who are excelling at school, have good social skills and seem extraordinarily happy and I am content with the balance I've achieved for them and me.'

7

Giving up work: Wendy Harmer's quantum leap

When popular comedian Wendy Harmer announced in November 2003 that she was giving up radio to become a stay-at-home mum her fans were stunned. One of Australia's most successful and highly paid broadcasters, with a salary package that had made her millions of dollars, it was impossible to imagine weekday mornings without her. After all, she had ruled the roost as Queen of Breakfast Radio for eleven years.

Wendy's contract prevented her from working in radio until 2005 so she had a year to sit down and 'play Barbie and Play Doh' with her two children, Marley, six, and Maeve, four. It has to be every working mother's dream come true – the chance to find out if she would be happier away from the workplace, swapping full-time work for full-time motherhood.

Within days of broadcasting her last show for 2DAY FM Wendy found herself on a sharp learning curve. 'Marley asked me if I was going to take Maeve to the park because, "She has to go and meet her friend there." I had absolutely no idea what park I needed to go to, let alone what the name of Maeve's friend might be. Our nanny always took her and she had gone home to Japan.'

Shortly after this exchange, Wendy drove Marley to kindergarten for the very first time in her life! 'I asked him if he wanted to buy his lunch and he said yes. When we got to school I went to give him some money but he just looked at me and said, "You have to look at the list to see what you can buy."

'I studied the list, thought it looked pretty good and asked him if he'd like some party pies. Marley said fine and I gave him the money. I'd packed him a few other little snacks and as he went to get out of the car he said, "I think I'll just have the snacks for my lunch."

' "Why would you do that?" I asked. "You have the money to buy something."

' "It's supposed to be in a paper bag with my name written on it."

'Well, I didn't know that! I had to ring his teacher and confess that I didn't *know* how to do a lunch order.'

Things took a turn for the better when Marley got home and asked Wendy, 'You like us more than you like making money, don't you Mum?' When she replied that she did, he said, 'Yeah, I knew that.'

Her son's rationalisation of the new family situation caught her off guard. 'I wouldn't have thought such a little boy would have been thinking through that scenario . . .'

It is said that behind every successful man there stands a woman. In her case, Wendy says the reverse is true. In some ways Brendan Donohoe, her husband of nine years, is a pioneer.

'I never could have worked the way I have if he hadn't been such a committed father. When we got together, Brendan told me, "I am a great 2IC. I'll stay home and be the backstop and you can be the breadwinner." '

As part of the couple's household budgeting arrangements, Brendan gets paid a wage. 'When the kids came along we were able to afford a nanny so that Brendan could do things that interest him outside the home and in the garden.' Again, it is the kind of arrangement many a working woman would love and couples often think about but lack the nerve to try, because it means breaking such new ground.

'We've succeeded because Brendan has this ability to take everything in his stride and be good-natured about other people's reactions. We'll go to some corporate do and someone will ask Brendan what he does. When he tells them he is a househusband, the blokes' eyes glaze over. I usually have to officiate at functions so Brendan is often left with the wives of all the big honchos and they talk about kids. Sometimes he finds out some amazing stuff. The wives love him.'

They live in the most incredible home that looks as if it has grown like topsy – there are large rooms, small rooms, additions, nooks and crannies, somehow all blending together, enhanced by a breathtaking cinemascope view of the Pacific Ocean. The house is perched high up on a hill overlooking Collaroy Beach on Sydney's northern beaches. Wendy's earnings have allowed them not only to buy the house they live in, but also the two closest properties, both of which are rented out. They have created a private compound, with a permaculture garden beautifully unkempt, not from neglect but by design. 'Brendan did the entire garden and we have frogs, chickens and ducks.'

When Marley's school wanted a frog pond Brendan had the time to put one in for them and they have won a regional Keep Australia Beautiful award. A town planner by profession, Brendan also works voluntarily for the Surfrider Foundation, a non-profit organisation dedicated to the protection and enhancement of Australia's oceans, waves and beaches. In 2003 he won the Foundation's

National Member of the Year award for his beach environmental work.

Brendan is the perfect neighbour too, always willing to lend a hand. If someone's house needs a coat of paint Brendan is there to help. When an elderly 92-year-old man living nearby needed home nursing care, Brendan visited him every day, dressed his wound and cut his toenails. 'If more men were prepared to stay home, they could do such things too. It's nice to have a good, strong man around the place . . .'

Brendan does sound a bit too good to be true and must be the closest thing to a wife that a woman could ever hope to find. Wendy is the first to admit she is fortunate. 'My situation is unique and it has worked well for us, but Brendan got handed a lot of shit from his mates when we first started down this road. One of them came along to see me, as head of a "delegation" and said, "We've all got together and I'm here to tell you that we are really worried that Brendan is losing his identity." I told him he should let us worry about that. I did feel a twinge of guilt at first . . . But when I told Brendan, he rolled around laughing for about an hour and I shook it off.'

～

But even such perfect childcare arrangements did not keep Motherguilt away. 'I think mothers suffer from guilt because we are hard-wired that way. A woman always feels responsible for the environment she creates for her children and the way they operate in it. If you are not walking around massively loaded down with guilt thinking I could do more, you probably are not female. I've had tons of guilt.'

Breakfast radio is a gruelling shift. For eleven years, Wendy was generally in bed by 8.30 p.m. and got up at 4 a.m. 'The kids used to kiss *me* good night! When I had holidays, they would ask why I was still up. Brendan was the one they called out for in the middle of the night. If they were sick, they always yelled, "Daddy". There were times when I felt "ouch" but, under the circumstances, it was the only thing that could happen. I needed my sleep.

'I felt guilty when I came home one day and discovered that Maeve knew all her nursery rhymes and I hadn't taught her any of them. I felt guilty when Marley's teacher told me that one of the other children had come up to her and asked, "Doesn't Marley have a mum?" I felt guilty when I would come home tired, feeling a bit snappy and bite the kids' heads off. And I used to feel really guilty because our nanny always took Maeve to the local playgroup and I only got to know other mothers because she would invite them home and introduce me to them. Did other mothers judge me? I am sure they did. I felt they did. I couldn't stand it. At times I felt terrible.

'I am so looking forward to spending the next twelve months with Maeve. There is so much for me to learn about her. I have no idea of Maeve's schedule at all. Once a week, she goes to the library where she is in a reading group. On what day? I have no idea. I don't know whether she is particularly good at reading. I know she is good at drawing but I have no idea whether she is good compared to anyone else. I don't know what songs she likes to sing. I had more input with Marley I guess – but as the years have gone by, I have become more and more tired. I owe Maeve.

'I do somehow feel that my best years with my kids are going to be when they are a little older. I think some mums are good at the baby years and not so good at the older years . . . although I know a mother has to be good at *everything*.

'To tell you the truth, when Marley was ten weeks I was bored out of my mind. I was looking at him once thinking, "For God's sake, do something," and then he kind of smiled and my mood was over at once. I've never been into the real baby thing. I have never regretted having my children though. Those women who say they aren't going to have children are utterly, utterly mad. The only thing I wish is that I had started sooner and I could have had four. I had my kids when I was forty-two and forty-four. I was stupid. I do get tired.'

⌒

Over the years Wendy has also felt the need to don her Superwoman cape as she packed her waking hours with all kinds of other commitments, such as writing, hosting awards, television appearances, and acting as MC at corporate and show-biz functions. Plus there were the trips to the United States for the Academy Awards, the Golden Globes, the Emmys, often taking Brendan and the kids with her. 'Our whole family has been "bent" towards my job. Whenever I had a break, we'd usually go overseas for holidays. Marley has been to London, Paris, to LA five times. Maeve has been to LA three times. They've been to Bali and we have just come back from Japan.

'There have been times when Brendan has had words with me telling me I am working too hard, that I should stay at home with the kids more – which always made me feel guilty. But I've worked really hard to make the circumstances right for the way that I wanted to live my life. I'm proud of what I've achieved and the money I've earned. I think I have done a tremendous job for my family.'

Wendy does sometime discuss her guilt feelings with her friend Laura, whom she used in a comedy routine once: 'My best girlfriend Laura rings up and says to me, "I have been singing the baby to sleep with the Louie the Fly commercial. Do you think they can come and take the baby off me?"'

Breastfeeding Maeve also provided some amusing moments. 'I was able to broadcast from home right after she was born. Sometimes I was breastfeeding when I was on air and the boys would be in the studio listening to Maeve's slurp, slurp, slurp and ask me if

I was topless. "Yeah, yeah, yeah," I'd tell them. One particular day we were interviewing someone famous person – I can't remember who now – and Maeve started to cry and I put my hand over her mouth. Then I thought, "What *am* I doing?" It was either truly professional or truly, truly bankrupt . . . But I like to think that the fact that I was sitting at a microphone breastfeeding my baby and working was some kind of encouragement for someone somewhere; proof that your brain doesn't go completely AWOL and it is possible to be a working, feeding mother. It was difficult though and I wouldn't recommend it to anybody because when you are breastfeeding, your brain is so often away with the pixies – it's like patting your head and rubbing your tummy.

'When I had to return to the studio and Maeve was still breastfeeding, I used to miss one feed. I would get up and feed her at 3.30 a.m. and then I would express milk for her 8 a.m. feed, and because radio is not a nine-to-five job, I was able to get home in time for her 11 a.m. feed. Then I was on tap all day. Brendan has never had to worry about what to cook for dinner. I've always done that.'

Wendy worked on air through both pregnancies. 'That was hard. They could have put Brad Pitt next to me and it wouldn't have meant a thing. If you have a baby inside kicking, all that's on your mind is what the baby is doing. I often felt, as I presume every mother does, that while external things were going on, the baby and I were having a much more interesting and important dialogue than I could have had with Brad!

'After the kids were born I would leave for work when the whole family was in the deepest, deepest slumber. The kids never woke up and said, "Mum, don't go." I'd get up, have a shower, get dressed and creep out. Brendan always made my lunch and left me a little note every morning. I have thousands of his love notes. They always begin, "I love you more than . . . " and it could be anything, like, "I love you more than ant's footprints." They are a record of the nine years we've been married.

'I would never have contemplated putting the children into outside care as little ones. I have strong opinions about people who go off to work and put babies into daycare. It is wicked and I don't hold with it at all. My kids are young now but in the blink of an eye they will be grown up. I know that one day I am going to look back and wish I had spent that time in the park with Maeve or that I'd had the monotony of Vegemite sandwiches. I used to look at Maeve when she was a baby for hours and hours, trying to soak her in. She slept with me every single night and I would cuddle her for hours – and it has all gone. Childhood is so ephemeral and it wouldn't matter if you were there 24/7, you'd still look back and think could I have done more? Did I make the most of that?

'There have been times when I've run away from the kids and punched the air as I've got into the car. I don't think I'm any different to other women in that regard. You can't tell me that most women, if given the chance, wouldn't run away from the pile of nappies, making the Vegemite toast and doing the washing. They would zoom out the door! Some of the most boring words in the world are, "Mum, will you play with me?" I'm being really honest. When Marley says, "Mum, you be a waterfall and I'll be a river," or "You be Superman and I'll be Batman and we'll fight," I just go "Oooh" and think, "God, the tedium of early childhood." I take my hat off to mothers who do all that stuff day after day. They are fantastic.

'I do feel guilty about the amount of times Marley and Maeve have come into the house to find me working on the computer in the back room and I've said, "Don't bother me, I'm busy." Even though Brendan has always been around, one of them would always ask, "Oh, are you going to work on the computer, Mum?" or Maeve would say, "Now, you are *really* going to play with me, aren't you? You're not going to work on the computer and pretend you are playing, are you?"'

In fact, Wendy has an entire list of guilts.

➤ On Friday nights, I get a bit pissed and I give them frozen food for dinner.

➤ Occasionally I forget to give them a bath.

➤ Sometimes, because I am really tired, I dodge family occasions that I should attend and pretend I have to work.

➤ There are times I buy them presents to compensate for the lack of time I have to spend with them.

➤ I often skip whole sections of books when I am reading to them because I want to go to sleep.

➤ I keep Maeve's hair short because I can't be bothered doing it – but it does suit her!

➤ Sometimes I park the kids in front of the TV (doesn't everyone?) when I should be doing something with them.

➤ I have invented the ultimate game to play with the children when I have a hangover. I make a cubbyhouse inside the house with brooms and blankets and then I crawl inside and pretend I'm sick. I lie there and they bring the 'patient' drinks of water and biscuits. It is dark and warm . . . and nice.

➤ I have never spent hours making one of those children's birthday cakes out of a *Women's Weekly* cookbook. Once I made the most crappy birthday cake ever. I bought about forty iced doughnuts, arranged them in a big pile, and stuck candles everywhere. It was a huge hit.

Like many working mothers, however, Wendy is quick to justify her decision to be a working mum by bragging about her children. 'My kids are really, really well behaved. Marley is one of the top kids at his school and has won three principal's awards. They both have good manners and have no behavioural problems at school. If they did, I would be mortified. I know plenty of women who are stay-at-home mums and I reckon their kids' conduct is far worse than my two.

'I don't believe that shit that many women go on with: "If I am happy and fulfilled my kids will be." That is just crap and the biggest excuse women have ever come up with to shirk their responsibilities. Kids don't really care if you get that promotion at work. It is good for a woman to be happy but you can't expect the kids to be thrilled for you in your career.'

Marley and Maeve are delighted to have their mother at home. 'For Maeve to get up in the morning and find me still here is an absolute treat. I have signed on for canteen duty. I want to make some clothes for Maeve – I can sew, but I've never had the time. I have a pile of new recipes to try out, I want to paint the house, clean out all the cupboards and spend more time reading to the kids. My friends say it will take only three months before I am screaming blue murder to go back to work.' Wendy doesn't share their misgivings. 'I am so looking forward to the year ahead.'

Footnote: Wendy had been home for a couple of months when 'Maeve and I were doing some drawing together when a replay of an interview I did with Bert Newton on *Good Morning Australia* came on television. Maeve insisted on watching it, then turned to me and said, "I like Mama at home much more than the Mama on television."'

8

Stay-at-home mums work full-time too

Nothing provokes the wrath of a stay-at-home mum more than the suggestion that, because she does not have a paid job, she is not a 'working' mother. Jean Kittson gets hot under the collar at the very idea! 'The term "working mother" is redundant,' she says. 'If you are a mother you are always working and at times it can be really hard work.'

Stay-at-home mothers lead lives that can be just as frantic as their office counterparts. As well as running their households and caring for their children they do hours of voluntary work for charities and the community generally. Schools would not be able to operate as efficiently as they do without them. Stay-at-home mums cheerfully do numerous chores, like canteen duty for example, that 'paid' working mothers are often 'too busy' to do, and help out with all kinds of things from barbecues to sports days, classroom reading and other curricular activities.

In the same way that society undervalues motherhood, it also seems to place little worth on the contribution of these unpaid volunteers, taking it for granted that stay-at-home mothers should be 'grateful' for having something to do! Whichever way you look at it, the input of women to the Australian way of life is consistently underrated.

'Motherhood isn't esteemed at all and yet doing a good job as a mother is no mean feat,' Jean says. 'We don't tell mothers often enough that they are doing a great job. I have a friend who frequently tells me I am a fantastic mother and it makes me feel really good. Mothers don't praise each other enough and when we do get together we talk about our problems and worries instead of the things that give us pleasure. We need to tell each other that motherhood is terrific more often than we do.' Why women don't do this is hard to understand – especially as nearly every woman says that the day she became a mother was the best day of her life – but it is possible that society's downsizing of the importance of mothering has resulted in women undervaluing it too.

However, there is never any shortage of people prepared to tell women that motherhood is boring. Some everyday jobs that mothers have to do can be mind numbing, especially when kids are little, but it is a temporary situation and soon passes. Many paid working mothers have jobs requiring them to perform repetitive, monotonous tasks every day too, but often are stuck with them for the rest of their working lives.

'At least when I have to do boring jobs around the home I can stop if I want to and read a magazine or play with my child. When a woman is in paid employment, whether as a checkout chick or a corporate executive, she loses control over her life. I'd hate to be like that.' Robbie Stewart has never regretted giving up her job as an executive assistant just before her daughter was born three years ago. 'Being a mother is the best job in the world and it can be magical. I was walking in the park with my little girl one afternoon when she spotted a cluster of dragonflies fluttering above a pond and thought they looked like fairies. I shared her delight.

It wouldn't have been the same if a nanny had told me after a long day at the office.'

'Working mothers, particularly ones with high-powered jobs such as lawyers, do like to patronise us,' says Kerrie, who loves being a stay-at-home mum. 'They think they are such "ace" mothers because they can give half an hour of "quality time" when they get home at 7:30 p.m. and that's absolute bullshit. Both parties are too tired to either give or accept "quality time" and little children should be in bed at that time.'

The expression 'quality time' is one that a lot of mothers in the paid workforce like to use because it helps ease their Motherguilt, but few children would have the faintest idea what the term means. Kids have a habit of demanding mum's attention when she least expects it, which makes it impossible for a woman to set an agenda for 'quality time' and keep to it. What mother has ever said her children understand her work pressures so well that they appreciate it when she can find some 'quality time' for them? Stay-at-home mums prefer to talk about 'quantity time' and, when they do, are often smugly judgemental about their employed sisters. Kids couldn't care less about the quality versus quantity debate; the only thing they care about is the way their mother listens to them.

'I value the time I can spend with my children when we are having a meal, swimming at the beach, or just doing something together with no particular timetable. The amount of time a mother can spend with her children *does* make a difference,' says Ann, who lives with her husband and three daughters in Perth. 'There are occasions when my children want my undivided attention and I think it's important they get it. I stopped work when my first child was born ten years ago and I'm glad I did. Nappies are definitely bad news but they're soon gone and forgotten, just like sleep deprivation. I get so cranky sometimes at the condescending attitude of some women. I can be at a party and someone asks me what I do and when I say I'm a busy full-time mother, some smartly dressed career witch asks scornfully, "What on earth do you *do* all day?" I always have enormous delight in saying that I have time to do whatever I want, that I even have time for me. Then I pause for a second before asking, "Do you?"'

Being a stay-at-home mother does not mean a woman is automatically safe in some kind of a guilt-free zone though. Mother-guilt can make them search their souls with the same intensity as employed mothers do.

'I popped in to see a friend on my way home from the supermarket and she'd just made blueberry muffins for her children's afternoon tea,' Tina says. 'She had some wonderful stew simmering on the stove, there were fresh flowers in the hallway, the whole place was immaculate – nothing like the chaos that I'd left behind at my place. As I drove home guilt sneaked up on me. Were my mothering skills up to scratch? Could I do better? When I got home I rang my mother but she soon straightened me out. "Answer me three questions," she said. "Are the kids happy? Is your husband happy? Are you happy?" When I answered yes to all three, Mum just laughed. "What more do you want?"'

It is just over forty years since Women's Liberation challenged, and then changed, accepted thinking about the traditional homemaker role expected of women by society. Two of the most significant social changes of the twentieth century were mothers leaving the home for the workforce, and the education of women, but 'liberation' has not been without a cost, particularly to women's health. Working women, especially those with children, are permanently tired. In order to get everything done women consistently short change themselves on sleep, when in fact they need more sleep than men because their biology is intrinsically more complex than men's.

When women are pregnant, breastfeeding or premenstrual they should be getting ten hours sleep a night. Which working mother ever gets that much sleep? There are greater numbers of women suffering from what were traditionally male conditions such as heart attacks, high blood pressure, ulcers, cirrhosis of the liver and executive burnout, and younger women are beginning to question whether their mothers got it right.

Trends emerging in the United States indicate that the winds of change are blowing and that the stay-at-home mother could be coming back into fashion. In March 2004, *Time* magazine published a cover story headlined 'The Case for Staying Home', in which it said there was a growing trend for new mothers to leave the workforce because women were tired of giving up the joys of motherhood for the rat race of the marketplace. Sociologists and family commentators have hailed the article as significant and a sign that the positive aspects of stay-at-home motherhood are at last being recognised.

Time's article reinforced American research that also shows this shift in women's thinking, perhaps signalling the beginning of a new movement of women choosing marriage and family over a job. In the same month that *Time* hit the streets, Susan Shapiro Barash told the ABC's Radio National Breakfast Show that her research indicates, 'Young women in America are saying that they don't want to repeat their baby boomer mothers' mistakes.' Author of *The New Wife: The Evolving Role of the American Wife* and gender studies professor at Marymount Manhattan College in New York, Susan says Generation Y women – the daughters of the baby boomers and born between 1977 and 1997 – are a new voice in the motherhood debate.

'These young women are educated [like Australian women they outnumber men at universities] and well equipped to go to the workplace. They're not saying they will never go, but rather they won't forfeit a successful marriage and having children at the appropriate time to do it. They are rationalising their choices and saying, "I went to medical school but I don't think I'll deliver babies. I'll become a dermatologist and work from ten until four and contour it around my children's schedule." This seems to suggest to me that the myth of "having it all" hasn't really worked, and that Generation Y women think there is another way to do it.

'They want a less stressful existence than their mothers, a more compelling, romantic marriage and one that doesn't end in divorce. Many of the Generation Y women have mothers whose marriages ended in divorce and, although their mothers might be satisfied in their careers, they're thinking that maybe they missed out by not having a successful marriage.'

It is not only women's thinking that is changing. Susan's research shows that men are reconsidering their choices, too. 'These twenty-first century wives and young women are saying to their partners and future partners that when the time comes to have children they want to stay home and look after them and they want their partners to be the sole provider. And the men are saying, "Yes, okay," because they're the children of baby boomer mothers as well and have endured the same disappointments with tired mothers who missed the important school play and so forth. They want a wife who is at home and available and not too stressed to nourish a marriage.'

Australian sociologists say they have seen no signs yet of this trend here, although research shows young women have observed the difficulties their mothers and fathers have in juggling work and kids. 'Australia often lags behind America but that doesn't mean it won't happen here eventually,' Ita says. 'I think there are signs that a change of thinking is in the air — only financial realities are stopping women from exercising this "new" choice. Our high cost of living means women have to work but, in their heart of hearts, many mothers would much rather stay at home with their kids.'

In 2003, *Pregnancy and Birth* magazine surveyed 500 working pregnant women and found that nine out of ten working pregnant women believed the Federal Government should give them more money to stay at home. Only 35 per cent of the women surveyed felt they could afford the child they were about to have, 60 per cent were planning to go back to work after the birth, and a further 20 per cent had still not made up their minds. Significantly, if money were no object, two-thirds said they would never return to work.

A PhD study, 'Mothers in conflict: expectation and experience', released in 2003 by Dr Wendy LeBlanc of Sydney's Macquarie Graduate School of Management, surveyed one hundred first-time mothers aged twenty-five and over from New South Wales and Queensland. It found that mothers who stayed at home with their children encountered increased isolation and felt undervalued by society. Of those who returned to work, more than 90 per cent said they experienced major conflict between their dual roles and found it extremely difficult to find a balance. More than half of these working mothers said they would far rather be home with their babies and young children. It appears these mothers' words are not falling on deaf ears. With its return to power in 2004, the Federal Government has committed itself to spending $1.1 billion on extra assistance for stay-at-home mothers.

Making the adjustment from being in the workforce to being a full-time mother is not as simple as it sounds. 'The thing I found difficult about staying home with my two girls was justifying what I did all day,' Karen says. 'As a lawyer, I was used to a full-on day at the office. Suddenly I had all this time. I worried that if I played with the kids too much people would consider me a loafer. Then I worried if I attended too many coffee and chat mornings that people would think I was neglecting my kids in some way and being selfish. My grandmother put me on the right track. She told me to relax and do what I thought was right. I have joined a mothers' club and, we have a terrific support network. When we meet for coffee, we talk about politics, the latest books, whatever is happening in the news and, yes, our kids. Just because we've chosen to be full-time mothers doesn't mean we're brain dead.'

Mothering does take time, the one thing employed mothers do not have in abundance, and all the justification in the world cannot disguise that fact. Stay-at-home mums say they do not expect their kids to fit into the demands of their lives; they organise their lives to suit the demands of their kids.

'Being a mother is *my* job and like *all* women with a job I take it seriously,' says Joselyn Van Fleet, a former Miss Queensland who has twelve-year-old twin boys. 'I can see working mothers thinking, "What *does* she do when her children are at school?" But, by the time I drop the boys off, go home, clean up after breakfast, make beds, buy groceries, plan meals, do the washing and odd jobs for my husband, it's time to pick them up again and ferry them to various sporting trainings, head home, help with homework and cook dinner. The working mothers I know cope by getting other people to do a lot of this stuff and most of them rely on me to let them know what's going on at school. I'm the one they all ring. I feel like getting an answering machine that says: "For homework information, dial one; for excursion enquiries, dial two; for examination timetables, dial three . . . and, most importantly, for location of desperate mothers' support group coffee, dial four!"'

Nanette Moulton stayed home until her three sons were all in primary school because, 'When you decide to be a mother, you get a new job and you are the only one who can do it properly. That's what people always think about their jobs in the paid workforce and it's what I believe about the job of mother. When a woman delegates her responsibility as a mother, guilt is automatically triggered because deep down she knows no one can do it as well as she can.'

Nearly all stay-at-home mums were in the workforce before having their children and there are days when they do think about their former jobs. Twenty-seven-year-old Sarah Hawker used to work in the South Australian hospitality industry in Adelaide. 'I miss the people, there was always something interesting happening. My darling children are *interesting* but I know most of their tricks – until they whip out a new one!' But the yearning is not so overwhelming that Sarah wants to return to paid employment. 'I don't agree with going out to work to pay someone an astronomical sum of money to care for my children. I've always wanted to be with them for their milestones – the first steps, that kind of thing.' When her de facto partner died suddenly four years ago, she was left to raise their two sons on the single mother's pension and took them home to live with her 'excellent parents who have been always there for me emotionally. I know working mums think I'm lazy and sponging off the Government, but I've made my choice just like they've made theirs.'

Sarah waxes lyrical about the time she has to do things that give her pleasure. 'I can crawl around with the kids and play. I've just built an obstacle course in the backyard with a tunnel and rope slung over a tree branch so that the boys can avoid the "sharks" swimming below. I'm going to show them how to swing on a rope. I've time to listen to my friend's problems for three hours and bring her six cuppas while she tells me about them. I've time to bake a cake – I don't think working mothers would – and to help at school.' She is on the Parents and Citizens' Committee, does subcommittee work when asked, lends a hand at sausage sizzles and with serving hot soup during winter, does class reading and works as a LAP volunteer, the Learning Assistance Program that assists children with learning or behavioural problems.

'Time can work against you if you let it. When your children are little and sleeping a lot, it can be demotivating and it's easy to fall into the trap of watching daytime television and snacking. It happened to me, but not for long. Once the kids got older I kept the TV off. Sometimes I feel guilty that other women go to work to pay taxes so I can have the privilege of staying home with my boys.'

Every now and again the media 'discovers' motherhood. In 2003 newspapers carried stories of 'yummy mummies' who were said to be shunning the notion that they had to have both career and family and were opting for homemaking full time – including making 'yummy' biscuits and cakes. The press made no mention of the fact that the women who were exercising this option could afford not to work because they were married to highly paid corporate executives. For many Australian families, the need to pay mortgages and school bills means mothers have to remain in the work force – they have no choice – and nearly all mothers who stay at home confess to suffering from guilt because they are not able to contribute financially to household expenses. As Joselyn Van Fleet says, 'I do feel guilty that I don't actually earn dollars and do my share of helping out with finances in the family; however, I do remind my husband that if he were paying me housekeeping rates of $300 per day, I *would* be earning dollars.'

'It can be a bit of struggle occasionally,' says Sarah Simic. 'Sometimes my mum buys my daughter's school shoes and I think, "I should be doing that," and then I feel guilty because I haven't been able to provide well enough for Tayla. My partner understands, though, that I was raised to be a mother. My own mum stayed at home and that has influenced me. Being a mother is very rewarding but it can be stressful too, because kids do push you to the limits. Sometimes I yell at my daughter and afterwards I am so annoyed for not controlling my anger. I tell myself, "Sarah you could have handled that *so* differently if you hadn't been so cross, if you'd just sat down with Tayla and talked with her, mother to daughter." '

Few people comment any longer about older women having babies because it is so commonplace. Having satisfied their career ambitions before motherhood these older mums often choose to stay at home quite happily, but statistics indicate that they are usually married, well-educated and affluent.

British studies show that the offspring of older parents do better at school than those born to the very young and that, statistically, older mothers are more likely to give birth to left-handed children. This is nothing to worry about. A London University College study showed that left-handed people achieve more than their right-handed counterparts and that their brains are structured differently to right-handers in a way that widens their range of abilities. The genes that determine left-handedness also govern the development of the language centres of the brain. Researchers say that the increase could produce a corresponding intellectual advance and a leap in the number of mathematical or artistic geniuses.

Caroline Eburn was thirty-seven when she had Annie. 'I led a nomadic kind of life before my marriage. I left Australia when I was in my twenties and travelled all over England and the Continent before going to America, where I got a job as a secretary at the IMF (International Monetary Fund) in Washington. For the next four and a half years, I was sent to different locations in South and Central America to do relief work for six to eight weeks at a time. By the time I married Bernie, who was a Qantas pilot, I was happy to settle down because I had done everything I wanted to do. My childhood ambition had been to see the world and I had done that. I feel sad that so many mothers have to go to work but understand their need for a career. If I'd had Annie when I was younger, I might have felt the same way. The best thing about being home is having time to do the things I want to do.'

Now fifty, Joselyn Van Fleet once had a high-profile job in public relations. 'When the boys were babies, I was the oldest mother, with more patience than anybody – and considering I had twins, I had to have not just "double patience" but "triple patience". The younger mothers in the various playgroups and mothers' groups couldn't believe how I handled every situation so calmly, but 50 per cent of the time it was a big act because I had the maturity to put on a brave face and not let on that sometimes I was really struggling. Now I'm still one of the older mums and I feel old, tired and not always in control. When I think back, I feel that running after twelve-month-old toddlers, who were always running in different directions – half the time with me not knowing which one was which – was easier than handling teenage boys who still run in different directions.'

In 2004 Joselyn sent the twins to boarding school. 'In my head I know my husband and I have done the best thing for the boys, but in my heart I worried that it would be difficult for them to cope without having me picking up their things and doing everything for them, like stay-at-home mums do.' Organising the boys' clothes was painful. 'When I was getting their uniforms ready, I sat down to sew on nametags. I pulled out one twin's gear and while I was sewing a tag on a shirt, something hit me – these are the most important labels I have ever sewn on – and I sobbed into the shirt for two hours and then had to hang it on the line to dry! I wondered if I should sew special little sentimental things on to their shirts, so they would know I was thinking of them. It's such a silly thing and reminded me of when my mother died and the sadness of losing someone you love so much. I was sure that the next day of labelling for the second twin would go better. I didn't do his shirts first, I did his socks, but I broke down again. I rang other mothers whose kids are at boarding school and was somewhat reassured when they told me my reaction was normal. One woman with three boys at boarding school said it didn't matter how old your children were when they went to boarding school, "When they leave you, they always leave a hole in your heart."'

Joselyn copped plenty of criticism from other stay-at-home mums. 'They made me feel so guilty by saying things like, "Isn't sending the boys to boarding school like sending them to prison?" "How could you *do* that?" and "What will you do without them?" Now the boys are settled at boarding school, my priority is to look after my health and have more time for me because I'm an insulin-dependent diabetic and my health suffers with the pressures of always putting everyone else first.'

~

Women's Liberation not only changed women's aspirations, it also gave them a voice. Up until then it was customary for women to keep their feelings about motherhood to themselves. 'You were a mother and that was that,' says 69-year-old Jean, who had her first child in 1956. 'Women put on a veneer that they were happy and what they were doing was the right thing to do, but no one ever delved too much below the surface. Our children might have been abominable but it was important to keep up appearances. That was so important. Women had very little real communication with each other. I don't remember many conversations with my husband then either. We never went to a movie or a concert; all that mattered was just getting through the day.

'Women are now far more out in the open – in fact too

much so. I think women are conditioned now to feel guilty about bloody well everything. They have to feel guilty about every damn thing they've ever done, even though at the time it was the only thing they could do. My expectations about how things would be when I became a mother were nothing like what happened in reality. I can remember thinking, "If this is my life, my God, I'd rather be dead." It was repetitive, boring drudgery and everything had to be done with the kids by the time your husband came home from work. You got up at the crack of dawn when the first child woke and went through the day like a robot. Getting into bed at night and going to sleep was heaven!'

Germaine Greer's *The Female Eunuch* changed Jan Murray's life. 'When I was first home with my children I adored it. I never felt my brain was going to mush because we didn't have feminism telling us we could do mothering alongside other occupations.' But Germaine's description of Australian women (most of whom were stay-at-home mothers) as 'stuffed, overfed white mice' struck Jan like a thunderbolt. 'Germaine was right! That's when I decided to get an education but once I started going to university, I began to feel guilt. I had left school at fourteen and no one in my family had had anything to do with higher education. I wanted it so much. My mother used to say to me, "Why do you need to go to university? You have a husband who loves you, beautiful children and a lovely home." No one could understand. My mother even suggested I take up cake decorating!'

Liberation has not 'freed' all women though. Kathy stays home not by choice but at her husband's insistence. She is thirty-two, has two children, a husband who runs his own successful business, and a home in one of Sydney's stunning waterfront suburbs – but Kathy feels miserable and lonely. 'I am not sure why. I think I'm bored. I am a wife and a mother, but after ten years I don't know who I am. I want to find me.'

Kerrie's husband – 'a typical Greek' – preferred her to stay home too, but she was happy to comply because it was what she wanted to do. Their four children are now twenty-three, twenty-one, twenty and sixteen. 'I didn't have a career before I married. I worked in travel but I didn't go to university and I've loved being at home. If my daughters decide to be working mothers, I won't judge them. It will be their decision but I'll help them. I think you can go out to work and still be a good mother. I do worry about my future, when the children are no longer at home. I put so much into them that I have nothing to fall back on. I don't even have a hobby. Sometimes, I think if I'd been a working mother and not there to run around after them all the time they might have been a little more self-sufficient, but they seem to have become independent people anyway.'

Being a stay-at-home mum is not without its frustrations. Mothering is a complex job and women learn as they go. Adorable though children may be they do also have their 'bad' days. Kathy is not the only stay-at-home mother to worry about losing her identity. Many women say that from being 'someone' at work they have become invisible, and there are times when – just like paid working mothers – they dream of having some time for themselves.

Camille says there are days when she envies her husband 'leaving home at his own pace, with one little briefcase, the radio on as loudly as he likes it, driving along by himself. Once you're a mother, you lose "ownership" of your movements. Even when I do the grocery shopping everything revolves around this little person. Now and again, I think I would like to be out of the "nappy zone" and in the adult world, so that I wouldn't feel so limited in my contribution to the evening discussion when my husband asks: "What have you done today?" And I reply, "Well, I took him (our son) to the doctor, then he had a swim, did three semi-bad nappies, had one extra large tantrum and got one, possibly too harsh, smack that made me feel guilty for half an hour."'

'Being at home is often viewed as a real luxury and it *is* – for my husband and our children. I get mad because I'm slave to everybody!' At thirty-two with two sons aged three and seventeen months and another baby on the way, Diane finds being a stay-at-home mum 'really hard work because I'm responsible for everything at home. I do all the housework, the ironing, look after the boys and, when they are finally in bed, my husband expects to have the "sex kitten" at home just like the good BC (before children) days!

'Going out to get takeaway can be a luxury for me, not because I don't have to cook but because I get in the car and can be by myself for ten minutes! Sometimes I resent my husband going off to golf. He doesn't seem to feel guilty about doing so but if I get a babysitter so that I can go and have my hair done, it is viewed differently.

'I don't necessarily envy my husband though. He has the ultimate financial responsibility and I wouldn't want to be in his shoes because there is a great deal of pressure on him. To be honest, parenting young children is a lot of hard work. I don't think it's easier for working mums with all the juggling they have to do but, you know, the grass is always greener . . .

I think it depends on what sort of day you are having. If it is a shocking one, the kids are sick or whiney, then I think I would like to be at work. But when I'm having a good day, I am very happy to be at home.'

Thirty-year-old Camille, mother of a toddler, says that being a stay-at-home mum means she is working in the unpaid workforce 24/7. 'I could change it if I wanted to but I love being at home. Perhaps I'd resent it if I didn't have a choice. This is a stage in my life that won't be there again and it will be gone in a flash.'

And it is. 'One minute your kids are little, happily holding your hand and looking up at you, and suddenly before you know it they are taller than you are and looking down on you, often in amusement,' says Ita.

~

Being a mother demands a great deal. It involves powerful love on the part of a woman for her child, and yet a mother's love must be strong and wise enough to allow that child to become independent from her. All mothers, whether at home or in paid employment, know what is required of them. 'I think the value that I can contribute, as a person and as a woman, is as a mother to my children and by helping them achieve their potential and their dreams,' Jean Kittson says. There does need to be a re-evaluation of motherhood. Children are a nation's future and raising them is the most important job in the world. Mothers understand how crucial their role is. Why is it so difficult for everyone else?

9

Our son has two mothers

'When people see me with a child they automatically assume I'm heterosexual and some of them start asking questions about my husband. I find that kind of reaction enormously difficult to handle. It began almost as soon as our son was born and made me feel so defensive, as if I needed to go through the whole process of "coming out" again.'

As a proud and, in her own words, 'powerful' lesbian, Brenda never imagined that motherhood would change her persona so dramatically. 'I didn't picture myself being the mother – I always thought I'd be involved as a parent but that my partner would have the baby. The idea of falling pregnant never occurred to me and didn't really appeal to me either.'

Brenda and her partner Lin had been in a long-term relationship for several years before they decided to become parents. It seems the female biological clock ticks on relentlessly whatever a woman's sexual preference, and by their mid-thirties they both yearned to be mothers. After much soul searching and extensive counselling, the pair decided to try to have a baby and, as Lin is

Chinese and Brenda Caucasian, they wanted their child to be Eurasian – 'a mix of both bloods'.

There was no shortage of volunteers wanting to donate sperm as both women had brothers who were prepared to be donors. Initially, Lin was going to be the birth mother but as Brenda's brother already had children of his own and had had a vasectomy the women felt it would be too complicated to use his sperm. They would have had to use IVF technology where doctors extract sperm from the testicle via a needle, get eggs from the mother, inject the sperm into the eggs, and then put the embryos back into the womb. It is an expensive, intricate procedure and had less chance of success than the method they finally chose, which involved using one of Lin's brothers as the donor.

'We chose the brother that I thought was most like me. He and I think the same way, his views on life are politically correct and he shares my values and ideas. He had no children of his own, which Brenda and I thought would be more emotionally uncomplicated, but most importantly he wanted to be an uncle and not a father so there would be no danger with legal challenges.'

However, as all mothers know, nothing about motherhood is ever that certain. Other lesbian mothers have thought they were 'safe' from paternal challenges only to find that male emotions (understandably) are capable of throwing a spanner in the works. Sometimes, despite any 'formal' family document he might have signed, a sperm donor changes his mind about not wanting to know 'his' child. 'Formal' agreements between a donor, the mother and co-mother are not recognised in law and complex legal issues can then arise. Both the judiciary and the gay and lesbian community are calling for law reform.

In 2002, in the Family Court, Judge Guest said, 'Despite recently enacted legislation recognising same-sex relationships there are many areas of state law that continue to discriminate against gay and lesbian Australians. It is time for state laws to be enacted to make available to lesbian women and their known donors a well-regulated scheme with all the safeguards, medical and otherwise, available to heterosexual couples.' The judge also said it was time that the legislature considered 'the nature of parenthood, the meaning of "family" and the role of the law in regulating arrangements within the gay and lesbian community'.

Gay and lesbian groups claim they are being denied their basic rights. While state laws vary across Australia, the raft of legal rights currently denied to gay people in New South Wales is extensive and includes the following limitations:

* Partners in gay and lesbian couples cannot both be legally recognised as parents.
* The non-biological parent cannot adopt the child without the birth parent giving up all parental rights.
* Access to donor insemination is not universally available from health clinics.
* The Human Tissue Act 1983 (NSW) prevents gay men from legally donating sperm.
* Adoption is not an option for lesbian and gay couples.
* Laws covering superannuation do not recognise the dependency of a child of a lesbian or gay couple when a contributor is a non-biological parent.

What will Brenda and Lin tell their son when he asks about his father? Brenda answers, 'We will tell him the truth but I think he will first ask, "How did you get me?" rather than, "Who is my father?" The latter is really more "adult" talk. Our son is of a new generation of kids. It's a mistake to assume automatically that his generation will have the same hang-ups as ours. It's not that we think our son doesn't have a biological father – he does – but the biological factors aren't as important as the two people who are rearing that child.

'I don't have any guilt about not providing him with a "daddy". He has many wonderful people in his life – some of them are women, some are men, some are kids and some are elderly. What children really need in this world are people who love them and an extended family. I don't believe children of lesbian mothers need a man just because traditionally the family unit has one. They need a man because about half of Australia's population is male and our kids need to know how to relate to men. These days many women are widowed, divorced, separated or single and they manage to bring up their children alone. I don't think kids necessarily suffer from this kind of upbringing, but of course it helps if the women have male friends so that children can learn to be comfortable in the company of men.'

'Of course, we have no desire to exclude men,' Lin says. 'All lesbian couples we know think the way we do. They want to include male friends and relatives in their child's upbringing and, like us, they have fathers and brothers who will have a role to play.'

Having selected the right sibling, Brenda timed her cycle carefully and when she determined she was ovulating, Lin's brother would provide them with semen – a masturbatory specimen that they injected into Brenda's vagina with a syringe. They were successful on the fourth attempt. 'Our baby was conceived in Room 412 at the Grand Hyatt Hotel in Canberra,' Brenda says. 'We injected the sperm and then made love. We wanted to be able to tell our baby he was a product of our love and that he was conceived – although with a few biological modifications – as part of our lovemaking.' When Brenda's pregnancy was confirmed, both mothers-to-be were ecstatic and, like most expectant women, their goal was to become 'perfect' mothers.

'We went to ante-natal classes – which were boring – but rather than attending how-to-parent classes we had therapy to help us get used to the idea of becoming parents. The baby was going to transform our lives and we wanted to know the best way to cope with the changes that were coming, the expectations that we had, and deal with them all. When our son was born neither of us had much guilt at the way he was conceived for instance or that he would have two mothers, because we had dealt with it all before-hand,' Lin says.

'Whatever our worries, we both were certain about one thing,' Brenda says. 'We *wanted* our baby. I didn't get pregnant because we slipped up one night when the condom broke. That's the thing about kids born from lesbian couples – you know there's no mistake involved, it was meant to happen. I think a lot of rela-tionships break down once a couple has had a child because there hasn't been any preparation.'

'From the moment we started talking about a child, we used to talk about a "her" and we were shocked when we found out we were having a boy,' Lin says. 'Initially we were disappointed and we felt guilty about that. It lasted for about forty-eight hours and then we got over it. I used to worry that because I wasn't car-rying our son and couldn't feel him kicking and get a sense of who he was that I wouldn't bond with him, but I did from the moment I saw him – it was an immediate bonding.'

Lin experienced more guilt when the time came to tell her parents 'we' were pregnant. 'I'd gone home to have lunch with them and I stood at the front door with my car keys in my hands, ready to make a quick escape but trying to get up the courage to go in. I was so nervous about telling them. I fully expected them to kick me out and disown me. I think they *were* stunned at first but after their first "Oh!" they have been supportive. My father did say, "I guess you don't want to consider adoption?" but when we announced "our" pregnancy he was like any other expectant grandfather and told me that he hoped everything would be okay and the baby healthy.'

As Lin is well aware, many Chinese parents might have reacted differently but she says her parents have never made an issue of her sexuality. When she told her mother she was gay, several years earlier, her mother took the news 'quite well – perhaps she had an inkling anyway. I've never discussed it with my father. He just seems to accept the situation and my relationship with Brenda.

'I don't feel guilty about my sexuality for myself but I do feel the need to protect my parents from any shame they might feel because of it. If they were made to suffer because of me, I would feel guilty. We were at a party recently and an elderly relative told my father that our son would never have a father. She said it twice. My father wouldn't have a bar of it but I was devastated. I thought, "How dare this person hurt my father?" I didn't worry about what she would say to me, only about what she would say to him. The personal growth in my father has been amazing. He has gone from objecting to my brother marrying someone from a different racial group to the stage where he is supportive and protective of Brenda and me – and our son. When he and I talked about our elderly relative my father just said, "She has old ideas." '

Lin says she now values her Chinese background much more than she did as a child. 'I did wish I wasn't Asian when I was growing up. I was so different and so was my family – different clothes, different food – I was embarrassed about everything. All I wanted was to be the same as everyone else. What I feel really guilty about now is not learning my own language. I regret this now but at the time I just wanted to be like all the other kids.'

The months of pregnancy were a continual learning experience for both women, affecting every aspect of their lives. 'Work was a huge issue for me,' Brenda says. 'Lin said it was my choice but the more I thought about it, the more I was convinced that any decision I made about work shouldn't be only my choice, because whatever I did would affect both of us. I did stop working after our son was born, and now I do feel guilty about not being able to contribute financially to the relationship. The other day I went into my former workplace and I came home on a real high. I was excited because I had been reminded how much of a buzz I got out of my work, but later preparing dinner, I felt guilty. I'd had an important management role and I felt I had deserted my colleagues, and that feeling of guilt was mixed up with my other guilt feelings about briefly enjoying being away from home so much.'

Brenda says pregnancy changed her mentally and Lin agrees. 'When she was pregnant, I was under a lot of pressure because Brenda was incapable of making any decisions. It was all down to me. I'd ask her about something and she'd say, "I don't care, you decide."'

'I think perhaps I "lost" my brain during the last three months of my pregnancy,' Brenda admits. 'It must have been my hormones! But Lin and I had quite a few arguments and sometimes when I was at board meetings I'd find myself saying, "Look, I don't think I can make this decision." One day a fellow director said, "I never thought I'd ever hear you say those words."

'My twin sister once asked me if I thought people at work had noticed I had lost my brain cells. I still feel guilty about how I changed and much of that guilt hasn't gone away. I know I'm a different person from what I used to be. I am definitely more sensitive and in many ways, I actually feel I've lost "myself" and I do have guilt about this. About three-quarters of me has changed back but there is a part of me that is vulnerable and defensive because I feel I need to protect our son from everything.'

As lesbian prejudice is widespread, that is understandable. Many people prefer not to think that intimacy between women exists and frown on lesbians raising children. In 2003, the Australian Family Association's spokesperson Bill Muehlenberg was quoted in the Melbourne *Age* as saying, 'Some people have said it's a form of child abuse to bring a child deliberately into the world without a mother and father. Every child has a right to its own mother and father, not two dads, not two mothers and not a committee.'

However, there is plenty of evidence to show that children born to lesbian women using donor sperm seem to be as well adjusted as those brought up by heterosexual couples. In 2002, scientists at the Dutch-speaking Free University in Brussels, Belgium, interviewed forty-one pre-adolescent children, whose average age was ten, brought up by lesbian couples. They concluded that the children were well adjusted, interacted with their family the same way as children growing up in heterosexual families did, and had no problems in accepting that they had two mothers. Around the same time Australia's IVF pioneer Dr Carl Wood released American research suggesting that lesbian couples made better parents because their children were more tolerant of diversity and more socially skilled. 'Women are more verbally skilled,' Professor Wood said, 'so with two women bringing up a child, it has a greater chance of developing better conversation skills.'

'All mothers want to give their children the best possible start in life and a lesbian couple is just as capable of providing a stable, supportive upbringing as any other mother, whether she is single – which society now accepts – or has a male partner,' Lin says. Some women envied the lesbian couple's pregnancy and female friends were lost on the way to motherhood. 'One of our friends was devastated when we became pregnant because she had been trying for ages – three years of heterosexual sex and no success – but it had taken us only a relatively short time,' Brenda says.

'Women are tough on other women, they are so judgemental. As lesbians, we didn't encounter it. We were seen as something "different" but we weren't in competition. After becoming mothers, though, we were on the same playing field and suddenly were being judged. We've fallen out with some of the important women in our lives, including my sister who is a stay-at-home mum living in a small country town. She had always begrudged me my busy life in the city and reckoned I "had it all". When we had our baby – the one thing I didn't have and she did, which made her feel special – a huge jealousy problem arose between us.'

Whatever people might think about lesbians having babies, good old Mother Nature is not at all judgemental and when the time came for Brenda to give birth, like many a heterosexual and gay mother before her, she had a difficult labour. 'I felt guilty but I don't know why. I've always been completely okay with the idea that there's nothing natural about childbirth – any more than you'd have open heart surgery without drugs – but I felt really bad that I couldn't deliver vaginally because I needed an emergency Caesar. My head knows differently, but my heart feels awful about this. Other people's actions added to the way I felt – especially Lin's dad who asked, "So, what was wrong with you?" Maybe I put my guilty interpretation on what was a harmless question but when my nephew then asked, "Is the baby all right?" I felt like I *had* done something wrong. Our son was born with jaundice and I thought I was responsible for that too. The entire time he was in my stomach I felt I was harming him in some way.'

She hadn't though and before long Brenda and the baby were at home with Lin juggling feeds, nappies and sleepless nights.

'Lin would usually get up when I fed him at night and get me a glass of water, and often we would lie together in bed when I fed him.' Like all couples with a new baby, their old way of living was no longer viable. 'Lin and I had no quality time together and I found that hard. By the time we had got him to sleep and then ate dinner, it was time to go to bed. There was quality time for him but none for our relationship.' Occasionally Lin felt frustrated when Brenda was feeding the baby because, 'I couldn't comfort him and that made me feel guilty.'

Brenda was mortified when 'our son had his first asthma attack, because I smoke. I never smoke around him, I always go outside – but I still felt guilty. I was upset with myself the other night too, because it was well past his bedtime and he wouldn't go to sleep, so I brought him downstairs and I said, "You just sit on the floor there," while I got myself a glass of water to calm down. And the first day he went to daycare, I cried and I rang his other mummy several times at work. I have become this "soppy" partner of the person at work and I can't bear that I've become like this and it does make me feel guilty.

'He has finally worked out that one mummy goes to work and he points to different places in our house and says, "Mum, mum, mum, mum," so I've been talking to him about this a lot lately and took him to visit Lin at work the other day. I know it's all a part of his development, but one morning he was so upset when she went to work that he pushed me away and he kicked me because he wanted her. My feelings *were* hurt.'

Lin and Brenda now find it hard to remember what life was like without their son, but becoming mothers has brought them contentment and happiness and cemented their relationship. 'We are a real family now,' Lin says, 'and the maternal instincts of two women will provide just as much love for our son as traditional parents could ever give him.'

They know that the road ahead will not be all smooth sailing. 'We worry about him going to school and that when the other kids find out there is a mummy and a mummy that he might be bullied,' Brenda says. 'We can assume that might happen and we can prepare for it.'

'Prepare for the worst and hope for the best,' Lin says. 'Two of our friends who have a child at school were concerned about their daughter when it became common knowledge that she had two mothers. Some snotty-nosed brat came up to her at lunchtime and said, "How can you love your mother? She's a lesbian." The little girl just looked at him and said, "You love your mother, don't you?" End of story. We thought that was beautiful.'

School is a few years away for Brenda and Lin's child, and for the moment they are enjoying the pleasure of his company. 'I love it now that he is talking,' Brenda says. 'He said "bubble" to me last week and my heart sort of grabbed. My joy is seeing him develop and hearing his words. It is one of the incredible things about motherhood – he can say the word "bubble" and I'm on a high all day.'

'The happiest motherhood experience for me was the day our son was born,' Lin says. 'I felt so completely at peace with myself and us as a family unit. I was voted the happiest parent in the ward and I didn't give a damn what other people felt about us having a child.'

10

Anything your child can do mine can do better

Like everyone else in society mothers have become caught up in the race to hurry children through childhood. In their efforts to make sure their kids are well equipped for the future, they jam their lives with all kinds of before and after school activities – all the while drumming in the 'winning is everything' philosophy that is so much a part of twenty-first century thinking. Childhood years must not be wasted taking part in activities merely for fun, but rather spent on honing skills and abilities that are the same as adults'. Studies show that in the past twenty years children have lost twelve hours of free time a week, and eight of those lost hours were once spent in unstructured play and outdoor pursuits.

So, how did this happen? Pushing children too soon was once frowned upon, but throughout the twentieth century attitudes to child rearing changed rapidly. Women's Liberation not only changed women's lives; it also altered the way families operated. Superwoman was also a Superparent raising Superkids. Children were encouraged by their time-stretched mothers to do chores that once their mums would have done – like starting dinner, putting away their clothes, minding their siblings. Adult responsibilities began to be pushed on to them.

About the same time there was all kinds of research promoting the benefits of early childhood learning, and parents began to believe that children should learn more and be exposed to more. Perhaps working mothers innocently helped push this line of thinking, as, while they wanted to believe it was best for their children, there was another benefit. Kids could go to pre-school to be cared for, freeing their mothers from the pressure of finding someone to look after them while they were at work. Children used to stay home with their mothers until they were five but now parents push and schedule their children as early as possible, anxious not to waste a second of their precious years when their learning capacity is said to be at its peak. But compelling medical evidence shows that this is harmful, both physically and emotionally for children.

All work and little spontaneous play is not good for children. They need time to enjoy their childhood – to play as they choose; to use their imagination; and sometimes just to gaze at the clouds drifting by, watch a butterfly flit around the garden or throw pebbles in a pond. As the traditional freedoms of children continue to be eroded, psychologists are warning that too much planned activity and not enough fun can be harmful to a child's development. The evidence is all around us if we choose to look. Tell today's children to go outside and play and many of them ask, 'But what will we do?' Children are so used to leading timetable lives and being entertained that they no longer know how to amuse themselves. They've lost the art of make-believe.

David Elkind, a professor at Tufts University's Department of Child Development, one of the world's leading centres for the study of how children grow and learn, based in Massachusetts, USA, has been writing about the dangers of forcing children to grow up too soon for many years. He first sounded the alarm in 1981 in his book *The Hurried Child: Growing Up Too Fast Too Soon*. A third edition of the bestseller was published in 2001, only to reveal that the child psychologist's call-to-arms had gone unheeded. Kids were being made to hurry even faster than before and the Hurried Child syndrome – a condition in which parents over-schedule their children's lives, push them hard for academic success and expect them to behave and react as miniature adults – has been identified.

'There's a lot of stress in children's lives, caused by a combination of factors – the mass media, the school system, new technologies, and parents who are overloading their children with lessons, extra tutoring and other activities,' Elkind says. 'Children are being "hurried" because parents aren't making the kinds of choices necessary for a fulfilling and protective family life. Instead, they pursue personal, material and status-oriented goods, very often to the detriment of the family. That is not to say parents don't care for their kids, but because our culture is so steeped in radical individualism and materialism, the very idea of what a family is supposed to be has been lost. It is not surprising that the children suffer as a result, in terms of both emotional and character development.'

Elkind believes the world is going through one of those periods in history, such as the early decades of the Industrial Revolution, when children become the unwilling victims of societal upheaval and change. 'It is a very difficult time in which to be a parent and it's getting more difficult,' he says. 'In their efforts to "prepare" their children for whatever lies ahead parents want to give them everything they can. But piling on too much too early not only takes away from time for free play, which is an important activity for children, it can also add strain that kids aren't ready to handle. Whenever you put a lot of pressures on kids and don't allow them enough time to play and relax, stress and stress symptoms come out.'

What alerted Elkind to the extent of the problem was the increase in the number of children suffering from stress at his clinical practice. The same thing is happening here in Australia. 'The number of kids I see suffering from anxiety disorders and depression these days is alarming, and the age of children with these problems is getting younger and younger,' says Penny. 'I'm seeing children as young as eight with recurrent abdominal pain or headaches and, while I'm obliged to run all the tests, I know that invariably they will turn out to be normal and stress will be identified as the problem. There is also an increasing number of children taking stimulant drugs for ADHD (Attention Deficit Hyperactivity Disorder). As a doctor, I'm the first to agree that children who really have this disorder need medicating – but the realist in me is concerned about the increasing numbers who are labelled with this problem. I often suggest to mothers that their children need to do less activities and have more time to relax, but my advice falls on deaf ears.'

$$\approx$$

Once parents used to strive to keep childhood a carefree golden age but now they propel their kids through it. Children cross adult boundaries long before they are ready and know too much too soon through exposure to television, movies and the Internet. Their innocence is disappearing as quickly as their childhood years. And on top of all this they have to cope with competitive mothers who use them to score points over other mothers.

Competition between mothers often begins almost straight after birth. Usually within a few weeks of leaving hospital, most first-time mothers visit their nearest baby health clinic where they are allocated to a group of ten or so other new mothers, who initially meet for morning tea so they can form friendships, compare ideas and support each other. This is sisterhood networking at its best. Many lifelong friendships had their beginnings at a mothers' group. This form of interaction is of particular value to those new mothers who do not have a large social network of family or friends to support them in the early days of motherhood when they are trying to 'learn the ropes'.

But some group members become so caught up in the race to motherhood perfection that new mothers can be made to feel utterly inadequate when seemingly innocent questions are tossed at them. 'Has your baby's head always been *that* shape?' 'Are you sure you're *trying* hard enough to breastfeed?' 'Isn't your baby rolling over *by now*?' 'My baby is *already* sleeping through the night.' 'I always make my *own* baby food – it's so much better for them.'

As their babies grow older, the competition between mothers intensifies. 'My Johnny was walking at eight months; your Jesse is fourteen months, why *isn't* he walking?' 'Isn't your child toilet trained *yet*?'

Sharon Freund calls this competitive phenomenon 'Baby Olympics'. 'It is truly nauseating and must be the bane of mothers' groups worldwide but otherwise I found my group to be a lifeline. First time around, I had no idea how to do anything. I found having a baby isolating and sometimes lonely and then there was the exhaustion and the hormones. Getting out, having a coffee and eating something sweet and chatting with other mums – invariably about our kids – made me feel I wasn't alone.'

In the twenty-first century, mothers' groups often meet on the Internet. Sally Burleigh found talking with other mums in her group a great way to relieve any anxiety she had. 'We would email each other about our problems and share information about how our kids were going. We exchanged photographs and when someone cooked something their baby loved, she passed on the recipe to the rest of us. We were all very supportive of each other and I loved our weekly sessions.'

Later, as babies become toddlers and then start school, mothers compete to have 'gifted and talented' children – kids who are so smart that their parents have to form a support group to discuss them. These mothers raise children who are immersed in all kinds of scheduled activities. They rattle off how many dance classes little Suzie goes to and how many awards Johnnie has won and how all their children are geniuses, which is why they have enrolled them in extra coaching classes to assist their 'brain power'. Mothers of 'normal' children – there are still some left – are left feeling inadequate. 'It's crazy, I know, but these women do make me feel guilty,' Mary Lou says. 'I can't help but think I'm failing in some way because I'm not offering *all* the opportunities that I should to my child and perhaps I'm not pushing her enough either.'

But David Elkind says that too many parents are intent on raising mini-adults rather than children. 'It is important to strike a balance for kids with artistic lessons, sports, school and family activities and to be careful not to squeeze out family time or take away children's thinking times – those quiet moments of the day when contemplation and creativity should be encouraged.'

'I think we've lost track of good old-fashioned play and letting kids use their imagination to make up a game without adults butting in to run it,' Rebecca Wilson says. 'And when kids have a dispute many parents rush to intervene there too. Kids have to sort out their own conflicts but I do sometimes think – should I feel guilty for not arbitrating?'

Rebecca tries not to be pushy with her kids. 'One of my boys is a good swimmer and I reckon a lot of mothers would have said, "Right, you're going in the swimming squad," but I told my son it was his call and that if he wanted to do it, then he could decide for himself.'

Rebecca's approach is an admirable one. When it comes

to sport and kids, pushy parents are anything but sporting as far as their children's choices are concerned. Hoping to raise athletic prodigies they commit them to tennis lessons, swimming classes, football, netball, gymnastics and other sports – and sometimes more than one – reminding their kids that sporting superstars can earn a lot of money. When Tiger Woods appeared on the world's sporting stage as a teenager, scores of young boys were seen in our public parks practising their putting under the encouraging eyes of their parents. Tiger is a superb golfer, but how many people know that he took up the sport when he was only two?

Mothers of 'accomplished children' often induce Mother-guilt in other mums. 'For years, I was tortured by a mother up the street,' says Mickie. 'Her kids were always doing extra before and after school activities. "Madeline is doing Suzuki violin," she announced one day, in her mother-of-accomplished-children voice. "Oh, when did she start?" I asked casually. "She's been learning for three years now and is already up to Book Four."

'My eight-year-old daughter and I had obviously missed the boat in the music department and she was never going to be a concert violinist. But I told myself that perhaps it wasn't too late. She might be a fast learner and so I signed her up. I can't remember if I asked my daughter if she actually wanted to learn the violin or not but really that didn't matter; she *had* to learn because I wanted to be a mother-of-accomplished-children. Of course, that meant we had to buy a violin and they come in various sizes, which means you have to keep buying new ones as your child grows. When I committed to (and paid for) the first term of lessons, what I didn't realise was that with this method of teaching the mother has to sit in on every lesson so that she can supervise practising sessions. We lasted about six months. There is only so much 'Twinkle Twinkle Little Star' played continuously in only one semi-tone that this mother could endure. The only person more delighted than me when I finally pulled the plug was my long-suffering daughter.'

Jean Kittson has watched many mothers become 'over focused' on their children. 'I know a number of women who have given up professional careers to concentrate entirely on their children. With little else to occupy them, everything about their kids' school life takes on a much more exaggerated importance. Their kids do debating, fencing, boxing, this thing, that thing, and the poor children have no time to do their own thing at all. That is just so wrong; kids need to be allowed to be kids.'

'What I notice is the way younger mothers are always telling their children to hurry up. What on earth makes them think that every moment of their children's waking lives must be crammed with things to do?' Ita asks. 'Have they really forgotten what their own childhood was like? I remember mine . . . climbing trees; having dirt bomb fights with my brothers; playing hide and seek; making lemonade and selling it for pocket money; going to the park and playing cricket; reading books for fun; putting on magic shows and concerts for my grandparents; going to Saturday matinees at the local picture show and watching Tom and Jerry cartoons before the main feature, which was usually a Western; and playing cowboys and Indians with my brothers – I was always an Indian and had to be captured!' ('Oh, how I know what it's like to be the only Indian,' Penny says. 'My two brothers always relegated me to that role too.')

'There is so much pressure on little children to do more, learn more, excel more, and it seems to me there is very little time for fun. These days children even fail kindergarten! What a dreadful cross to bear through life. My young nephew was tested twice for his mathematics skills while he was still in kindergarten. Why are we subjecting little children to this kind of nonsense, because that's what it is,' says Ita.

David Elkind believes schools tend to label children too quickly and too early and usually for management requirement reasons rather than for reasons related to the effective teaching of children. Understandably mothers are eager to see their children succeed, but allowing children some time to explore and satisfy their curiosity is another good way to acquire knowledge.

Mothers may also try to make up for their own shortcomings through their children's studies. One little boy complained to his best friend how he was stuck doing Kumon – a maths tuition program – two afternoons a week, which he hated. Why was he doing it? Because his mother had been bad at maths when she was at school.

'I see these poor little darlings in the surgery,' Penny says, 'with big black rings under their eyes. It would be bad enough if they were allowed to stay up so late playing but it's rarely that. They've been burning the midnight oil doing extra maths, extra languages, extra music or the excessive amounts of homework they have been set. Quite frankly, it's unhealthy.' Too much too soon does not always add up. Force-feeding children with learning can affect their mental wellbeing.

School projects can often be just as much of a challenge to the parents as they are for the kids. In fact, they can often be the bane of a mother's life and present the ultimate dilemma. 'If I do help I feel guilty for not letting Emma develop initiative,' says Charlotte. 'If I don't help her enough, I feel I have abandoned her to the scorn of her peers for letting her turn up with a dud effort. The biggest guilt of all is how irritated I feel when she brings home the prospective project. All I can think is, "Oh no," at the prospect of all that cutting and pasting.'

Sarah, an advertising executive, had a busy weekend planned working on a concept for a new client when her daughter arrived home with her latest school project on glaciers. 'It was the last thing I needed. Lara had to research four of the wretched things and build a model of her favourite one. What ten-year-old has a favourite glacier? I reckon teachers decide that if their weekend is going to be messed up by marking and lesson planning, that they may as well ruin parents' weekends too. I can think of no other reason for them organising such a wicked form of revenge as the "school project". They try to disguise the torture at times with subtle name changes like "Extension Activity" or "Weekly Task Card", but as an experienced mother, I can sniff out a project a mile off.

'I know projects are supposed to be done by the children, but when your kid turns up with his coloured pencil sketch of the pyramids done all by himself, he can't help but be a little underwhelmed when it's displayed next to the 3D cross-sectional diorama smugly presented as his own effort by some kid whose father coincidentally has a PhD in archaeological architecture. No mother who wants the best for her child would let them suffer that kind of humiliation. The teachers know the parents help the kids with them; the mothers do too. And I know that if I don't help with school projects I will feel guilt because my kid will look stupid, neglected or both.'

As children learn by example, we can only wonder what their minds make of cheating parents and condoning teachers.

Canteen duty is another fertile source of Motherguilt. Some mothers like to rub the guilt in by mentioning casually just how often they do canteen duty. Others like to lay guilt trips on non-canteen duty mums by saying things like, 'Of course, it's the very mothers who don't help at canteen because they are out somewhere being paid to work that use the canteen the most for their kids.'

However, canteen duty is a vocation and not all women have the calling. Rebecca Wilson decided long ago that her contribution to her sons' education would not be via the canteen. 'I work between forty and sixty hours a week and I can't contemplate doing canteen duty – but I do feel guilty about it.' Joy Smithers found the canteen hierarchy daunting. 'It was such a competitive place. I remember one humourless mother chiding me for laying the hot dogs in the wrong direction!'

'But canteen duty *is* an excellent way to find out what's really going on at your children's school,' Beth says. Melbourne mum Anne Brennan did canteen duty once and had a ball, but a return appearance was vetoed by her six-year-old daughter. 'She told me never to come back because I was the only mum with bright red lipstick and the shortest skirt!'

Robyn had paid for a babysitter to mind her younger two children so that she could put in an appearance for her oldest son. 'The usual long queues of rowdy kids were surging up to the counter. A particularly arrogant fourteen-year-old boy gabbled out an inordinately long list of what he wanted and as I was painstakingly assembling them while keeping a running total in my head, he started to drum his impatient little fingers on the counter. So I smiled at him sweetly and leant over the counter and said quietly, "I am a lawyer and I've spent a fortune having my other kids babysat so that I could come and work in this hell-hole today and I don't need any garbage from you!" My queue was very short after that.'

Many children consider canteen duty an affirmation of their parents' love for them. Mary Lou's son saw it as proof his mother was prepared to take some time off work in order to give to him. 'He wanted assurance that he was an important part of my life. I explained there were some things I was good at and some things, like canteen duty, at which I was hopeless but that I'd be happy to do other things. So I was roped into doing the scoring for basketball even though I know nothing about the game at all – but at least my son was happy.'

Adele Horin tried to allay her canteen duty guilt by using her 'other' talents and agreed to coach the school's debating team. 'Because I'm a newspaper columnist they thought I'd be good and that I'd be able to marshal arguments. However after the team lost every single debate I wasn't asked back the following year.'

Men are beginning to do canteen duty these days. 'My kids are always pleased to see me and come up to say hello with big grins on their faces,' Charles says. 'I'm usually the only dad on duty and treated just like everyone else on the team. I do it because my job entails shift-work so I have days off during the week whereas my wife works full-time. When the mothers ask me if I'd like a cup of tea, I ask them if they'd like a cappuccino and when they say yes, I drive up to the shops and bring us all back one – and win a few brownie points.'

Some fathers who front up for canteen duty at other schools are treated like deities by their female co-workers and bask in the glow of praise that greets them: 'Aren't you a wonderful dad?' 'Isn't your wife lucky?' 'How do you like your tea?'

George, a partner in a major legal firm, has been taking time off work for the past four years to do canteen duty. He insists he was not pressured to do this, but that he volunteered because his wife challenged him to do so. His all-male roster includes a surgeon, a merchant banker and an entrepreneur. The mothers refer to them as 'token canteen males'.

After his first day on duty, George told his wife that his all-bloke team was so well organised that the four of them had been able to slip away between morning tea and lunch for a coffee and a business discussion for an hour and a half. His wife, a canteen veteran, could not figure out how they had managed it until the canteen supervisor later revealed to her that, unlike the mothers, the fathers' team had conveniently overlooked the annoying cleaning up part of the job. Of course!

Even when not associated with canteen duty, food still can be used to prove a mother's worth. 'I remember having to bring "a plate" to my daughter's kindergarten Christmas party,' Joy Smithers says. 'I didn't have time to make anything and there were quite a few raised eyebrows when I humbly placed a large bucket of Kentucky Fried Chicken among the lovingly prepared butterfly cakes and other home-cooked goodies – but hey, whose food got eaten first!'

Rebecca Wilson says stay-at-home mothers made her feel guilty when her children were at kindergarten. 'When I'd drop the kids off on my way to work, they'd say disapprovingly, "You haven't baked a cake for today's stall." It wasn't good enough that I'd give them a plate with a five-dollar bill sticky taped on it, which they'd then sell for $2.50 – I hadn't made a proper cake. I'd stand in front of them feeling like a naughty child.

'I think I've failed the school lunch competition too. I make my children's lunches and they buy their lunch once or twice a week. They have the most basic sandwich – jam or honey, that's it – and I give them a piece of fruit and perhaps a biscuit or some other treat. When I see some of the kids with their amazing lunches – some kids even take sushi – I feel guilty, but I remember when I was little and my mother was a working mum I used to have Vegemite sandwiches every day. I was always so envious of the kids who had packets of dried apricots, nuts and homemade cakes.'

Ita remembers tinned spaghetti sandwiches, 'which I loved and still do. I offered them to my children once and they turned up their noses. I used to swap them for the kosher lunches that the Jewish girls brought to school. Their food was always delicious and they thought the same way about my spaghetti sandwiches.'

⌒

Birthday parties are now also a huge source of stress. Once upon a time, children's birthday parties were simple affairs, not annual *events* that cost parents a fortune. 'When I was little, kids had a party when they were six, another when they were twelve and finally one when they were eighteen or twenty-one, unless their parents gave them an overseas trip instead,' Vicki says. 'One of the mothers in my son's class recently spent $50 000 on a birthday party for her five-year-old. She had three jumping castles, donkey rides and clowns, every kid in the class was invited – even Batman made an appearance. It was a fabulous party but spending that kind of money on a little child's party is ridiculous.'

'We have a rule about birthday parties – only every second year and a maximum of five kids,' Tanya says. 'Mine are restricted to two hours and I never have them at home,' says Rebecca Wilson, who says she hates birthday parties. 'The best one we ever had was for my son's tenth birthday when we asked thirteen kids because that's a rugby league team size. We also invited the football great Laurie Daly, and he showed the boys how to tackle, run, etc., and then we had the birthday cake in the grandstand. I can't stand these women who have birthday parties from eleven until four on a Sunday, because that's the day I like to spend doing my own thing. You have to drop your children off at eleven and then hang around in some impossible place where you can never park.'

'Probably the best party we ever had was for my son Tom when he turned seven,' Penny says. 'We reserved a table in the local national park, which cost only $14.50. We had brought along a whole lot of takeaway food containers so that Tom and his mates could catch tadpoles. It was the sort of stuff we did as kids back in the good old days when we were allowed to explore and have fun and learn all sorts of things without constant and intense adult supervision. The kids had a wonderful time and went home happily with their tadpoles – the more scientifically minded of them later watched theirs metamorphose into frogs. The party was an immense success and it didn't cost a fortune. We didn't have to play all those awful games either. However, we subsequently found out that tadpoles and frogs are protected species and the boys' tadpole hunt had been illegal and ecologically incorrect.'

'You only enjoy kids' birthday parties if you have a shit-load full of wine before everyone gets to your place,' Neroli says. 'But there was one I will always remember. It was my eldest son's second birthday and we'd invited all our adult friends who also had small children. When I brought out the cake – just a simple choco-late cake, nothing fancy – my son suddenly realised it was for him and there was a little look on his face that was lovely.'

'Adults always seem to be invited to the birthday parties my daughter gives her children,' Mary says. 'It was much easier in the days when I gave her birthday parties. First of all, we didn't start having parties until she turned five and had begun school. I'd ask about six or eight of her friends who would be dropped off by their mothers at about two in the afternoon, returning at five to pick them up. We played a few games like pass the parcel; the kids had sandwiches and jelly in oranges, plus a birthday cake. Each child went home with a balloon on a string, a piece of cake wrapped up in a paper napkin and if any of them had a brother or sister there was a slice for them too.

'The other day my daughter, who works full-time, gave her two-year-old twins a birthday party and invited thirty of their friends – I ask you, what two-year-old has thirty friends? – plus their parents. Of course, she hired entertainment and even had caterers. "Mum," she said, "I thought it would be better for the kids to have some entertainment and to keep them amused and not have them running through the house so that their parents would be relaxed." What does a children's birthday party have to do with "relaxed" parents?'

Ita confesses to a touch of extravaganza with her chil-dren's parties. 'Humphrey B Bear came to one and he was a smash hit. Another time, because my daughter was born on Christmas Eve, we had Santa Claus as a special guest. Perhaps we full-time working mothers give our kids fabulous birthdays to calm any guilt feelings we might have about the amount of time we spend away from them.'

'I think it has a lot to do with time,' Sharon Freund says. 'Working mothers always have less of it but a greater disposable income, and try to assuage their guilt by making it up to their kids in material things, whether it's the latest in dolls, clothes or automobiles.' But Alex thinks that is only part of the reason. 'We mothers do want to make up for lost time – but really, kids don't give a damn. It is mothers who want to outdo each other and I really don't know why. Perhaps it has something to do with the modern-day obsession with money and flaunting it for all to see.'

⁀

Children and parents now find themselves locked in a competitive, fast-paced existence, always trying to squeeze every productive moment out of their lives. But, what *is* the big rush? All children have the right to be children during childhood, but the early forcing of so many choices on them is denying them that prerogative. Children are not meant to behave like mini-adults – they need to play and indulge in childlike behaviour and just enjoy life. It is what children are meant to do.

Childhood is not meant to be some kind of competition but a rite of passage to be enjoyed by both mother and child. 'I encourage mothers to let their kids be kids,' Penny says. ' Play should be "their work". They learn so much from their own games, and seeing their excited, happy faces when they're doing their own thing gives a mother such a high.'

'I couldn't agree more,' Ita says. 'Childhood passes quickly and special moments are rare, coming when a mother least expects them. She needs to grab hold of them when they happen because seeing things through a child's eyes is one of the greatest joys of motherhood and the stuff of which memories are made.'

11

Different cultures, different times

There is nothing new about children claiming their parents do not understand them, and when couples have settled in Australia from another country and their children are born here it is not uncommon for the kids to declare their parents are from a 'different' world. This is more a cultural clash then a generational difference and does not mean that these children want to deny their heritage, but rather that their parents' 'old country' culture does not fit into the new culture of Australia.

When love enters the picture the situation can become even more sensitive. Australia is proud of its attitude to multiculturalism but its success has also encouraged cross-cultural relationships and, ultimately, intermarriage. Research from Melbourne's Monash University shows that second-generation Australians – children of immigrants – are increasingly marrying people from other ethnic groups, and their relationships are happy and successful. However, some immigrant parents, even though they might have lived here for years, are apprehensive about 'mixed marriages' and the possible loss of their traditional cultural values. Sometimes they can be so strict and rigid in their expectations that children keep their feelings from them.

Kevin and Anthia fell in love almost at first sight. She is Australian-born of Greek parents, he is from Adelaide, and they met in Newcastle where they were both working and living independently from each other. Kevin is a hairdresser and Anthia is a naturopath.

'Anthia's parents weren't accepting of me at all,' Kevin says. 'They rejected me because I wasn't Greek even without meeting me. Her parents wanted her to marry a Greek boy, preferably one from Cyprus where they both came from. They didn't want to arrange Anthia's marriage; they just wanted to control who she met. Yet she has never been out with a Greek boy in her life and before we started seeing each other she had been in a relationship with an Italian.' Anthia was then twenty-eight and Kevin, thirty-seven, had been married before. 'My divorce was another black mark against me as far as her parents were concerned,' he says.

'I used to tell my parents, "If you could see the way he loves me you'd understand,"' Anthia says. 'But they were determined that I should marry someone of the same religion and nationality. I did feel a little guilty that I was so angry and I kept telling myself that I didn't want to judge them as they were judging me. I knew they were trying to maintain a culture the way it was when they grew up in Cyprus, but this old way of life didn't fit in with the one we had in Australia.'

'We had been seeing each other for eight months when Anthia moved back to Sydney for work purposes,' Kevin says. 'Her parents came to help her move furniture and so did I and we met for the first time at Anthia's apartment. They said hello but with their heads down – it was a sort of "if you don't see him he's not there" attitude. Still, that was mild compared to what happened when I first met Anthia's *yaya* (grandmother). She threw herself on the floor and wailed, "Who is he? How could you do this?" She absolutely freaked out. We left with Anthia in tears.'

Anthia's parents were delighted to have their daughter back in Sydney and would visit every second night and drop off food. 'In Greek households everything leads back to food,' Kevin says. 'Anthia's mother believes food is to share with others and to celebrate life.'

Before long he was on his way to Sydney too. 'I moved some of my things to Anthia's place, but before moving in had to return to Newcastle to finalise some business matters. Of course, Anthia hadn't told her parents that we were going to live together so when they came over on one of their regular visits and saw my furniture they bombarded her with questions. "Whose is all this? Whose bed? Whose TV?" Anthia said nothing. "It's *his*, isn't it?" her mother said. When Anthia replied yes they stormed off. "How could you do this to your father?" her mother yelled. "You're not our daughter any more!"

'Although we lived there for about eight months they never came back. But other family members, including Anthia's favourite aunties, were more accepting and had begun asking me over. Without telling me, Anthia asked two of her aunts and her eldest brother to try to persuade her parents to accept me and an invitation to lunch at their home soon followed. We arrived at one p.m. to find the meat had been barbecued and was ready to be served. We sat down at once – just me, Anthia and them – and ate lunch, amid a lot of silence. We didn't stay long.

'I kept seeing them at other family functions and they continued saying hello with their heads down. This treatment continued for eighteen months by which time Anthia and I had decided to get married. When we went over to tell her parents, the atmosphere was tense and Anthia was nervous. She called her mother from the kitchen – her favourite place – and

I simply announced, "I've asked Anthia to marry me and she's accepted."

'After what seemed like a deafening silence her father asked, "How does your family feel about you marrying a Greek girl?" I told him they loved Anthia. Then her mother asked what religion I was. To be married in the Greek Orthodox Church you have to be Christian and although I'd never been christened I satisfied them that my beliefs were Christian. From this time onwards I was invited to family functions at their home but it wasn't until we were formally engaged that I was finally accepted.

'The engagement party could have been straight out of the movie *My Big Fat Greek Wedding*. Anthia's parents invited at least 250 members of their family and friends, all of whom brought gifts. The "event" was held at their home and included a formal ceremony where the priest blessed our wedding bands and we made a commitment to get married. The engagement changed everything. I think Anthia's parents were worried I'd take advantage of her, but once I'd made a commitment before God to marry her their attitude changed.'

And when, before the wedding, Kevin decided to get baptised in the Greek Orthodox Church Anthia's parents were overjoyed. 'I decided that as I was going to marry in the Greek Orthodox Church and raise our children in the faith I might as well get baptised. I had several sessions with the priest and felt very comfortable making this decision. The only person who wasn't happy was Anthia, who always claimed that the one thing that had made her life miserable was her religion – she resented always being told she couldn't do this or that because of it. Her parents had always wanted her to marry a good Greek Orthodox boy and the one person she thought would never be that was me.' 'I was afraid that he would become like them and I didn't want that,' Anthia says.

There were times, Kevin says, when he thought of giving

up his fight for Anthia. 'But we all get on well now and I call my mother-in-law Mum. I love the Greek sense of family and the way everyone respects each other. My in-laws come over once a week. Mum cleans, rearranges everything, takes the dishes out of the dishwasher and washes them and takes our dirty washing home with her to do.' Other couples might consider such 'help' interference but it doesn't worry Kevin or Anthia because it is the Greek way.

～

When her eldest son told Eleni that he was marrying an Australian girl her reaction was similar to that of Anthia's parents. 'I was very upset. She seemed like a nice enough girl but what did I know about her or her family. There were big arguments that lasted for days. I told my son I wouldn't come to his wedding and I told his fiancée that I had nothing against her but I wanted a Greek girl for my son.'

Eleni reasoned that a Greek girl would understand how hard it had been for her when she came to Australia as a young bride from Greece, when only twenty-one, with her husband Peter, who was forty-five, and that she would have been brought up to have the same 'family-centred' values. She would bring her family to Eleni's home – they would all speak Greek and Eleni would finally have the extended Greek family she so often yearned for. Now it looked like her dream was not to be.

Eleni has never forgotten how difficult her life was when she first came here. 'Australia is different now, but back then many Australians didn't want to know us. They called us "dagos" and said things like, "Go back to where you came from."' Peter had been living in Australia for twenty years before they married in 1950. 'He came back to Greece for a holiday and to see his mother. He asked my father if he could marry one of his daughters and chose me. One of ten children, Eleni grew up on her parents' farm, leaving school when she was twelve to help at home. Marriage to an older man was considered more secure, she says. Eleni had no say in the matter even though she barely knew Peter and had seen him only a couple of times before they married, but she says, 'My husband was a good man and I respected him.' The day after their wedding they sailed for Australia. 'I never saw my mother again. She died eight years later.'

Peter owned a milk bar in the Sydney seaside suburb of Manly and the couple lived in a small two-bedroom apartment nearby. 'I was desperately lonely and homesick. I had no one to talk to except my husband who left at 9 a.m. to open the milk bar, which didn't close until ten at night. I used to ask myself, "Why did I come here? Why? Why? It has ruined my life." I felt like killing myself. I had no relatives, no friends and I couldn't speak English.'

Within three-and-a-half years Eleni was the mother of three children. 'When I came home from hospital with my first baby, someone from my church put me in touch with a Greek woman whom Peter paid to stay with us for a few weeks to teach me how to look after my baby. I started to see myself in a different way once I had my children. Although I was lonely, I had something to live for and, slowly, I started to feel happier.' She also began to meet people through her church. Her faith is important to Eleni and she still goes to the same church every Sunday. 'I had been in Australia for ten years when my brothers started to emigrate – that made a big difference because I had some more family and I didn't feel so alone any more.'

Hard though those early motherhood years were Eleni insists she never experienced motherguilt. 'My family came first. I did everything for them. I only felt guilty about not seeing my mother before she died. I would have liked to have shared my being a mother with her and for her to see my children and them to see her.' She feels no guilt about the way she felt when her son said he wanted to marry a non-Greek Australian girl. 'I always wanted my children to have Greek values. I sent them to Greek school on Saturdays. I wanted them to marry Greeks. I spoke to them in Greek, cooked them Greek food and took them to Greek dances in the city. Being Greek was special to me. I had grown up in a good family and I wanted my family to be like mine and to experience the happiness I had when I was growing up.'

But in the end, nothing Eleni said or did could persuade her son not to marry Angela. 'He told me, "I love this girl and I am going to marry her and that is that." So, I changed my mind and went to the wedding. I had a good time too!' Eleni says.

For her daughter-in-law, Eleni represented the ultimate challenge. 'I knew I had to prove to her I was good enough for her son,' Angela says. 'I was determined to give her a completely different impression of Australian girls.' Eleni's view had been coloured by the girls she had observed in the apartment block where she lived. 'It seemed to me they drank a lot and that young men visited them frequently. I thought all Australian girls were like this,' she says.

'I knew I would fit the bill and that I wanted to be the sort of mother who put family first,' Angela says. 'Before we were married, she bought me a beautiful coffee set for my birthday. I loved it and I felt she had accepted me.' But Eleni says acceptance really began with the birth of her first grandchild – Angela's daughter. 'Now I know her, I am very close to Angela,' she says. 'I love her and think of her as my own daughter. She is a good family girl.'

⁓

It is not only Greek mothers who are protective of their sons when they want to marry outside of their culture. Italian mothers have similar traits, as Paula discovered when she fell in love with John. 'I am definitely not what my mother-in-law wanted or envisaged for her eldest son's wife. I think she is bitterly disappointed I was not Italian or, at least, a traditional wife and by that I mean one who cooks, looks after the children and obeys her mother-in-law. The Italians know, socialise with and virtually live with every second cousin in a warm and friendly way, and when I married John it was particularly difficult for me because I am not close to my own immediate family and the introduction of dozens of inherited cousins was a very daunting experience.

'I distinctly remember the first "family" lunch I was invited to as a girlfriend. There were at least twenty people around the dining room table and I was the object of much curiosity, questioning and general probing. The $64 million dollar question – had I passed the test? Fortunately, I am dark and look Mediterranean so it took a number of relatives several years to work out that when they spoke to me in Italian I didn't have a clue what was being said. I just nodded a lot and said, "*Si*!"

'Like a movie script, my mother-in-law and I came to loggerheads over the wedding plans. She wanted lace tablecloths; I wanted white linen. I think all her frustration and disappointment about her eldest son's choice of bride-to-be came to the surface in the "war" over the lace tablecloths. It was at this point in our relationship that I discovered if things did not work out the way she intended, or anyone challenged her, she took to her bed, said she was sick and stayed there for anything up to a week, refusing to talk to anyone or see anyone. I have the type of personality that gets mad, yells and then it's all over in a few minutes – no grudges. So I actually thought this type of behaviour was very funny, which of course just annoyed her even more. She has done it several times since we have been married but not lately, so she has clearly decided this is one tactic that doesn't work.

'The turning point in my relationship with the Italian culture came when I had children and I realised that should anything happen to me, my husband and my daughters would never be alone. The support, love and caring that all the family and relatives have shown my children has been wonderful and something I would never take away from them. Their grandmother adores them, fusses over them, loves them to bits and they her. There have been odd moments of frustration when she has done something that annoys me – for example, cut their hair without my knowledge (she did it once but would never do it again!) – but they have a remarkable, close and gorgeous relationship with her.

'My attitude has also changed over the years. While we now keep a friendly distance, I often wonder what type of life she would have led had she been given the opportunities that I have taken for granted. She came to far north Queensland from Sicily as a very young girl and has never had an education to speak of. She is amazingly creative and very talented, so had she been encouraged to expand her horizons and not been forced to accept the traditional Italian culture, she is a woman who would have made her mark on the world. Unfortunately, she is, as many in her generation of Italian women are, a lost soul, caught between two cultures and unable through circumstance to settle comfortably in either of them. I am sure she is very envious of the life women now lead and would love to live her life again and take advantage of the opportunities offered to her.

'Although I am still an outsider with my nose pressed against the window of Italian culture, and always will be because I am Australian-born, marriage into such a vibrant, dynamic, loud, happy, joyous race of people has been an interesting, often challenging, but incredible experience. No doubt, my mother-in-law and I will find something else to argue about in the future but, the next time we don't agree, one of us will probably back down and agree to live and let live. After fourteen years of marriage to her son, we have reached what I now call an uneasy truce. We have reached a certain level of tolerance and acceptance in our relationship and an understanding that, while we are different, we both love her eldest son and two granddaughters more than life itself.'

~

Richard's 'Italian experience' was not quite as successful as Paula's. He met Maria when she started working for his father in the family medical practice in suburban Melbourne in the mid-seventies. One day he asked her to a party and they were soon inseparable. Then it was time for Richard to meet Maria's family. She was the eldest of four and had a sister and two boisterous brothers. Her parents were Italian immigrants from a small town in the north-western region close to Milan. Her father worked in the building industry and the family lived in a house Maria's father Gino built with other Italians soon after arriving among the wave of immigrants after the Second World War. Mealtimes were noisy affairs around a large table in the kitchen, a far cry from the gentle, almost academic, conversations at a dining-room table in Richard's home.

'About six months after we began dating, Maria and her nearest brother kept a promise to their parents to visit Italy and their grandparents who still lived there. She said she would be gone for three months. We wrote to each other at least once a week and because our letters overlapped, answers and comments came erratically. After two months I sent Maria a letter asking her to marry me. However, her next letter told of a trip to the lakes of the far north of Italy and the following letter told of her search for a church and a priest. I didn't know what to think. Was she telling me she'd met someone else? Three letters after my proposal, I finally received the definitive reply I wanted.

'My parents were delighted. I negotiated with Maria's second brother to make sure he and his young sister were out of the house on the evening I was going to ask her parents. They were in the kitchen as usual after the evening meal, mother Theresa sewing and father Gino reading. I told them of our desire to marry and asked them for their approval. They were polite but for once Maria's father did the talking. They liked me very much, I was a fine young man, but I was not Italian and, more important, I was not Catholic. I was devastated.

'Gino suggested we go to their parish priest together so that the issue of Catholicism could be explained. I grasped at this very thin straw. The meeting with the parish priest was brief. I explained my relationship with Maria and our love for each another. The priest asked me to leave the room while he talked with Gino. While I have no idea what was said in that meeting, it later became clear the priest explained to Gino that old practices could not continue, that my apparent impediments were no grounds for the priest not to marry us.'

The months that followed were strained as Gino in particular struggled to accept Richard as a prospective son-in-law, but when Maria returned from Italy wedding plans were implemented. 'It would be a Catholic Church wedding, of course, and I was required to attend lectures with the priest to learn about the faith and to promise that any child would be brought up in the Catholic faith,' Richard says. 'Whenever we visited her parents they were always welcoming and polite, but the exuberance that had characterised the household during our early months of courting was gone.'

Three years later a series of events occurred that highlighted the tensions Richard and Maria's marriage had generated. First, Maria became pregnant. His parents were delighted with the news. Then, six months later, the elder of Maria's two brothers, Antonio, got a girl pregnant. She was a blonde, white, Anglo-Saxon Protestant. Marriage plans were rushed into place. 'When we had a beautiful girl both our families celebrated,' Richard says. 'But when

Antonio's new wife had a son it seemed as if all of Gino's frustrations at seeing his children marry outside his system were dissolved in that child. He turned his focus, his attention and his generosity onto the "new" family. If they wanted or needed anything he found it for them. Maria and I – and our daughter – were all but forgotten because Gino had a grandson and heir.'

Over the next five years, Maria's two other siblings also married outside Gino's system with no ill effects. 'Maria and I had broken a dam wall and, while her siblings took advantage of the break, we were never forgiven for our actions,' Richard says.

Among all the cultural stereotypes, the Jewish mother is legendary and in some families the cliché of the 'Jewish mother' is a larger-than-life fact, so much so that it is not uncommon for a Jewish daughter to vow she never wants to be anything like her mother when she marries and has children of her own. 'The thing about the stereotypical Jewish mother is that she can be *very* real,' Roelene Markson says. 'Take my mother for instance. The other night I was in bed when she rang and our conversation went something like:

'"I am sick."

'"I'll come over."

'"No, don't do anything . . . but I feel ill."

'"What can I do?"

'"Nothing. You lead your life."

'"I'll come now."

'"Don't worry. I'll get better . . . but I am sick."

'What else could I do but get up, put on some clothes, grab some chicken soup and whatever else I could bloody find and rush right over to her! When it comes to laying on guilt my mother is in a class of her own.'

'The last thing I wanted to be when I grew up was a

"Jewish mother",' Rachel Goodman says. 'I was never going to get married and have children. My mother had turned me off from ever wanting to do that. She was constantly critical but not in a constructive way, and I used to worry that if I had children I'd treat them the same way.' Love changed her thinking completely however, and 36-year-old Rachel is now married to a Jewish businessman! 'He has helped me get back my confidence, as did a year working overseas where – somewhat like Samson – I was able to grow my hair for the first time with impunity, as my mother, who was unquestionably obeyed, always insisted that I have fortnightly haircuts when I was a child and a teenager. Growing my hair long brought with it an independence and confidence that as a teenager I only dreamed about.' Rachel and her husband now have two children and a third on the way. 'I discipline my kids but I never criticise them,' she says.

'Do I love my mother? Some days I don't think so. The domineering Jewish mother is meant to be a stereotype but she actually exists in my mother who is a powerful figure in my life. My mother has strong views on nutrition, health and education, especially when it concerns her grandchildren. Because her milk dried up she wasn't able to breastfeed me and as she watched me breastfeed my first child she let rip. "Why are you breastfeeding? You have no idea how much milk that child is getting. How do you know he isn't still hungry?" The fact that my son was gaining weight and sleeping well didn't wash with her at all. Three months later when I weaned him and my mother saw me giving him a bottle, she was so happy. "A nice big bottle of milk, *now* you can see how much he is eating." And she actually smiled at me in approval.

'When my son was older, my mother still thought I wasn't feeding him properly. "What do you mean you gave him one chop? I always gave you two. You are not giving him enough to eat." My mother on health goes something like: "That child is constantly sick, he always has a cold. What are you doing wrong? If you kept him warm – a child should always be warm – he wouldn't get sick." She even gave me the dunce's hat for education. "You were reading by the time you were four, your child isn't. You are not doing something right. I was a better mother than you."

'I've never been able to please my mother. She heaped guilt on me whenever she could and she still does. When I was in my teens, I was terrified of my own shadow and had the lowest self-esteem, and I blame my mother with her constant criticism for the state I was in. She had the ability to make me feel two inches tall and didn't just lay guilt on me, but smothered me with it – as my grandmother did to her. I have no intention of continuing that particular "tradition" with my children.

'The other night, she in effect told me that I wasn't a good daughter, that I was too cold-hearted, and all the while she was sitting at my table, in my home, eating the food I had cooked! Sometimes she tells me even my husband isn't good enough. The *only* thing she doesn't criticise is my being a working mother, although she does think I do too much. In a quiet moment, I find myself thinking about my mother, trying to work out why she finds fault with me all the time. I do feel guilt about her.'

Annie would love to have a closer relationship with her mother but she 'brushes away any help I might be able to give her, even when I think she might be dying. Does my mother lay on guilt? Oh, yes! She did it five minutes ago on the phone. She didn't even say hello but got stuck right into me. "Don't you ever dare call an ambulance for me again. If I need one, I will make the call." She was referring to an incident – well a major happening is more like it – when she called me at the office recently saying she didn't feel well. Her speech was slurred. I was terribly worried. She sounded awful and so I called an ambulance to take her to hospital and it turned out she'd had a stroke. Afterwards she was furious with me. "If I am supposed to die, let me die." I felt so guilty. What was I supposed to do?'

Roelene Markson is a fellow sufferer. 'I'm forty-seven for God's sake and I feel guilt about everything. My grandmother laid it on my mother who laid it on me and always told me, "You can never be perfect, you must do everything for your children." I am doing my darndest not to lay guilt on my daughters. I have made a conscious decision not to do it.'

Diane, who is thirty with two young children, is 'not sure about laying on guilt – perhaps it's "expectations". Then again, perhaps that's a euphemism for laying on guilt. I think it has lessened a little for the younger generation, and I include myself in that, because we are not Holocaust survivors. My mother's generation, for instance, tends to feel guilty about not suffering the pain and horror that their parents experienced. Sometimes I think my generation feels guilty for not being able to feel anything about it because it is too far removed.'

Rabbi Allison Conyer, one of three female rabbis in Australia, says she believes the 'tradition' of passing on guilt will continue to lessen because younger Jewish mothers do not spend as much time in the home as their mothers and grandmothers did. 'Children are not their single focus because many of them are now in the workforce and have other things to occupy their minds.'

'Jewish mothers have incredible problems letting go of their children and, when they finally do, complain that it has taken years off their lives,' John Symonds says. 'When I left home, Mum said, "That is one year less I have to live." He is twenty-eight and his relationship with his mother Helen has been uneasy since his last year at school. She came to Australia when she was ten with her parents, who had survived the Holocaust. 'John has always had the ability to say exactly what he thinks but he does tend to exaggerate.

He has a thing about me making him feel guilty – not me *and* his father; just me,' Helen says.

'She does make me feel guilty,' John says. 'I've felt the effect of her laying on guilt but I am not sure what is behind her desire to do it. She says things like, '*Ben* is a PhD,' implying there is something wrong with me and that I've disappointed her because I don't have one yet – *and* as a result have taken years off her life. Or she says, "He's a doctor, he's a lawyer," implying that I should have been a good Jewish boy and become a doctor or a lawyer. The problem with stating that opinion, over and over and over again for years, is that if I don't do amazingly well then I'm not living up to my potential and I end up feeling guilty.'

'That is John's interpretation,' Helen says. 'I don't want him to feel guilty. I have no desire and no intention of doing that to him. I do want him to *be* however. He has the capacity, the ability and the potential. When he was five I did want him to become a doctor, but when it became apparent he was not going to become one I wanted him to be a professional and go to university to succeed there. I may occasionally say, "What have I done to deserve this?" and when I do, I am *taking on* guilt, not laying it on John!'

Helen is not the first Jewish mother to urge her son to become a doctor. Her own mother also wanted her to be a doctor but, like John, the thought of a career in medicine had no appeal. However, many Jewish doctors do admit they took up medicine because they were 'prompted' to do so by their mothers. 'This is a culturally inherited value that has nothing to do with the prestige of being a doctor; it's more a means of survival,' Helen says. 'Education is seen as the best means of escape from and/or coping with the persecution that Jewish people and their ancestors have endured for thousands of years – and still endure – often resulting in them moving from country to country. In order to make a living, medicine – or a trade that does not require language for success or survival – cannot be bettered. This is one of the main legacies that each generation of Jews inherits, even in the twenty-first century, and is as much relevant today as in the past.'

Anita, a 'professional' with a PhD in chemistry, agrees. 'My mother brought me up to value education because in the past Jews couldn't own land, were only permitted to do certain jobs, and over the centuries have become used to things being taken away from them,' she says. 'But no one can take education away from you. As a Jewish mother, I feel responsible for seeing that my family follows the cultural customs and that includes "pushing" education.'

In his book *Let Us Praise Jewish Mothers*, French Jewish doctor and author Bruno Halioua studied the lives of mothers of famous Jews – including Albert Einstein, Karl Marx, Marcel Proust, Sigmund Freud, Sarah Bernhardt and Anne Frank. He concluded that none of them would have become the successes they were without the mothers they had. 'The secret of Jewish mothers is that they give not only love like all mothers to their children but also tremendous self assurance,' Dr Halioua says. Einstein proudly acknowledged his mother's effort when he won the Nobel Prize in 1921 by sending her a telegram that read: 'Mother – *WE* won the Nobel Prize.'

'The role of the Jewish son and his mother is unique; their relationship is an unbreakable bond,' Roelene Markson says. 'She worships her son and in return he worships his mother. If she tells him to do something, he does it. When we had our second daughter, my mother-in-law said, "What a shame she's not a boy."'

'I know that my mother would have liked a son, although she never made me feel unwanted and gave me the very best of everything, but when I married and my first child was a son, she was overjoyed,' Naomi says.

Unlike many other religions, perhaps because it is more

than a religion, Judaism is passed on through the mother. Orthodox Judaism, which many Jews believe is diminishing but is by no means dying out, assigns a woman a definite place in her home over which she reigns supreme. A prayer in appreciation of her role as a wife and mother is always said on the Sabbath. Although she is mistress of the household, a Jewish woman can still combine motherhood and career. Her right to do that (because of her good education) is taken for granted, but it does emphasise the pivotal role a mother plays in the success and survival of the Jewish family.

'What I like about Judaism is the sense of family. I am not religious but I like the traditions, like the Friday night dinner marking the Sabbath,' says lawyer Sharon Freund. 'Our three children will be given a Jewish education so they know their background, culture and traditions. I would feel guilty if I didn't do this.' Before she married, Sharon says she dated lots of non-Jewish boys. 'But at the back of my mind I always knew I'd marry another Jew. Marriage is hard enough not to marry a man who understands the Jewish traditions.'

Helen would prefer John to marry a Jewish girl for much the same reason. 'If you have a lot of things in common with your spouse then half your battles have been won. It's not that I think Jews make good or better husbands and wives; the key issue is the similar background and the "bond" that Jewish people have shared for thousands of years.'

Conflicts with traditions of culture and the demands of modern life are not confined to particular ethnic groups. Asian mothers often feel very isolated because of their cultural customs. Emmelyn is a stay-at-home mother of two boys, aged fourteen and sixteen. She and her husband are both Singaporean Chinese and have moved home many times because of the demands of his job with a large multinational company. He once lived in Sydney full-time with his family but a major promotion resulted in him transferring to Shanghai where his head office is based. Emmelyn lives in Sydney with their sons while her husband 'commutes' four times a year from Shanghai. 'We didn't want the boys' education to be disrupted once they were in secondary school so it was best I stay here,' she says.

Emmelyn, who is forty-three, accepts this lonely arrangement because she says it is her duty. 'My role is to take care of the household. The ultimate responsibility for the children and the home is mine, not my husband's. This is the way I was raised and if anything goes wrong, I will feel guilty.' Sydney has the reputation of being a tough city to crack socially. When you are an Asian mother on your own it is even harder. Emmelyn has plenty to do – her two sons see to that – but she has suffered from loneliness and cultural isolation and has missed not having a sense of community, belonging and friendship.

'Looking back, Australia has been good for all of us, but we don't have that extended family or the support that people who have lived here all their lives tend to take for granted, and at times we do feel a bit lonely,' she says. Her greatest source of support has been the Chinese Christian Church, which provides an extended community for the family. She and the boys attend church every Sunday and take part in social activities that the church organises throughout the week. 'It's a relief to be able to talk to other mothers who are also away from their family and home and who understand my cultural background,' Emmelyn says.

The greatest difficulty she's faced in bringing up her sons in Australia is the clash of cultures. 'Australian working mothers sometimes feel guilty because they're not at home with their children 100 per cent of the time, but I feel guilty because I am not able to be a role model for my sons according to Western standards. If we were back in Asia, my role would be acceptable, but my sons are Australians now yet I am giving them an Asian role model that might create problems for them in the future. For instance, they might expect their wives to be like me. They have seen their grand-mothers serve male members of the family, waiting on them hand and foot, and here I am, doing much the same thing although I try not to. I'm trying to make my sons more independent but it's hard because it is not the way I was brought up to think. I know there are times when I do mother them too much and it's hard to change my ways – but I am trying.'

Loneliness seems to be a big problem for many women from other countries when they come to Australia. Ten days after her marriage to Gerald in Malaysia, Esther arrived here to make her new home. 'I found living in a strange country without family and friends had some lonely moments,' she says. Both Malaysian Indians, their marriage was an arranged one. 'I had the right of veto but I found Gerald interesting from the day we met over lunch at my auntie's home,' says Esther, who feels she has been 'very, very blessed' as the couple eventually fell in love and enjoy a warm and happy relationship.

Like Eleni and Emmelyn, she looked to her religion for assistance in helping her adjust to the Australian way of life and had not been here long before she made contact with her local Anglican Church where, she says, 'Everyone was so friendly and welcoming.' But because she was used to having a large extended family there were still some very lonely moments. 'I wasn't working either and Gerald's job as a management consultant meant he had to travel a great deal. In the first three years of our marriage he was away for 370 days!

'I didn't know how to cook "normal food" either. When I was growing up we had a cook at home. I only knew how to bake cakes. I didn't even know how to *buy* food. In Malaysia, when we wanted to buy meat, we would go to the market and point to a carcass and say, "I want this part." When I first arrived in Australia, I would take my recipe book to the butcher and he would help me work out what cuts of meat I needed.' Ironically, Esther is now a caterer!

She and Gerald have prospered in Australia. They have a comfortable lifestyle and live with their fourteen-year-old son Dinesh in a beautiful home with sweeping views of Sydney Harbour. 'We'd have liked four children but I suffered from severe endometriosis and it was considered a miracle that I even managed to have one child. But I do feel guilty that I haven't been able to give my son any siblings, and I also occasionally feel guilty that he doesn't have all his extended family living closer.'

The first sign of a cultural difference of opinion between Dinesh and his parents happened when he was about ten and they forbade him to watch *The Simpsons,* a television show that was popular with his classmates. 'A combination of our family beliefs and religion made me feel I didn't want my son exposed to certain attitudes that might influence his behaviour and his patterns of thinking. There were mixed feelings within our Anglican Church about this show. I wanted Dinesh to be old enough to understand the satire in it. He obeyed us, but was angry about it because he didn't want to be different to the other kids.'

Now that he is a teenager more complex issues are emerging, such as dating, for instance. 'When I was a girl I didn't go out with boys,' Esther says. 'I was asked, but my Mum didn't think I should go out with boys on a one-on-one basis. I wouldn't say no to Dinesh about dating, but I wouldn't encourage it at a young age and certainly not before he is sixteen. I have no issues about my son having to marry an Indian, however — a partner from any racial group will be okay, as long as she shares his faith and principles. I don't want to "arrange" a marriage for him but should he ask me to help him meet someone, I will do so.'

While there are many differences among the cultures and clashes are sometimes inevitable, on one point there is no disparity at all. Universally, the motherhood bond is strong and common to all mothers. It cannot be broken by language difficulties or differing cultural points of view. Most mothers, wherever they come from, want only the best for their children. As Emmelyn says, 'Mothers can't lead their children's lives for them. It is their journey, not ours. We can only guide them.' Most mothers learn to do that very skilfully.

12

Tackling the teen years – triumphantly

There is so much negativity about the teenage years that many mothers dread the thought of them. They expect the worst, only to be pleasantly surprised at getting through this stage with only occasional difficult periods – and this is the norm rather than the exception. Teenagers can be challenging, but they are also delightful human beings, enormous fun and full of ideas for changing the world. Their minds are constantly processing a multitude of thoughts. One moment they want to tell their mothers everything, and the next, they want her to mind her own business. Attitudes to teenagers are usually coloured by the negative press they so often receive. If one teenager does something wrong, all are tarred with the same brush.

In the same way that little children are being hurried through childhood, teenagers are being subjected to similar pressures and pushed into adult roles too early. They may be called teenagers but they are expected to be adult-children. Once teenagers used to look to their elders for the answers to their questions, but now they can find out whatever they want to know via the Internet.

The influence of movies and television on their lives is significant too. Through these mediums boys and girls learn about violence, drugs, rape, gang mentality – and adult madness. They learn much of what they know about sex from Hollywood where film-makers produce films that are so sexually explicit nothing is left to imagination and sex between a man and a woman is often shown as a violent act. In the past, kids were sheltered from this kind of material. It was private, strictly adults-only material, but not any longer. Children used to be protected from death and serious illness too, but television brings this kind of information into their homes on a regular basis – including such things as the deplorable 2004 photographs of naked Iraqi prisoners who were tortured by US Army personnel. Children know too much too soon. They are unprotected. 'I consider myself to be very broadminded but even I am shocked at times by what some kids say, including my own,' Penny says.

Everywhere you look children are mimicking adult behaviour. Kids swear like troopers these days – another Hollywood influence helped by parents who think nothing of swearing in front of their children whereas once they would not have done so. Even the physical appearance of adults and children is becoming similar. At the 2004 Australian Fashion Week young teenage girls performing as models were stars at the opening day. The *Daily Telegraph* reporter David Penberthy described them as 'barely pubescent teenagers' and that one of them wore a 'Liz Hurley-style dress cut down to her navel'. She was photographed for the paper and looked pathetic and out of place. It could be argued that this half-naked little girl was in need of help from the child protection authorities. Where were they? Naomi Toy, another *Telegraph* reporter observed, 'Not only were these girls dressed as grown-ups, they played at grown-ups by refusing the offer of finger food by joking about not being able to fit into their dresses . . .'

Just like adults in the workforce, teenagers are expected to put in long hours at school and then do hours of homework each day and on weekends. Their final school year is so pressure packed that if a boy or girl fails they believe their chances for a successful future could be gone forever. That might sound somewhat melodramatic but teenagers' thinking is often over the top.

'My kids had many anxious moments during their last year at school. I've thought for some time that schools put too much pressure on children,' says Ita. 'They really need their parents at this time of their lives. I cancelled most evening engagements during my kids' respective HSC years so I could be home in time to cook dinner as many nights as possible and we could have a relaxed meal around the table. I managed to fit in a walk with Kate before dinner because she found it helped her unwind.

'They both laughed at me later, but I was always telling them that some of the world's most successful people had once been told they were failures. Beethoven's music teacher told him he was hopeless as a composer; a newspaper editor fired Walt Disney because he didn't have ideas; when Edison was a boy his teacher told him he was too stupid to learn anything; and Einstein's grades were so poor his teacher told him he would never amount to anything. I think the point I was trying to make sank in.'

As she navigates the capricious pubescent zone a mother must remember two things: what it was like to be a teenager and never to lose her sense of humour. Maternal cunning is also crucial. From time to time mothers do have to go into bat for their adolescent children without their knowledge, because a teenager's natural instinct is never – well, hardly ever – to do as his or her mother wants. 'When I realised my son was smoking – most of the fourteen- and fifteen-year-old boys at his school did – I went and talked with his house master, the football coach and even the dentist (nicotine stains the back of people's teeth) begging them to deliver anti-smoking messages in the hope that he and the other boys would give up,' Ita says. 'Ben never knew I'd done this and the boys did stop, but only temporarily because they wanted to win the football competition and the coach mounted a persuasive argument.'

Mothers often forbid their teenagers to do things because they are frightened they might make the same mistakes they did, but kids need to be allowed to explore new ideas and boundaries. While it is natural to worry about a teenager's growing independence, letting go comes with the job of being a mother. 'Teenagers do go through a sort of rejection of parents, which I think is understandable, because they do have to create their own personality,' Carla Zampatti says.

'My son is just entering the teenage years and what he really wants is more geographical independence – to be able to walk up the road, to ride his bike. I know that, but I still feel anxious,' Mary Lou says. 'If I let him and something happens, I'll feel terribly guilty because it would be my fault for letting him have too much freedom. And when I don't I also feel guilt because I'm impacting on his ability to grow and to become independent.'

From time to time teenagers sorely test their parents' patience, as they always have over the generations. In every one of them there is the child who still wants to be nurtured and told what to do, but there is also the budding adult who wants to make his or her own decisions, to break away and to take risks. These two personalities are understandably at odds with each other. A classic example of this is in the title of psychologist Anthony Wolff's book on teenagers called *Get Out of My Life but First Could You Drive Me and Cheryl to the Mall.*

As with everything to do with raising children, attitudes have changed markedly. Once children were seen and not heard.

Not any longer. Children are brought up to give their opinions and have their say, and when they are teenagers they not only like this, they demand it – just like adults. This does not mean mothers agree with everything they say, but bringing up teenagers today involves a lot more discussion and negotiation than in the past when parents drew a line in the sand and if children stepped over it they were in big trouble. Nowadays parents draw a line in the sand from which they constantly retreat. This constant 'negotiation' can be tiring, frustrating, uncertain, and not without guilt.

'During Melysha's HSC year, it was necessary for her father and I to go away for two weeks,' Pauline Markwell says. 'I had been so concerned about doing this that earlier in the year, I'd asked her permission – would it be all right with her? "Who is going to look after me?" she asked. When I told her that she was okay at cooking meals herself she then asked, "But who is going to make sure I have the right meals and the right balance?" I offered to arrange to have her grandmother come down from Brisbane, suggested she might like to have a friend over to stay or perhaps that she go and stay with a family friend. She didn't want any of these things and so, when the time came, her father and I went away as planned. But no sooner was I home than she ticked me off for leaving her.

During the actual HSC exams, I was back at work and she was not happy about this either. Even though her father drove her to school, she told me all the other mothers took their girls to school on HSC days. She accused me of not looking after her well enough because while the other girls' mothers cooked them "proper meals" I didn't. Her father couldn't help with meals – he never does any-thing in the kitchen – but of course I made sure she was well fed. She was exaggerating.' In fact, seventeen-year-old Melysha was just twisting the knife, something teenagers do with consummate ease.

In their struggle to be independent, teenagers can be

extremely cruel to their mothers, trying out all sorts of different techniques to see what sort of response they create. They know so well how to push their mother's guilt buttons. Belinda bought a mobile phone for her fifteen-year-old daughter so she could phone her when she was out to check that she was okay. 'But whenever I try to ring she either doesn't answer my calls or has her phone turned off, but when she wants me, she calls and says, "Where are you, Mum? I need a lift."'

Teenagers dye their hair weird colours, have Mohawks, dreadlocks, shaved heads, tattoos, body piercing – all in an attempt to be different. This kind of experimentation horrifies their mothers, who watch their once beautiful child evolve into a grunge, a goth, a tart or some other grooming nightmare. Yet, ironically, these kinds of cosmetic changes make them all look the same. The truth is that teenagers like to be different from their parents but they do not want to be different from their peers. Teenagers whose parents are high profile are just as conformist and, while they love their parents, are self-conscious when, because of them, they stand out in the crowd. Former politician Ros Kelly used to do the morning teas at her teenage kids' sporting events, 'pretending *not* to be Ros Kelly but just being a mum. I thought that was important, because the one thing kids don't want is a "personality" mother.'

The son of a prominent television journalist was upset when his father was sent to New York to cover the 9/11 tragedy, and when the terrorist attack was discussed as a group in class he broke down and cried. Shortly afterwards, his mother received a call from his class teacher asking her to come and collect her son because he was upset after being attacked by a gang of boys, which the teacher described as 'a pack of animals', teasing him about his father. One classmate even said, 'Your dad will probably die.' The boy was extremely upset and his mother eventually organised a change of schools.

Bullying is not confined to the children of high profile parents. Research shows that one in six Australian students is bullied every week. Boys are usually bullied by one person, and girls by groups. In April 2004 three teenage girls were expelled from Ascham, one of Sydney's most prestigious girls' schools, for bullying a fellow student. They were accused of defacing her locker and putting mouldy food and an offensive handwritten note inside. Most schools now have written policies regarding bullying and children learn about it in their Personal Development classes. 'Parents need to not only ask themselves what makes a bully but also what makes a victim,' Penny says.

'I'm not aware that either of my kids "suffered" because of my profile,' Ita says. 'I have asked them about this and they have said not, but I was always conscious of the need to let them enjoy their anonymity. It helped because I kept my maiden name, which meant their surname wasn't the same as mine, and I rarely allowed them to be photographed. When he was in his teens, there were times Ben found my presence "embarrassing" and I was aware of that. I drove him to football one Saturday and told him I'd go to the supermarket and pick him up afterwards. However, when I returned, he told me the coach had asked him to play another game. "That's fine," I said, "I'll watch. Where will I go?" He pointed to some trees that were miles away in the distance. "Gosh, darling," I said, "that's a long way away. I don't think I'll be able to see the game well enough." He just looked at me. I knew at once what his problem was. "Look," I said, "there's an antique shop down the street. I'll go and browse and be back when the game is over." He was so happy. I drove around the corner and sat in the car reading the newspapers until it was time to collect him. At my daughter's school I was seen as something of a role model, not so much because of my career achievements but because I didn't learn to drive until I was forty. I was the only mother on P-plates and Kate told me the girls were impressed.

'Probably my biggest challenge during my kids' teenage years happened when Kate was fourteen and she was diagnosed with a rare form of juvenile arthritis. It took some time before the doctors were able to diagnose what was wrong with her. She underwent many tests and we both went out to the Prince of Wales Children's Hospital in Sydney, where we answered questions put to us by a round-table of doctors and specialists. It was an unsettling time. One evening as I was kissing her goodnight, she asked me if she was going to die. The poor little thing – it was a terrible moment. It never crossed my mind that she was thinking such thoughts, which only goes to show how hard it is for parents to fathom what is going on in the teenage brain. Although I reassured her that she was not going to die and she believed me, it was hard for her at school – because she was "different", she couldn't do what the other girls did. She had to give up piano and tennis for instance, and had to endure severe pain in her hands among other things. She needed a lot of love and encouragement. Fortunately her story has a happy ending. We did everything the doctors said and today Kate is cured – well, her specialist says 98 per cent cured. I don't think doctors ever like to over-commit themselves!'

While the majority of teenagers grow up to be productive, happy adults there are signs that for increasing numbers of teenagers all is not well. For one thing, they are drinking too much. The number of teenagers suffering from depression is escalating. Mental illness and youth suicide is rising. So is teenage crime. So are obesity and anorexia. Why are these things happening to our teenagers? Expecting them to be mini-adults while still children is a major factor, and a society that promotes a 'must-have' culture is another. Parents spend a great deal of time working to pay for material things and many teenagers grow up thinking 'things' matter more than people.

There is another possible cause that cannot be ruled out. This growth in children's illnesses and mood disturbances has occurred in line with mothers' greater participation in the workforce. Could this be coincidental? Can any intelligent woman seriously believe such a thing without doubt of any kind? Surely, it is impossible to overlook something many mothers would prefer to close their eyes to – that perhaps children have become the 'victims' of the female ambition to have it all.

'It would be so much easier to pretend this is not the case, but I think we have to face facts,' Ita says. 'Maybe women got it wrong, and I include myself in this indictment. It is all too obvious that children need more of their mother's time than we have been able to give them. Kids need to be supervised, and teenagers in particular need more of their mother's listening time. Perhaps, most of all, they need their mums to be in less of a hurry. We can't turn back the clock but we have to find a better way to raise children. We can no longer close our eyes to the reality that there are many teenagers in need of help. In the past, women have undervalued their role as a mother, and children have been the losers. Keeping our heads in the sand in the hope that what is happening will go away is not the solution. If, as mothers, women need to feel guilty about anything it is children. We have short-changed them. They have been sending out signals for years now but we have preferred to be blind to what has been going on.'

Consider the evidence. Fifty per cent of Australian fifteen to seventeen-year-olds drink alcohol, and the last time they consumed alcohol 25 per cent of these teenagers had more than seven drinks. 'Parents often express surprise at the amount their children drink but forget that they are their children's role models,' Penny says. 'Teenagers copy their parents. They watch them consume four or five glasses of wine each night.' Many mothers admit to having their first glass of wine at 6 p.m., which they knock off as they get dinner ready. In many European countries, where wine is served with most meals but taken only in moderation, teenagers do not have such a problem with binge drinking.

Mothers of teenagers often discuss among themselves how best to react when they catch their kids out, and have discovered that behaving as their children least expect can have unexpectedly good results. When another boy's mother rang Tessa to complain about her son's drinking, she blamed herself for 'going wrong somewhere. He was with a group of boys at this other mother's home and they decided to have a beer – heaven knows where she was. They were only fifteen and, as far as I knew, my son didn't drink. With a couple of beers on board, he behaved like a bloody idiot and somehow damaged a curtain. When he got home, I was ready to read the riot act but then I changed my mind. I quietly told him I'd trusted him and that he had let me down. The look on his face told me that my tactic had hit home. I never had a problem with him and alcohol again. Our natural reaction as mothers is to yell at our kids because we are so worried but I think sometimes the softly, softly approach works better.'

Jane's fourteen-year-old daughter Jessica had invited a boarder from school to spend the weekend at her home and the girls had permission to go to a neighbourhood party. She and her husband were having dinner with friends when their son rang to say Jessica's school friend had been sick and would not wake up. They rushed home to discover the girl sitting on their front veranda and semi-conscious. 'I really had to shake her to get her talking but it didn't take me too long to realise that she'd had too much to drink,' Jane says. 'I told my daughter, "This is your friend and you

watched her get like this so you clean her up and take care of her."
I made Jessica undress her friend, make her have a shower and put
her putrid clothes in the washing machine. Then I said she would
have to lie in bed with her – all night – watching her, with a bucket
just in case she was sick again. I also insisted the girl had to tell her
mother what had happened. I'm sure Jessica has a drink at parties,
but I think this experience has taught her not to overdo it.'

Marion caught her son smoking so made him eat a huge
roast lamb dinner with lots of vegetables and gravy and then smoke
an entire pack of menthol cigarettes. 'He was as sick as a dog and
has never smoked since,' she says. 'I don't believe in being laid back
at times like this. Cigarettes are the enemy, attack is the best plan!'

One of the fears most mothers share is the threat illicit
drugs represent. Many kids will try them at some time or other
during their teen years, but youthful experimentation is generally
a passing phase and the majority of teenagers usually do not have
major problems. However, some teenagers are more susceptible
than others and kill themselves from drug overdoses. While fathers
often think, 'How did my child get into this?', women invariably
ask themselves, 'Where did I go wrong as a mother?' Amanda had
two daughters: one is a successful doctor, the other died of a drug
overdose. 'I don't know what I didn't do right that caused this to
happen. They were both raised the same way but she seemed hell
bent on this path of self-destruction and now I don't know which is
worse, the grief or the guilt.'

Janet's son Denis started smoking marijuana when he was
fourteen. 'We used to find bongs hidden around the house. Every
time I found one I would rant and rave and go berserk at him and
throw them out. Last year, when Denis was nineteen, I found one
again. When he came home, I told him he had to move out. He
became teary and asked where was he supposed to go. I told him
he should have thought of that before he broke our rules again. He

packed a few things and left. I felt sick. He was away for three days and it seemed like an eternity. He kept sending me text messages saying, "I do love you, Mum." Four days later, I came home from shopping and found him in his bedroom doing an assignment on the computer. We had a serious talk about the rules of the house. I had felt guilty when I made him leave but I knew we couldn't keep going the way we were. I haven't found a bong since.' 'This kind of "tough love" approach can work,' Penny says. 'I've seen other mothers use it successfully too.'

⁓

In the past parents could say with reasonable certainty whether or not their daughters were virgins up to a certain age – say eighteen. Even though it is against the law to have sexual relations with a girl or boy under sixteen, many underage teenagers are sexually active. 'It's normal for teenagers to be thinking about sex and their sexuality; their hormones are flooding their body. But the age at which they are putting their thoughts into actions is getting younger and younger,' Penny says. 'Issues such as sexually transmitted diseases and contraception are breezed over by teenagers, as are important issues such as self-respect and valuing relationships.'

This relaxing of sexual standards has continued in spite of the threat of HIV/AIDS and, because teenagers are often unsupervised while their mothers are at work, it is easy for them to experiment in their own homes. Some teenagers have no difficulties discussing sex with their parents while others find it impossible, but because it is so easy to find out about sex through the media, they no longer rely on their mothers and fathers for this kind of information.

'But parents should not ignore the fact that many of their teenagers are sexually active,' Penny says. 'Their value systems are different and trying to force our moral code on them will only lead to a breakdown in communication. That's not to say we shouldn't tell them our beliefs, but it is equally important to provide them with accurate information about contraception and safe sexual practices. These discussions increasingly seem to be the responsibility of mothers.'

Nothing quite prepares a mum for the first time she finds her teenager in bed with a member of the opposite sex. 'I went to wake up my son for breakfast,' Janie says, 'but when I opened his door there was a girl in bed with him. They were both fast asleep. I closed the door at once and returned to the kitchen. His sister was making the tea. "Your brother has a girl in his bed. What will I say to her when she gets up?" "What about good morning?" my daughter said.'

'Every mother reacts to this kind of situation differently,' Penny says. 'Sometimes they think they've failed in dealing with the issue of sex and feel guilty about it. I had a woman as a patient who had found a condom in her son's jeans. He was only sixteen and she was worried, not only about whether her son was old enough to deal emotionally with a sexual relationship but also the age of his girlfriend who was only fifteen. When she spoke to her son he wasn't aware that he was breaking the law and could be charged with carnal knowledge because until the condom discovery she'd never discussed this issue with him.'

Oral sex presents an even bigger problem. Like former United States president Bill Clinton, many teenagers think that oral sex is not really sex and have no idea that sexually transmitted infections such as herpes, chlamydia, gonorrhoea and even HIV can be spread this way. 'Many teenage girls like to think they can remain virgins, and avoid pregnancy, not realising that just as they should use condoms for vaginal sex, they should also do so for oral sex,' Penny says. 'Lots of mothers are embarrassed, or don't even think to talk about oral sex, but they must because teenagers have to understand that, like every form of sex, it carries risks.'

'When my teenage daughter was going overseas at nineteen I talked to her about the importance of safe sex,' Michelle says. 'She rolled her eyes . . . she knew all about sex . . . what was I going on about. "There's no need to look at me like that," I told her. "I'm aware that you think you know everything *but* when a big passion hits you every piece of advice I've ever given you will go from your head. That's what passion does. Put some condoms in your wallet and make sure you always have them with you."'

Teenagers do feel emotions deeply, just as adults do. 'When my seventeen-year-old daughter was dumped by her first boyfriend, after going out with him for a year, she was devastated,' Helen says. She just sat in her room for hours sobbing. Her pain was clear but what surprised me was how I felt – it brought back all those painful feelings I'd experienced when I'd broken up with a boyfriend in the past. I wished I had somehow prepared her better for this.'

'I used to creep past my son's bedroom in the morning before he woke up,' Suzanne says. 'Usually he'd thrown off most of his bedding and the thought used to cross my mind that physically my beautiful boy had the body of a man but mentally he was still a child. He was almost eighteen and I'd wonder how he managed to study as well as he did while his adolescent hormones were in turmoil. Poor bugger. I think growing up is very difficult for boys. One day his girlfriend broke off with him and I heard him say, as he hung up the phone, "It's okay, I'm used to rejection." Then he went to his room and didn't come out for hours. I wanted to go and hug him but I knew he would have hated that. His "broken heart" was a personal matter. I think it is important to give your teenage son space to handle his emotions and not to crowd him. Mothers don't need to know every intimate detail of our children's lives but that doesn't mean we shouldn't be aware of what's going on in their lives.'

Mood swings and teenagers go hand in hand. Puberty blues are commonplace and rarely harmful, but sometimes teenagers develop more serious problems, like depression. About one in eight Australian teenagers suffers from it and depression is on the increase. Australia's suicide rates are also disturbing. We have the highest youth suicide rate in the world and suicide follows motor accidents as the second most common cause of death in male teenagers. Girls attempt suicide more frequently than boys, but boys succeed more often.

'I do worry about kids and suicide,' Rebecca Mowbray says. 'And because children spend more time with their mothers, they tell them more and unburden a lot on them. Sam (aged eighteen) tells me his problems and I spend all night thinking about them and don't sleep a wink. In the morning, he's forgotten all about them – while I am exhausted.'

Depression is not always easy to pick. An Adelaide GP was shocked when she failed to diagnose her fifteen-year-old daughter's problem, although she was worried enough to seek professional help. 'The psychiatrist told me that she had obviously been suffering from a significant depressive illness for at least nine months. Of course it was obvious, now. In retrospect, all the signs were there. The sullen face, withdrawal from her friends and family, the weight loss, the falling grades at school – why didn't I see it? It wasn't until I noticed my daughter sitting on her bed staring out the window one night and she said, "I may not be here tomorrow . . . " that the penny finally dropped. Depression! The despair I felt over her suffering was equalled only by the guilt at not having realised what she was going through. It was my worst experience as a mother.'

Once her daughter was diagnosed the depression worsened. 'There were three stages to it,' the GP says. 'Initially she was withdrawn and suicidal. She couldn't eat and lost ten kilos over two months and barely spoke. The second stage was anger, mainly directed at me, and the third stage was "acting out" – doing silly things like wagging school and regularly being caught smoking. She missed about six months of school and the whole illness lasted about eighteen months.

'She would never connect with any of the therapists – we went through six of them – and refused to take medication. In her withdrawal stage, I felt I had to be with her all the time or else my mother came over to be with her. I took a lot of time off work. She would be awake almost all night and her brother and I took turns sleeping with her because she found nights terrifying.

'During the anger stage, I had to keep telling myself that it was her illness talking. She'd say the vilest things like, "Any last remnants of feeling I have for you I have tossed in a room, locked the door and thrown away the key." During this time, I went to a counsellor myself to learn some ways of dealing with her. When she started "acting out" it was hard to work out what was illness behaviour and what was teenage rebellion. Eventually, I had to be very strict with her and set rigid boundaries. I don't remember a particular day when she "came out of it" but I remember that the first time she laughed again, I cried.'

'Depression is an illness and not something that a child – or an adult – can just snap out of,' Penny says. 'It's important that mothers get professional help for their children and support for themselves, including learning strategies to help their depressed teenagers. Good medication is available and it's worth trying but they often won't take it. The vast majority of teenagers suffering from depression will get better and mothers should hold onto that thought.

'However, I am seeing more and more unhappy teenagers and the way they project this tends to follow rather classic male/female lines,' Penny says. 'The girls, usually younger to mid teens, demonstrate their pain with eating disorders, or non-life-threatening acts of self-harm, such as cutting the skin on their arms. When I asked one teenager why she had made so many superficial cuts on her forearm she, rather poignantly I thought, told me, "Because I want some outward physical sign to show the pain that I feel inside me." Teenage boys, usually mid to late teens, tend to display their pain by either "acting out" in an antisocial way, often with an excess of alcohol on board or smoking excessive amounts of marijuana, and moving into a state of total apathy.'

Eating disorders such as anorexia nervosa and bulimia are increasingly common among teenagers of both sexes in Australia, but they affect girls in greater numbers than boys at a rate of about ten to one. Currently one in every one hundred adolescent girls develops anorexia nervosa and up to three in one hundred develop bulimia. Disturbingly, 68 per cent of fifteen-year-old girls admit to being on a diet.

The causes for eating disorders are not known but there are many theories about this complex group of illnesses. The most widely held medical opinion is that they develop out of a need for a girl to 'be in control'. In past times, when food was scarce, putting on weight was seen as a form of social status. In today's society of 'excess', rigid self-control is seen as virtuous, especially by the media. Australia's biggest-selling women's magazines are fixated with weight loss and diets, and regularly feature some of the world's so-called most beautiful – yet skeletal-looking – women, as if they were the ideal for others to emulate.

Many impressionable teenage girls see these abnormal body images as their ultimate goal and sometimes mothers inadvertently encourage this line of thought. For instance, a woman's dissatisfaction with her own body shape can influence her daughter. Other women constantly diet – something that can also affect the way their daughters think about food. With all these pressures manipulating them, girls soon get the message that female beauty is linked to being slim.

There is widespread concern throughout Australia about girls' unhealthy eating habits. In June 2004 the Victorian Government released a manual, *Eating Disorders Resources for Schools*, aimed at helping teachers to recognise and provide early intervention assistance for students who may have some form of eating disorder. Research has revealed that families often do not realise a child has such a problem because they are too close.

Victoria's Youth Affairs Minister, Jacinta Allan, believes the constant pressure on young people to be perfect and to perform in every arena has much to do with the problem. 'Girls especially grow up in a cultural context that equates a woman's success with adherence to often unrealistic standards for weight, shape and appearance,' she says.

'With more and more of our teenage girls starving themselves because they feel so "out of control", it's just possible they're trying to send us a message,' Penny says. 'I think they're bewildered by today's fast and materialistic world and have lost a true sense of who they are.'

Some teenagers are so angry they carry out senseless acts. 'Acting out' is often labelled as 'attention seeking', but as Penny says, 'If a teenager goes to such extremes they surely need attention.' Alison was woken by the police at three in the morning to say they had picked up her son doing graffiti with some of his mates. At first she refused to believe it, insisting her son, who was fourteen, was in bed asleep. 'My husband and I went to collect him. It was my first visit to a police station and I was shaking. Our son was sitting in a room at the back of the station without his shoes and belt, as the police had confiscated them. After giving him a serious talk they allowed us to take him home. He wasn't fined and nothing was recorded against his name. So I gave him my own punishment.

I made him go to all the places he had defaced and scrub them clean. I sat in the car reading a book while he did it. Several times when he said he'd finished cleaning a particular wall, I told him it wasn't good enough and made him clean it again, but to this day I have no idea what made him do it in the first place.'

When a teenager has a mental illness everyone in the household is affected. Mothers (and fathers) are often ill prepared to deal with the emotional challenges that they have to confront. 'These upward trends in adolescent mental illness are disturbing,' Penny says. 'Recently I tried to organise an emergency appointment with a psychiatrist for a fifteen-year-old girl who was suicidal. The secretary told me there was an eight-week wait because this specialist in adolescent psychiatry was flooded with referrals. I have patients as young as twelve on antidepressants.

'I wonder whether our current generation of "mothers seeking perfection" is making the mistake of giving their teenagers more and more material things and greater freedom, when what they need and unconsciously want is more attention and boundaries. And while parenting teenagers can be difficult for both mothers and fathers, it seems that mothers carry an additional burden when their adolescents are unwell. In almost twenty years of seeing teenagers with mental health problems, they usually are brought to see me by their mothers. In fact, I can count the number of times fathers have brought them in on one hand.'

Problems with children can happen whether a mother is full-time at home or at work. No mother expects to lead a carefree life but there are times when things go haywire and situations occur over which she has no control. Most women try to carry out their mother role as best they can at the time. It is not a job that is taught to them, and usually their instincts guide them as to the right way to handle matters.

Jan Murray says she had a dream run with her five children

when they were teenagers and that 'only my daughter was a bit of a problem'. When she 'lost' her for a couple of years after her daughter turned sixteen, she says it took her a while to come up with the solution. 'She would tell me that everybody else could do *everything* better than I could. When she was eighteen, her father and I took her to London. We arranged a job and accommodation for her and we left her there. It was the makings of her and gave her the space between us that she needed in order to be who she wanted to be. It was a scary thing, leaving her in big, bad London and I cried all the way home, but we both benefited from the experience. The daughter who lobbed home two years later became, and still is, my best girlfriend. Guilt can be cathartic.'

The teenage years can be the most demanding part of mothering but they also provide some of the unforgettable moments too – like the first time a teenage daughter walks out in a formal dress looking like a princess, or seeing a teenage son resplendent in his first suit. 'They look at you with their eager young faces, pleased as punch with how they look, their eyes bright with excitement, wanting your praise and approval while elated and apprehensive as to how their night will turn out,' Ita says. 'You want their lives to be so good, so wonderful. You wish there was some way to spare them from the detours that life is bound to throw in their way – if only it were possible.'

It is not, of course, and in the meantime the pressure on teenagers to rush into adulthood is relentless. The teen phase is just seven short years – such a brief period – when adolescents need to be nurtured not pushed, when their wellbeing has to be a priority, allowing them time to enjoy this transition period of their childhood.

Geraldine Doogue says she often discussed teenagers with her listeners when she hosted *Life Matters*, on the ABC's Radio

National. 'More often than not the caller would say, "She was a lovely girl until thirteen or fourteen, now I can't talk to her," and I'd ask, "Do you take her out for a cup of coffee on her own?" The caller usually replied, "No." That's when I'd say, "Well do try it."

'I've always believed if you enjoy your children – I don't mean tolerate and I don't mean survive, I mean *enjoy* – usually everything comes right.'

13

When a mother gives up her child

'I don't know what was going through my mother's mind when she gave me up for adoption, but when I left my son I felt a deep loss and an ache that has never gone away.' Lynley Sutherland is fifty-eight. When she was only two days old she was adopted from the hospital where she'd been born. Twenty-seven years later, Lynley left her marriage and her seven-year-old son with his father to make a new life for herself without them. 'It wasn't easy to walk away from my child. I felt guilt and every other kind of emotion. I cried for the first three months, but at the time I thought my decision was in my son's best interests and that his father would be able to give him the kind of security I couldn't.'

It has never worried her that she herself was adopted. 'Mum and Dad never hid the truth from me and they each gave me a piece of their Christian names so I would feel a part of them. Mum was Lynette; Dad was Lesley – hence Lynley. They said I was very special and a gift from God and I always thought I was. Mum had a huge guilt complex about not being able to have children because she felt a failure as a woman and a wife – and that she had even failed as a mother because she couldn't have children of her own. I once asked Dad if he felt a failure like Mum did and he said, "What *are* you talking about? I am a father." '

Lynley and her brother, who was also adopted, grew up in the small Victorian country town of Nagambie in a happy family environment. 'I was blessed to have the parents I had,' she says. At seventeen, she left home to become a nurse and by the time she was twenty had married Greg, a share farmer who had a second job at a dairy factory at Cobram on the Murray River. At twenty-two, Lynley gave birth to Jack and life seemed perfect. 'I've always thought of birth as a miracle, and when Jack was born on Christmas Eve I fell instantly in love with him the moment he was put in my arms.'

So why and how could she leave him? 'When Jack was five his father had a serious accident at work and has never walked since. Living with a paraplegic was a strain. Our whole life changed and Greg was in the spinal unit at the Austin Hospital in Melbourne for twelve months. When a tragedy like this happens, your mind plays all sorts of funny games. Greg had intensive therapy, we both had counselling and marriage guidance and, before he could come home, the house had to be revamped to handle a wheelchair.'

The couple decided their best bet was to go into business for themselves so they sold their home and bought a motel. In whatever spare time she had Lynley played A-grade squash. 'I wasn't always around and one day I came home and discovered that my girlfriend's daughter was looking after my husband better than I was. "Enough is enough," I thought, but boy, was I angry! However, we parted friends and we are still friends. Leaving Jack was the second hardest thing I've had to do – the first was telling him his dad would never walk again.

'About six months before I left, Jack had actually asked me if I still loved his dad. I told him I did but in a different way.

When I made the decision to leave he said, "What about me, Mum?" I explained that I thought his dad needed him more than I did because he was disabled. Jack liked his school and was doing well there, and all his mates lived nearby. I didn't want to disrupt his life and I didn't know what I was going to be doing either. I can't really describe how I felt leaving him. It broke my heart and soul in two because we were so close. I was "Mum" and I was always there no matter what. When I came back a few weeks later to collect some of my things, I made sure Jack wasn't home because I didn't want to distress him all over again. I felt terrible.'

Lynley didn't see her son again for four years and their first meeting was 'a disaster, because Jack was still coming to terms with me leaving and demanding to know *why* I left. The question was always on his mind.' He was then eleven. A couple of years later Jack visited his mother again, but the experience was just as painful as the first time. By now, Lynley had remarried, but her second husband turned out to be a habitual liar, an alcoholic and violent. 'This didn't come out until we had the marriage certificate and, so I wouldn't find out about the debts he was accumulating, we moved around a lot to country towns in Victoria and New South Wales. He was a pub chef and I worked as a waitress, a cleaner, front of house, whatever . . .

'He was possessive, resented anyone who took my attention away from him and was also abusive – there were times when he beat me black and blue. Jack hated the way he treated me and I felt so guilty when he saw my husband hit me that after only two days I sent Jack back to his father. Why didn't I leave this man? Fear made me stay. I feared for my life but I was frightened to leave.'

Eventually the ill-matched couple made their way back to Nagambie, where he found a job – but not for long. When her husband announced he was off again, Lynley seized her chance to get out of the relationship. 'I told him I was staying put because my parents needed me and, as it turned out, they did because Dad was in the early stages of Alzheimer's.' Lynley has never heard from her second husband again.

Almost all adopted children want to know why their birth mother gave them up. 'I used to wonder if mine ever thought of me on my birthday,' Lynley says. When her second husband left her, she was thirty-eight and her relationship with Jack tenuous. Lynley felt alone and suddenly apprehensive about what the future might hold for her. She became obsessed with the urge to find out more about her past. 'I had to find my birth mother. I had her blood in my veins. I wanted to see what she was like.' With the approval of her adoptive parents Lynley eventually tracked down her mother, who did not welcome her with open arms let alone an open door! 'When I went to her home she didn't want to see me.' Undeterred, Lynley returned to Nagambie and kept trying to make contact. Finally, her mother agreed to talk to her on the phone. 'I told her I wasn't angry and I wasn't bitter – I just wanted to know *why*.'

It was a sad story and says much about how tough life must have been for some mothers living in the bush not long after the end of the Second World War. 'My birth mother was a shearer's cook and my birth father was a drover. Shortly before I was born my father's horse threw him, his leg was broken and he was unable to work. When my mother was in hospital having me he shot through leaving her with no money – just a flock of sheep, my sister who was then three, and me. My mother said that back in 1946 no one would have employed a woman on her own with two kids, so she gave me up for adoption and took my sister away with her to Sydney, only to put her in an orphanage there.

'She told me all this in an unemotional matter-of-fact way and didn't seem interested in finding out anything much about my life. I don't know if she felt guilty about giving me up but she never said sorry. Now that I'm older, I can understand why she did what she did – I am sure that in the same way I wanted Jack to have a better kind of life than I could give him, she wanted the same thing for me. When I got home, I sent her a photograph of Jack but I've never heard a word from her.'

Lynley's search for her sister had a happier outcome. 'It was Mum who kept at me to find her but I was worried about causing any upset in my sister's life – adopted people don't always want to be found – and she wasn't easy to find either. It took years and I was forty-six when I finally rang her. Her first words were, "Bloody hell! I have a sister!"

'It turned out she'd had a terrible life. A judge and his wife adopted her when she was eight but they wanted a child who was seen but not heard and her mother was very strict. When my sister was sixteen she went out, got pregnant and then put her child up for adoption as some kind of "payback" to the judge and his wife. It isn't something that makes her feel guilty but "terrific", so she says. I often ask her what she'll do if her daughter comes knocking on the door. She says if and when that happens she'll handle it. I don't know how my sister could have given her child up for adoption. I know I could never do such a thing – at least when I left Jack he was with his father.

'My sister and I have a wonderful relationship although I do think she is very confused, and when she tells me about the things that happened to her during her childhood I realise how lucky I was to have Mum and Dad. They were always there for me and Mum was so loving and wise. After my second marriage ended, she knew I was longing to see Jack and kept gently pushing me to make contact. I agonised about doing this because I was scared he'd reject me. It took me ages to get up the courage to phone but, when I did, Jack simply asked where I was and said he wanted to see me.' It wasn't all smooth sailing however. At eighteen, Jack was an angry young man and Lynley copped an onslaught of accusations. 'You left Dad, he was disabled. You left me. How was I meant to grow up? What was I supposed to feel? All the other kids at school had mums and I didn't.'

'He wasn't only angry with me, he was angry at life,' Lynley says. 'I actually think he was on the verge of suicide but we were able to sit and talk about his anger towards me, and my grief at leaving him. We sorted it out the best we could but afterwards I couldn't help but think I had done the wrong thing all those years ago.' Gradually, mother and son began to see each other on a regular basis. 'We had wonderful times together and did lots of silly little things that we missed out on when he was a child.'

Their relationship is now strong and healthy and in good shape. 'I couldn't love him any more than I do. If he is in strife, he calls me. He has a good job as a spray painter and still looks after his father. We talk on the phone three or four times a week and I always end by saying, "Love you, son," and he always replies, "Love you, Mum." Even though he is in his thirties, when he comes to stay I tuck him into bed, kiss him goodnight and tell him I love him. Underneath I have a real fear of losing him again and I don't know if that comes from me leaving him when he was a child or whether all mothers have that fear. Perhaps the fact Jack is an only child magnifies the way I feel.

'I'm sure guilt comes with being a mother and is part and parcel of raising children. I still question if I did the right thing in leaving Jack and whether I should have stayed in that marriage and sorted it out with more guidance. The guilt never leaves you. It's the same when you lose a child, you never forget. I had five miscarriages after Jack and I know the sex of each one – three girls, two boys. I missed so much of Jack's life. His father was terrific and brought him up well. I could not have asked for more except to have been there with him. But when you leave a child part of you dies. You grieve and you continue to grieve over and over again, and the grief and underlying guilt stay with you for the rest of your life.'

Somewhat tragically, it seems family history is repeating itself. Jack is now a father but has little contact with his three-year-old daughter because he and his partner no longer live together. He only sees her every two weeks. 'Jack idolises his daughter,' Lynley says. 'I would imagine he'd be feeling guilty at having to walk away from her.' Lynley admits to feeling a tad guilty at not seeing her granddaughter more often but this has much to do with the fact that she works on weekends when Jack has access. She didn't find the job that keeps her so busy though – it 'found' her and, like everything to do with Lynley and her extraordinary life, was completely unexpected.

'It's hard to describe, impossible really,' she says. 'I was called by God to serve Him. When it happened I was at a Good Friday service. I had this spiritual experience and I *knew* that God wanted me to serve Him in Ministry.' Even though she was raised an Anglican it took her by surprise because Lynley says she was not particularly religious and had only resumed going to church – after a twenty-year gap – when she began caring for her elderly parents. 'At first I resisted the call. I didn't want to start studying at forty-seven and least of all theology, but the calling was too strong.' In January 2004 after ten years of external studies with the College of Theology and School of Christian Studies, Lynley received word that she had graduated. She has since been ordained as a deacon in the Anglican Church.

'I have no idea where my life's journey will take me now – that's up to God – but I do know that Jack will be a part of it. I have learned not to dwell on the bad things that have happened in my life because it only makes you bitter. I am still trying to work through my guilt and maybe I will never manage to do that completely. Being a mother is one of the best things that can happen to a woman. I wasn't a particularly good mother because I left Jack, but I never gave up loving him and I now know that God never gave up loving me either.'

~

Many adopted children seek out their birth mothers, like Lynley did, to find out why they were given up, but large numbers of them have no desire to know at all and never bother to seek out their natural parents because they are so content with their adoptive ones. For some, the reunion with their birth mother is a happy meeting; for others, an opportunity to learn about their biological family history. But for some adopted children it can be a distressing experience.

Jennifer was very excited at the prospect of meeting her birth mother. 'I had always wondered who I really came from and what I might look like when I got older, but because our reunion was strained and upsetting I now wish I'd left well enough alone. It was good finding out more about myself, especially my health background, but the whole encounter left me feeling sad. My birth mother wasn't particularly pleased to see me. She didn't want to tell her other three daughters about me and didn't seem the slightest bit interested in finding out much about me. She said that over the years she'd thought of me as dead – which shattered me somewhat – but later, when I was calmer, I understood it was her way of coping with something that was painful for her. Well, I like to think it was.'

Jennifer's relationship with her adoptive mother, whom she thinks of as 'Mum', is close and loving. 'I was able to tell her how I felt about my birth mother's reaction to me and we talked through the reasons that might have made her respond to me the way she did. Mum's sound reasoning was comforting. I remember reading somewhere that being adopted means that you grew in your mother's heart instead of her stomach. That's exactly the way I feel about my mum.'

❧

When Andrea and Craig were unable to conceive after three years of trying, adoption seemed the natural option. 'I'd even taken fertility drugs with no success and the doctors could find no reason why we were unable to have children. I felt sad about this but never guilty,' Andrea says. 'We applied for a baby through a private agency and waited for two years before Deborah arrived. She was just ten days old. It was an amazing, wonderful thing to finally have a baby – at last we were a family. Of course, we realised the birth mother had four weeks in which to change her mind and we were very aware of this but presumed it wouldn't happen.

'We were so happy to have Deborah, but in the early months I used to ache for her birth mother and thought about her a great deal. The social worker told me that Deborah's birth mother had been given some clothes for her baby and wondered if we would use them. I naturally said that of course we'd love to have them.

'We'd always hoped to have three children, but once we'd decided to go down the adoption path I was concerned that if we did conceive a child naturally that they may feel a difference in their relationship to each other and us. Once we had Deborah the concern just slipped away, as we could not imagine any difference. We immediately applied for our next baby and, when Deborah was two, Maryanne joined our family.

'We would have liked to adopt again but in those two years between Deborah and Maryanne everything changed and it was then not possible to apply for a third child. It was the early 1970s. In the beginning of that decade 80 per cent of unmarried women were giving up their babies but by the time we got Maryanne the situation was reversed – only 20 per cent of them were giving up their children because the stigma of being an "unmarried mother" had gone.' Women's Liberation was a factor in changing attitudes, coupled with the introduction of the Federal Government's Supporting Mothers' Benefit payments for single mothers.

Andrea says she never gave the likelihood of either of the girls' mothers getting in touch much thought. 'As the law stood at the time of our adopting the girls, there was not any possibility of either party finding each other. We always told them they were adopted and they accepted the situation as just our particular family history. The girls were very relaxed about it and never embarrassed to tell people. Neither of them ever expressed any desire to find out about their birth mothers, and when the law was changed enabling adopted children and their birth mothers to contact each other they were in their mid teens and weren't interested.'

But then, when Deborah was twenty-five, a letter arrived for her with other mail. 'I put it in her room and thought nothing more about it. Next morning she handed it to me and said, "Read this." The opening sentence went, "You don't know me but I am your birth mother."

'Deborah seemed dazed as she watched me read it. We talked about it and as far as I was concerned it was her call. I told her if she wanted to make contact it was fine with me, but if she didn't that would be okay too. I also said that, if she did make contact, when she was ready I would like to make contact too if she agreed for me to do so.

'Several weeks went by before she casually told me that she had made contact and it was all right for me to get in touch with her birth mother if I wanted to. She told me bits and pieces about what had passed between them but I didn't pry because it was an unsettling time for my daughter. I think she talked to a counsellor at the university where she was studying about some of the issues that concerned her. However, I really appreciated having the opportunity of writing a letter to say "thank you for Deborah who has given us so much joy and pleasure". I sent her birth mother all kinds of photographs that we'd taken of Deborah since babyhood. At the same time, I told my daughter there was a ticket available for her whenever she wanted to meet her birth mother.

'About six or seven months later she flew to Melbourne. It was an emotional time for everyone, including me. I knew that Deborah was a bit apprehensive, which was understandable, and I couldn't stop thinking about her and what she might be doing. Later, her birth mother wrote me a letter appreciative of my understanding of her situation and assuring me that she would always see Deborah as my daughter. I think – and hope – any guilt she might have had about giving Deborah up evaporated on meeting her and seeing how well she has turned out.

'Of course I've suffered all kinds of guilt for my shortcomings as a mother – but not about adopting and raising my girls. If we had been able to create children they would have been Deborah and Maryanne, and I don't think my feelings would have been any different if I had given birth to them myself. I'm very proud of my girls.'

Susan and Steve made the decision to adopt when they were unable to have their own biological children, but faced a ten-year wait to adopt a child in Australia. 'We were desperately keen to be parents,' Susan says. When they were in their mid thirties they adopted Sam from Bogotá, in Colombia. He is now eighteen and Susan still gets emotional remembering the first time she held him. 'He was ten weeks old and we took part in a special "handing over ceremony". It was amazing, although a little scary. We stayed in accommodation that had been specially set up in Bogotá for adoptive families. People from all over the world were there wanting to adopt children. We stayed for three weeks and were shown how to look after our babies, something I found very helpful. When we came home everyone was thrilled for us and, for a little while, Sam was like a mini-celebrity in our local community. It seemed that everyone wanted to come and see him and I received presents from so many people, some of whom I barely knew.'

When Sam was three the family returned to Bogotá and Susan and Steve adopted Laura. 'The experience was equally wonderful, but less stressful this time as, second time round, we knew something about parenting.'

Susan has found that her worst moments are happening now that the children are in their teens. 'Guiding them through their teenage years has some challenging moments and other people's insensitivity and their racist views often create problems,' she says. 'Recently Laura and I were visiting a friend when her elderly mother asked Laura, more than once, "Did you know your *real* mother?" I was so taken aback. My friend immediately said, "Sue *is* Laura's real mother." We left shortly after, and when we were in the car Laura burst into tears.

'Of course we've told her and Sam about their culture and heritage and regularly mix with other families who have adopted Colombian children, but teenagers hate being seen as different. I felt guilty that Laura had been hurt this way and also angry. There was perhaps one positive aspect – when we told Sam what had happened, he told us that he had been taunted by kids at school when he was about the same age. He'd never mentioned it before and I think it was a relief for him to finally share that experience with his family.'

It is estimated that up to 40 000 children are adopted around the world each year, but in 2003 only 278 children were adopted from a limited number of countries into Australia. In August 2004, Channel Nine's *Sunday* show reported on the difficulties childless couples faced when it came to adopting a child from overseas. The program featured an interview with Ricky Brisson, Executive Officer of Australian Families for Children, who said there are thousands of children waiting overseas for families, but was critical of a lack of political will by Federal and State Governments to make overseas adoption work.

As *Sunday* reporter Helen Dalley pointed out, 'This is happening at a time when the Federal Government is actively encouraging couples to have children – handing out $3000 baby bonuses to new mothers, boosting family payments and subsidising expensive infertility treatments like IVF through the Medicare safety net. Many adoptive parents who commit to the lengthy and expensive process of inter-country adoption claim the financial, legal and bureaucratic hurdles forced on them by governments show there's one standard for biological parents, but quite another when it comes to those who want to adopt.'

Forty-five-year-old Louise remembers the huge amount of paperwork involved when she adopted her daughter Alice from Cambodia. 'Plus medical reports, psychological reports, a home study done by a social worker, references, criminal clearance and a "biographical statement" on how I planned to raise my daughter and how I would deal with interracial issues,' she says. Louise also had to do a lot of personal soul searching, as she was adopting Alice as a single mother – 'Could I afford to do this? How would I do it? How would I manage work and a baby as a single mum?'

A schoolteacher, Louise had lived and worked in Asia for twelve years and was deputy principal of an Asian school. She travelled regularly to Cambodia to do volunteer work at an AIDS hospice run by Mother Teresa's Sisters of Charity. 'I saw Alice, who was seven months old, and fell in love with her instantly. Her father was unknown and her mother had died from AIDS but thankfully had not transmitted the virus to her baby. I decided to see if

I could adopt her. I'd always wanted to have children, but I was too busy – I left it too late. I kept putting off having a baby because of my career. I had a long-term partner but he died when I was thirty-six and I buried myself in my career.'

When she made the decision to adopt Alice, Louise had already accepted a job back in Australia as deputy principal of a large private school in the city where her parents and sister live. 'I realise now if I'd stayed in Asia, it would have been much easier financially,' she says. 'Domestic help is cheap in Asia and I wouldn't have had to pay $80 a day for Alice's daycare as I do here.' She finds her parents' support invaluable and says that once she had assured them she had thought through all the issues thoroughly, they backed her decision without hesitation. A female missionary in Cambodia gave Louise some advice that also helped. 'She told me, "Stop using your head. Use your heart and you will make it work."'

'There hasn't been a day when I wished I didn't have Alice but I've been on a steep learning curve,' Louise says. 'When you get pregnant, there is a nine-month lead up. I didn't have that. I only had two weeks off work before I had to pack up my Asian home and return to my new full-time job in Australia.' It has not been an easy transition either. 'I found it hard to settle back into Australia because I'd lived in Asia for a long time and all my friends were there. But my parents have been wonderful and so has my sister. Alice is the first and probably only grandchild and they adore her.

'Sometimes people ask what nationality my husband is but I've never experienced any racial prejudice with Alice,' Louise says. 'As much as I hate the expression, she is seen as "a little Asian doll". Being a single mother is probably the greatest challenge.' As deputy principal her job includes attending a great many evening and weekend functions, which means she cannot always be with Alice as much as she would like. 'I feel guilty about working long hours, especially in Alice's early years, but I have a contract to honour and I've worked hard for twenty-five years to achieve such a senior level in my career.'

Louise says she also suffers major guilt about attachment issues. The first three years of a child's life are an important time in which they learn how to relate to those around them. When there are multiple carers rather than one who is there most of the time, a child may not develop a normal sense of trust in people and can have problems with relationships and trust in the future. 'Alice was ten months and crawling when I finally became her mother and many different people have looked after her since then. I am always looking to see if she has signs of an attachment disorder – things like indiscriminate affection, total clinging, lack of eye contact, or being over-the-top vivacious.

'It's hard for me to know what normal two-year-old behaviour is and I don't want to be intellectualising all the time – thinking perhaps this or that is a signal that I have a problem. But I do worry that her first ten months may affect her future relationships.' Louise also worries that Alice has no father. 'She is beginning to call other people "Daddy". She thinks of my father as a "Big Daddy" and calls him Bill.'

It would be easier for mothers in her situation, Louise says, if adoption advice from experts was more readily available – not just about legal matters but also the issues in parenting that are specific to inter-country adoptive parents. 'The major studies on inter-country adoption have come from the United States, where the large number of Vietnamese children adopted after the Vietnam War are now in their late twenties and early thirties. As adults, many have described uncertain feelings that emerged during adolescence that were specific to their life events. Not only did they have a sense of "genealogical bewilderment", the term used to describe feelings that any person who is adopted may have when they don't know their biological parents, but also that in losing their culture and heritage, they have lost part of themselves.'

It concerns Louise that Alice might suffer this way too. 'But from the time of my first visit, I've always felt an affinity with Cambodia and I have no problems with it always being a part of Alice's life. I have videos of the orphanage where she first lived and she loves seeing me with "baby Alice". She was baptised a Catholic by the nuns but she can also recognise Buddha, monks and temples and she greets Cambodian people in the traditional way with her hands together as if she is praying and her head bowed. I am also teaching her the small amount of her native language (Khmer) that I know and I plan to take her back to Cambodia every year.'

Louise is critical of new laws recently enacted in New South Wales that prevent children who are adopted from overseas having their name changed. This was not an issue for her as she adopted Alice as an ex-pat, under Commonwealth jurisdiction; however, it is a decision that she thinks is wrong nonetheless. 'I believe that it is very important that these children maintain their cultural identity and heritage but governments should not take away a basic parental right to give a child a name of the parents' own choosing. The adoptive community is up in arms about this'.

Louise says she never imagined motherhood would have such an impact on her life. 'I never thought I'd feel this way about having a child as part of my life. My career was always the most important thing to me and I can't believe how much my priorities have changed in such a short time. I haven't been out socially by myself since I came back to live in Australia. It is my choice. I want to be here for Alice as much as I can until she becomes an adult. I would love to have a partner to share this with, but somehow I can't see how this will ever happen because with my school duties and caring for Alice I rarely go out anywhere where I might meet a potential prospect.'

An adoptive mother needs to have not only all the natural instincts of a biological mother but also a good understanding of the circumstances that made her a mother and brought a child into her life. Above all, adoptive mothers must accept a child's past and heritage. Every night Louise thinks about some special lines from a book that an adoption agency gave her and says they give her strength and encouragement. 'They are simple but true,' she says. '"I don't have your eyes but I have your way of looking at things." I hope Alice will always be able to say that about me.'

14

Is sex ever the same after children?

In 2003, 150 women attending a mothers' sexual health seminar in Sydney were asked how many of them had thought about sex in the past twenty-four hours — not necessarily participated, just thought about it. Not one hand went up, although there was much laughter. When it comes to sex, Australian mothers are good at talking about it with their close girlfriends but rarely get around to actually doing it. Juggling work with family and household tasks has taken its toll on women in the bedroom.

The plain, simple fact of the matter is that many mothers are just too worn out to have sex or even to desire any kind of physical contact with their partners. When mothers discuss their sex lives the problem of tiredness comes up time and time again. Dr Barbara Pocock, the Director of Adelaide University's Centre for Labour Studies, released findings of a 2001 study that originally sought to uncover how work affected the lives of 150 women, but the topic of sex kept cropping up. Many of the women spoke about sex in the past tense simply saying there was just no room for it in their overloaded lives.

'The hidden cost of work could be measured in a loss of intimacy,' Dr Pocock says. 'Women find they can't be terrific workers, wonderful mothers and have great sex because too many of them are struggling under the double burden of paid work and running a home.' Tiredness was not the only turn-off factor. Many mothers told researchers they were angry that their partners did not help them more in the home. Dr Pocock describes anger and resentment as 'the enemies of intimacy'.

For many couples sleep is the new sex. 'It's the only thing that turns me on,' Alice says. 'I'm seldom home before seven because I pick the kids up from after-school care on the way, then it's time to cook dinner, before sorting out the washing and whatever else has to be done, and my husband thinks he is doing me a favour if he makes the coffee! Sometimes I let him have sex and fake an orgasm because I can't be bothered having to fob him off during the night, as I don't want my sleep interrupted. I'd rather get it over and done with – if only he didn't think I must always have an orgasm I think my sex life would be more enjoyable. I feel guilty about being so uninterested but sometimes I get bloody mad because of my husband's indifference to helping around the house.'

Weary they may be but women have not completely lost their sense of humour. 'There is only thing I want in bed – breakfast, and I mean bacon and eggs,' says Melissa. Another working mother of three says her idea of perfect foreplay is for her husband to clear up after dinner, help get the kids into bed and then give her a glass of wine. 'That's my recipe for great sex.'

Everything that happens in a woman's day after she becomes a mother, whether she is a stay-at-home mum or out in the paid workforce, affects her levels of desire and arousal. Doing the laundry, changing numerous nappies, being smudged with Vegemite, smelling of vomit, coping with toddler tantrums, helping with homework, and surviving emotional arguments with teenagers do tend to dampen a mother's sexual appetite. If she also has a full-time paid job, exhaustion usually switches off her libido completely. Stay-at-home mums suffer a decline in libido too, but not as great as mothers who work outside the home. On his Foxtel television show, Dr Phil often talks about 'sexless marriages' and claims they are 'an undeniable epidemic'.

～

Some men are beginning to understand that the best way to keep romance alive in a relationship is by sharing the household chores. A better appreciation of how much a mother packs into her day is underway – albeit slowly – perhaps caused by men taking on the role of househusband. When he was temporarily unemployed for three months, Robert became a househusband. 'I had to do all the so-called traditional female chores as well as the bloke ones, like mowing the lawns and taking out the garbage. I was tired, although of course I am physically much stronger than my wife so it wasn't anything I couldn't handle. Now that we're both working full-time again I always help her clean the house without her having to ask, do the ironing and, two weekends out of four, I take the kids out for the day, so she can have a bit of time for herself. It has made a big difference to our sex lives and we are both much happier. I tell all my mates who complain about not getting enough sex that their problems would be over if they shared the household chores.'

Other evidence confirms that men who help with the housework have found the best way to get women in the mood for love! In 2004, researchers at America's Brown University studied 265 married couples where both partners worked and asked them who did the cooking, shopping, cleaning and other chores. They found households where the husband does at least half the house-work were significantly more likely to have a second child. It was a hot topic on talkback radio and one husband rang 702 ABC Sydney radio host Richard Glover to say that he always helped his wife with the housework, often unasked – which he claimed was a real plus in his wife's eyes – and then bragged that he had five children. During the segment Glover joked that if men doused their bodies with Fabulon it would turn women on. He may well be right.

But even if men do help in the house this does not mean that a woman's sexual desire can be switched on at a moment's notice. During pregnancy, doctors usually tell women that their uterus will return to normal six weeks after the baby is born but hardly ever mention that their sexual desire may take more than six months to return. Sometimes mothers get so wrapped up in their babies that their partner feels left out. 'I wouldn't blame my husband if he had an affair, it would be entirely my fault,' one mum says. 'Before the baby came, we used to have a great sex life. We did it almost every night and just couldn't get enough of each other. Now when we go to bed my eyes are closed before my head hits the pillow.'

'Even when my kids were out of babyhood and aged about ten and eight, I was forever tired,' Sue says. 'I remember we were driving home one night after having dinner with his parents when I nodded off in the car – I often did, I just couldn't help myself. My husband began to stop and start the car by putting his foot on the brakes. I woke with a fright. "What's wrong?" I asked. "Can't you ever bloody stay awake?" he replied. He was furious with me, but had conveniently forgotten that my day had started when I got up early to do a load of washing and the ironing – I always had to iron his shirts because he didn't like the way the laundry did them – while he slept on for another hour. As he showered and dressed, I made the school lunches, fed the dog, served breakfast, tested my son's spelling, showered and dressed in a flash, drove the kids to school and made it to the office at nine by the skin of my teeth. I don't know why he bothered to wake me. I was so pissed off I didn't talk to him for the rest of the trip home.'

Thirty-two-year-old Sally, a stay-at-home mum with two daughters aged four and two, finds that at the end of the day the thought of sex is the furthest thing from her mind. 'I feel guilty about this but I just can't get turned on. He has been at work all day, interacting with adults and attractive female colleagues, while I've looked after the kids, been to playgroup, cleaned the house, swept the garden path, done a huge load of washing, usually have mashed food smeared over my clothes, and the only adults I've spoken to all day have been the greengrocer and the butcher. My husband comes home, relaxed after having a drink with the boys after work and wanting dinner, and after I've done the dishes and we finally get to bed, he wonders why I'm not in the mood.'

It is only to be expected that occasionally women bring their work problems home but stay-at-home mums can become weighed down by their many tasks too, to the detriment of their sex lives. Often the thought of her many household responsibilities can 'take over' a stay-at-home mother. 'I used to find myself waking up in the middle of the night thinking through all the things I had to do,' Fran said. 'I would lie there making mental checklists and going over them again and again. I'd look at my husband and he'd be fast asleep with not a worry in the world.

'We rarely had sex because we went to bed at different times. I'd go earlier than him because I was tired from waking up in the night so often and he liked to have a beer in front of the tellie. One of my girlfriends suggested that we try going to bed together earlier than usual so we could just talk. It made such a difference and one thing led to another. Neither of us ever wants to go to bed without the other now.'

Intimacy for men usually means erotica, orgasms and intercourse, while for women intimacy is about affection and romance – something many men fail to grasp. It is common for women to talk about feeling 'starved' of affection, of how when it comes to sex men prefer to 'take' rather than 'give' – an approach that rarely arouses the kind of response men are hoping for. Most women like a little romance in their relationships. 'I remember saying to a man who was interested in me that I needed to be wooed,' a divorced mother of two says. 'And he replied, "Whoo, whoo." He thought it was a big joke but I didn't laugh.'

‌

There are times in a mother's life, of course, when simple physiology interferes with her sexual desire, which inevitably alters as a woman's physical state changes. Two of the most significant of these are after childbirth and at menopause. When a woman is breastfeeding, high levels of the hormone prolactin can reduce sexual desire. Mother Nature, who is not called 'Mother' for nothing, does this deliberately because she wants a woman to devote herself to her new baby. 'If men were injected with an equivalent amount of the hormone prolactin, not only would their sexual desire levels decrease dramatically, they would be semi-comatose,' Penny says. Tempting though the idea may be the authors do not recommend this course of action.

Then there is the psychological impact a woman's changed physical shape has on her. A woman's body does alter after she has a baby and few women can jump straight back into their pre-birth jeans. They may have stretch marks, flabby tummies and/or pigmentation marks. All these things come as a bit of a shock and none of them helps a woman to feel sexual. Neither does a drastically altered routine coupled with severe, sometimes prolonged, sleep deprivation and leaking breasts. It is not that a woman does not feel desire but rather that she does not feel desirable.

First-time mothers can be extremely sensitive about their physical appearance. Daphne's son was delivered by Caesarean section. 'I had a horrible scar and stretch marks and I didn't think I was at all attractive. I didn't want to be touched let alone have sex because I couldn't believe that my husband could possibly find me desirable. I tried to explain this to him but I didn't think I had done so very well. However, the following night he came home from the office with a gorgeous black lacy silk nightgown and lots of candles. Later that night, we had the best sex by candlelight. It was wonderful and I felt so seductive in my black nightie that my husband told me he wished he'd bought me one years ago.'

Menopause is often another time when mothers experience diminished sexual desire for physiological reasons. At menopause, women again have low levels of oestrogen and they can have problems with vaginal dryness and/or mood swings. If they are having multiple hot flushes, women might also suffer from lack of sleep. Insomnia is one of the nastier little tricks menopause likes to play on women and is not a great recipe for desire. As Germaine Greer once said, 'No one warned me about the dreadful insomnia I would have to go through.' In the past, mothers usually had a bit of 'breathing space' as they were going through menopause, because this tended to coincide with their partner's first experience with impotency problems, which can happen to men as they get older. With the advent of effective drugs to treat this condition and an increasing tendency to treat men with testosterone if they feel their libido changing, women now have no respite and not all of them are pleased about it.

Julie was in her early fifties when her menopause began. 'One morning I looked at my diary and saw that it was my turn for canteen duty and my head felt so fuzzy that I didn't think I'd be able to remember anyone's order let alone concentrate on working out their change. Then I had to visit Mum who was in hospital with a broken hip, before going to see Dad who is in the early stages of Alzheimer's. I bought some food for him and did the supermarket shopping for the family at the same time, before having a cup of tea with Dad. Then I went home where I was greeted by my sullen fifteen-year-old daughter who wanted to know where I'd been. She accused me of never being home, that I was always out playing tennis or having lunch with the girls. I had bought her a pair of jeans I'd seen on sale that I knew she really wanted. She tossed them back at me saying I'd have to take them back because she was "*so* over this label now".

'As I was making dinner, my husband came home, poured himself a drink, talked about himself for about ten minutes and then sat down in front of the television. After all, he had been *working* all day and I'd had the day off. After dinner, I cleared away the dishes and went to the laundry to sort out the washing and finish off the ironing. Finally, I dragged my weary body and my dry vagina upstairs to go to bed but when I got there my husband was lying back on the pillows with a big grin on his face. He had taken one of those new, long-lasting impotence drugs. "Darling," he said, "if we don't get lucky tonight there's always tomorrow morning, tomorrow night, or even Sunday morning!"'

There is a lot of discussion about 'normal' sexual desire but it is probably debatable as to whether there is such a thing. *Forum* magazine published the results of a survey it carried out a couple of years ago that revealed four out of five people think other people have more sex than they do and that couples have a lot less sex than most people imagine.

In 2003, researchers from Melbourne's La Trobe University and the Universities of Sydney and New South Wales released the results of a phone survey of more than 19 000 men and women aged sixteen to fifty-nine carried out during the years 2000 and 2001. This study was the largest and most comprehensive survey of sexual behaviour and attitudes ever undertaken in Australia. It showed that, on average, couples have sex less than twice a week, with three times as many men as women expressing a desire to have sex daily. Common sexual difficulties experienced for at least one month in the last year of the survey were reported at least twice as often – and up to more than five times as often – by women than by men. These difficulties included a lack of interest in sexual activity, not having an orgasm and not enjoying sex.

Sydney sex therapist Dr Rosie King says women do not know what is normal and when they present with sexual difficulties it is usually out of ignorance. 'They often have unrealistic expectations and expect far too much from their sexual function. They have seen movies like *When Harry Met Sally* and watched Meg Ryan do her version of a female orgasm and they think, "Well gosh, mine's not like that," and they perceive themselves as having a problem when maybe they don't. The other aspect is that female sexuality is very much linked with relationship wellbeing, and a lot of women who experience loss of sexual interest or have problems getting turned on or with orgasm simply don't like the man they are in bed with. It is virtually impossible to have sustained good sex over a long period of time if you don't have a good relationship.'

'I'm so tired of those sexual researchers who keep branding women as "sexually dysfunctional",' Eva says. 'Women are not programmed hormone-driven creatures and we do find it difficult to feel loving and demonstrative towards our men if they neglect us and only expect us to fulfil practical purposes outside the bed, like taking the kids to school and cooking their meals. This feeling to me is absolutely "normal" rather than "dysfunctional". Has anyone ever heard of a "sexually dysfunctional" woman when couples are courting? Not often, I bet. Whatever I'm doing, I always make sure I give my husband a kiss and cuddle when he comes home and before the kids descend on him – because I am pleased to see him.'

'Most women suffer from sexual dissatisfaction not sexual dysfunction,' Rosie King says. 'They get no pleasure from sex because they don't enjoy it and often this is because they don't discuss the things they like in their lovemaking with their partners. A woman finds it hard to tell a man such things and, even if she does, he often forgets. Sex is a taboo subject between lovers. No one is to blame. It is an equal responsibility. We need to educate men and women to talk about sex more openly.'

~

Most women insist they do enjoy an excellent relationship with their partners but once the daily routine includes children they simply feel too exhausted for sex. There seems to be no escaping what appears to be a chronic maternal condition. Dr Caroline West who writes for *Good Medicine* magazine says, 'Research suggests that working women who are managing dual-income families are losing their libido at a greater rate than their mothers or grandmothers.' The signs that women are disillusioned with the struggle of juggling home and work lives are starting to show up in research not only in Australia, but in England and the United States – all countries where women embraced the 'you can have it all' line of thought. These rumblings of discontent are getting louder. Women are asking if this is as good as it gets – and if it is, perhaps it is not good enough. They are regretting not having more time for their children, not being able to lead a relaxed social life, and always being too tired to enjoy sex.

'There isn't any time for a relationship at all,' Mary Lou says. 'I didn't start having children until I was thirty-six and I didn't get married until I was thirty-five so I've really had no time for a relationship at all – it's all been parenting. I certainly worry about this because when the children are older and doing their own thing will I turn around and think to myself, "Do I *know* this man? What have I been doing with him all these years?" And I won't have the faintest idea.

'Every time I try to have a conversation with my husband,

the children interrupt just as they did when they were little and always managed to find me whenever I went to the toilet or got in the shower, wanting something at that very moment. Now when they hear me talking to him on the phone or if we try to have a conversation at home it's their cue to come and interrupt. I resent it and feel guilty of course because I seem to be neglecting this other human being as well. I think, well, he is an adult and should be able to look after himself but our relationship is my responsibility – but I am so overwhelmed by all my other responsibilities.'

'This happens to many couples,' says Penny, 'and it's not just their sex life that suffers but the whole relationship. Women often ask me how to handle this. I tell them that couples need "couple time". They need to go out for dinner by themselves. If babysitters are beyond their budgets, they should organise a child-minding swap with friends who need couple time too. Or just go for a walk together, holding hands and talking about anything other than the kids and the finances, maybe even why they got together in the first place – it can be very romantic.'

Raising children is hard work. It can be physically and emotionally draining but children are not meant to take over their parents' lives. They need to learn that their parents need time for themselves and that they cannot constantly interrupt when they feel like it. Mothers should never be reluctant to enforce this because children need rules and boundaries. That old saying 'children should be seen and not heard' had a lot going for it, and making time for herself is as important to a mother's equilibrium as loving the children and not something a woman should ever feel guilty about.

Eventually, most couples do successfully navigate their way through the sexual hiatus of the early childhood years – some manage to do this within weeks, others take up to two years – and happily resume their lovemaking before reaching the 'not in front of the children' obstacle. No matter how careful parents are, children have a habit of turning up when they are least expected – as Jennifer discovered the night her fourteen-year-old daughter invited two girlfriends home for a sleepover. 'Her bedroom is next to ours. I was hazily aware of the arm coming over in the middle of the night for a bit of action – you know that type of sex, where you wonder next morning, did we do it last night? I had drifted back to sleep when I became aware of a presence in the room. I opened my eyes to see my daughter standing by the bed sobbing. I sat up and asked her what was wrong. In a most accusatory tone, she said, "We *heard* you!" I will never forget the look on her face. I did vaguely remember hearing the radio in the next room suddenly going on rather loudly "mid act" but goodness, it was pretty tame stuff; we were hardly hanging from the chandelier.

'I explained that her friends probably didn't hear what was going on and she should be reassured that it was normal for parents to have sex. It meant we loved each other, our relationship was secure, which meant she was secure. Finally she calmed down and returned to bed. I gratefully went back to sleep only to be woken sometime later by her once more. "What now?" I asked somewhat tersely, and she replied, "I'm just standing here to make sure you don't do it again."'

Some parents enjoy the challenge of finding ways to keep their kids occupied so they can enjoy time alone, and enterprising mothers go to great lengths to find ingenious solutions. Simone's husband is an airline pilot. 'When he gets home from a long-haul trip I buy at least twenty or so bags of lollies and hide them in the backyard and tell our three kids that we're celebrating Daddy's return with a special lolly hunt. They spend ages searching for all the sweets and we are able to have time to ourselves, and because the sex always seems somewhat clandestine – like that furtive sex you had with boyfriends when your parents were out – it adds to the excitement.'

'We always looked forward to our Sunday siesta and built it up to such a fun regular event the kids looked forward to it,' Claire says. 'We always had a slap-up afternoon tea after siesta and they loved that. The rule was no one could leave their room until the alarm clock went off. We always gave ourselves an hour and would make wonderful love before dozing off in each other's arms. It was a bit rushed perhaps but that made it seem naughty and we rather liked that.'

Occasionally children broaden their mother's sex education . . . 'When I was nineteen I crept in the backdoor at six in the morning only to run into Mum on the way to the bathroom,' Angela says. 'With a coy smile she asked me, "Is it any different with a different partner?" She was only forty-three at the time, and I guess because she had only ever had sex with one man, she had a natural curiosity about whether other lovers were different. When I told her it was kind of a variation on a theme, she just nodded.'

Angela's experience was role reversal of the most unexpected kind because, as a rule, most mothers educate their children about sex. 'Whether together or separated, many partners delegate this role to mothers,' Penny says. 'Men are happy to tell a few jokes about sex with their mates over a beer, but when it comes to explaining "the nuts and bolts" to their offspring, they suddenly become reticent preferring to leave all this to mum.'

Chrissie, a divorcee, was quite happy to do this until the time came to tell her son the facts of life. 'My boy was about eleven or twelve and starting to develop,' Chrissie says. 'I waited until after dinner before going to his room to explain what was what. When I'd finished he just looked at me and there was dead silence for what seemed ages. Then he muttered, "Pervert!" I didn't know what to say. I mumbled something about getting his father to have a word with him and left the room.

'About an hour or so later I went to say goodnight only to find that he'd fallen asleep on his bed while reading his book. He still had his clothes on. As I began to pull off his shorts so that I could put on his pyjamas, he stirred, put both his hands over his penis, shouted, "Pervert!" and promptly fell back asleep. I covered him with the doona and fled, feeling mortified. In the end I asked one of my brothers to have a man-to-man talk with him and my son has never mentioned the word pervert again.'

It is amazing how children always manage to find items their parents think are well hidden; they seem to be born with some kind of inbuilt seek-and-find radar detection. Mary came home one night after work to discover her three kids had found a large box of condoms that she and her husband had stashed in the wardrobe. 'My husband is a journalist and someone had sent him a boxful of samples for a story he was doing. When I saw the kids with them I thought, "Oh dear, I am going to have to tell them about sex." "Mum," said my ten-year-old, "those balloons you and Dad have are hopeless. We've been trying to blow them up for hours and they don't work. You should take them back."'

So can sex ever be the same after children? There are plenty of parents who can answer that question in the affirmative – including the authors – but it is inevitable that scheduled encounters sometimes have to be abandoned because one of the kids throws up or the baby will not stop crying. Children are unpredictable and nothing will ever change that about them. Perhaps some of the spontaneity of sex might vanish, but that does not mean it has to be any less exciting or satisfying than the sex a couple enjoyed before kids came along. Couples do need to plan ahead and use their imagination.

For instance, showering together before going to work can be a lot of fun.

Realistically though, mothers' sex lives will not improve until they do something about reducing the demands on their time – and maybe men need to do some rethinking because it seems quite a few of them are complaining of tiredness too. The Australian Council of Trade Unions (ACTU) has been running a 'reasonable working hours' campaign since 2001 and has been calling for an urgent review of the long number of hours Australian men and women are expected to put in at their workplace. It argues that unrealistic work demands are having a detrimental impact on people's lives. Their researchers have reported that men and women complain that 'unreasonable' hours mean they are constantly tired, a condition that is affecting their sexual intimacy. Common gripes include: 'Our sex life doesn't exist.' 'We're so tired we just want to sleep.' 'We have sex on the run.'

'As doctors, we are probably the last profession who should be lecturing about long working hours, but we are concerned that the current "average working hours" are ballooning out alarmingly and considered as "normal" by so many people," Penny says. 'When they do finally get home women and men have little energy left to do much else but collapse in front of the television. Exhaustion levels are so high that if they are parents it's often a major effort to tend to their kids' needs first.

'I don't think twenty-first century women are suffering from some terrible physical "sexual dysfunction"; they are simply too tired for sex. Many women say they would love to be having regular intimacy, whether it's once a week or three times a month – there is no formula that must be followed. Sexual satisfaction with or without orgasm is important to a woman's emotional wellbeing and it's not really so much about intercourse but about being physically close, skin on skin. Some women actually say they are suffering from "skin hunger" – the need to just touch their partners. I never thought I'd be seeing the numbers of patients I do who tell me they just don't have the energy for sex. It is not just mothers – in about one third of cases, it's fathers who have lost "the urge". The fact that so many working women, and mothers in particular, are leading intimacy-free lives is a cause for concern. We really do need to address our lifestyles and start putting our relationships and our families first.'

Once people used to work to live, now they live to work. Caught up in this flawed modern thinking are mothers who are missing out on sexual satisfaction and, in some cases, their husband's fidelity. Just how bad the situation is becoming is illustrated by a man who wishes to remain anonymous. 'My wife goes to work, she is always tired and by eight at night is asleep on the couch. You learn to live with it. Once you have kids and your wife has a job as well, sex goes out the window. If I am lucky, I might get one when we go on holidays but usually she's too busy ringing home to see how the kids are. We blokes talk about this at work all the time. Those of us with working wives always find they are tired, but the men that have wives who stay at home say they're always tired too . . . because they have to make breakfast, pick up the kids, go to netball, basketball, football, ballet . . . there's always something. Do I ever ask my wife for sex? What, put the acid on her? Oh yes, but if I don't get one, I just roll over and go to sleep. It's almost mechanical.

'Most of us have sex on the side. You'd go mad if you didn't have a girlfriend. You tend to do more exciting things with your girlfriend than you do with you wife and you can relax with her and talk about other things apart from family, children, school and how much we spent at the supermarket on the weekend. If a girlfriend knows you are married and have kids she makes no demands on you. She knows the rules and is happy because she has her freedom and gets a regular good root!'

The authors would not wish to be seen as judgemental, but would like to point out that a man is four times more likely to die of a heart attack if he is having sex with someone other than his wife.

Cheating husbands might find that their need to look elsewhere for sexual satisfaction could diminish if they were to take up vacuuming and understand that it takes two to do the housework if a couple wants to tango. That Brown University survey makes so much sense. Of course a woman is going to feel that her partner appreciates her and all that she contributes to the household and family if he is prepared to give her a hand – unasked – with cooking, cleaning and caring for the children. Sometimes the answers to society's problems are staring us in the face but we are too blind to see them! There can be no escaping the fact that housework, sex and fertility are intimately connected. The ball is now in the male court in more ways than one.

15

Why doesn't Mum love Dad any more?

The ending of a marriage is rarely without heartache, especially when children are involved. Telling her children that she and their father are breaking up is one of the toughest things a mother ever has to do, and the possibility that this might happen is one of a child's worst fears. Just like adults, children undergo a wide range of emotions when their family disintegrates. 'My daughter was eight when I left her father after an eleven-year marriage,' Vicki says. 'I sat her down in the lounge room, put my arms around her and quietly explained that Daddy and Mummy were no longer going to live together. Her anguished, "Oh no!" stabbed me through the heart. I shall never forget it as long as I live.'

Rebecca says she will always remember the day when she and her three-year-old daughter were in the delicatessen waiting to be served. 'Her father and I had separated six months previously. The woman behind the counter asked, "Can I help you?" to which my daughter replied, "Why doesn't my mummy love my daddy any more?" I felt overwhelmingly guilty. Some eighteen years later, I still do.'

Michelle's daughter crept into her mother's bed at night and whispered, 'Mum, will I ever see Daddy again?' Because her father's work required him to travel outside of Australia several times a year the little girl feared he might never return. 'I allowed her to ring her father on a regular basis whenever he was away, and that helped allay her fears. I'd told him how worried she was about not seeing him and he always made a point of saying, "I'll be home on such and such a day and I'll come and see you."

'There are times when I think perhaps I should have stayed with him until she was older, that maybe as a mother I owed my daughter that much. He was a nice enough man but the passion had long gone out of our relationship and he was lousy in bed. Premature ejaculation has a lot to answer for in unhappy marriages! I used to think there must be something wrong with me but later, when I began dating again, I discovered I was in top-notch working order.'

Michelle's guilt over her daughter's reaction is not an isolated case. Many women say their sense of failure – sometimes mixed with feelings of relief, sadness and anxiety about the future – is invariably outweighed by the anguish and guilt regarding the effect of the divorce on their children. Given the high rate of divorce in Australia, it is unlikely that the situation will change much in the near future. Forty per cent of marriages end in divorce and of these 80 per cent involve children. In the majority of cases, women instigate divorce proceedings.

The stigma once associated with divorce vanished almost overnight with the introduction of the Australian Family Law Act in 1975. Since then no-fault divorce has had a significant impact not only on women's lives but also on families. Most couples manage to work out their divorces amicably enough and are usually able to make arrangements for residency and child contact. Of all couples who separate only half require Family Court intervention and of these only 6 per cent go before a judge because mediation did not work. Few couples feel the need to stay together for the sake of their children any longer. But while most adults five or six years after they separate say they are happy being divorced, their children often are not and in their heart of hearts hope a miracle will happen and their parents will get back together again.

'It was a reflective moment for me when a George Negus researcher gathering facts on my mothering abilities for George's TV show asked my daughter in 2004 if there was anything she would have changed about her childhood,' Ita says. 'Kate replied that the only thing she'd ever wished for was that we'd been a complete family. It wasn't a criticism, just a heartfelt statement of fact and she was then thirty-five. I've read reports from "experts" about divorce having little effect on children and I've wanted to believe them to help ease my own conscience. But, as the child of divorced parents and the mother of divorced children, I know such views to be absolute poppycock and no research will make me believe otherwise. I was certainly affected by my parents' divorce, and no matter how hard I tried to make their lives as perfect as I possibly could, I know my children were too when their father and I split up.'

Kirsten agrees with Ita about children suffering emotionally after divorce. 'My parents got divorced when I was fourteen. They fought a great deal but they were Mum and Dad and all I knew. I really can't remember when they didn't fight. Sometimes they were very funny and my sisters and I used to giggle at the way they went on. When they did decide to separate we were heartbroken because we used to do everything as a family – swim at the beach, have barbecues, go to the movies, and Dad and Mum always managed to get to our school concerts and sports days. It was nice to see them both sitting in the hall looking pleased and proud and it didn't worry us if sometimes Mum and Dad weren't talking to each other.

'After they finally did call it a day, Mum became bitter and twisted about Dad when he started going out with a woman he'd met through his sister. Then when he married her, Mum used to turn feral if any of us saw our father. I remember her pinching my little sister once when she told Mum what a good time she'd had on an outing with Dad. We soon learned never to talk about him in front of her. Later on I know my mother did have regrets about her behaviour, but she never said sorry. Something else I've never forgotten – my little sister once said to me that Mum and Dad never asked her who she would like to live with when they divorced. They didn't ask me either.'

Children are seldom consulted about which parent they would like to live with and usually have to put up with being shunted back and forth to suit their parents' requirements. In more than 70 per cent of divorces primary care custody is awarded to the mother, and many fathers believe this to be unfair. In 2003, Prime Minister John Howard announced that the Federal Government would hold a parliamentary enquiry into the merits of fathers being given automatic joint custody. It might keep the politicians and parents happy but has anyone thought of asking kids what they think?

Former Family Court Chief Justice Alastair Nicholson remarks that, 'If what is being asked for is a presumption that children spend approximately equal proportions of time with both parents, this will work to the detriment of many children for whom such an arrangement is inappropriate or impractical.' Obviously if parents can not agree on arrangements a shared regime could be disastrous for children, and if parents could not agree on much when they were married, why suppose that they will be able to agree when they get divorced?

'Children shouldn't be made to pay the price for their

parents' stupidity and mistakes,' Kirsten says. When her own marriage ended in divorce she says, 'I vowed that I'd never do to my kids what Mum did to my sisters and me. I feel really guilty about my kids because I know what it was like for me when my parents divorced. It was awful and no one should ever think children are immune from the emotional impact of divorce. I don't believe it's possible. You don't expect your parents to break up and when they do it seems like the end of the world.'

Relationships Australia CEO Anne Holland says children can react in very different ways to separation and divorce. 'The way they do depends on a number of issues, including their age at the time and the degree of conflict or animosity between parents. This is a stressful period for children but most recover and end up leading normal healthy lives. Their adjustment is enhanced when parents remain sensitive to the children's needs.'

'When I left my husband our three-year-old son started wetting his bed again. He was that upset. It was my son's way of telling me he missed his father and that he was feeling shocked and confused. I was wracked with guilt,' says Donna, a middle management executive with a major Australian public company. 'Don't anyone ever try telling me divorce isn't a crisis in a kid's life. It also affected me – and for the first twelve months I just wasn't myself at all. I often tell my friends who have separated never to make any important decisions in their life for the first year, that there is a grief period to get through.'

Although they might have initiated the break-up, it comes as something of a surprise to women how much they do grieve after their marriage or relationship ends. 'Even when our marriage was at its worst I was still able to talk to my husband about everyday worries or problems with the kids,' Rosemary says. 'There was another person to share the load. But all of a sudden the buck now stopped with me. I was scared.'

The thought of starting over again is frightening, as is having to accept the need to rethink the future because a woman's dreams and hopes have been destroyed. Anne Holland says it usually takes two or three years for a couple whose relationship has broken up to put their lives back together again. 'It sometimes takes five years for individuals and families to get over the emotional pain and trauma and many people can have serious health and emotional problems during this time.'

Most mothers do not leave marriages lightly and often have contemplated doing so for years. Many have also sought counselling. In many cases the culprit is time and lack of it. Couples grow apart because they are too busy to talk to each other about everyday matters let alone their desires and emotions. They tell each other things in passing. A friend of Ita's told her that she and her husband used to have what she called 'corridor conversations' until they both realised that they were no longer really talking to each other. This type of conversation only leads to mixed communication signals. Couples misinterpret what each of them is saying because they do not discuss anything – 'You said this.' 'Yes, but that's not what I meant.' That kind of miscommunication is dangerous to the wellbeing of a relationship.

In 25 per cent of cases, and even after many warning signals, husbands have no idea their marriages are in trouble until their wives tell them they want out. Kay's husband had always played around. 'I was pregnant with our first child when I discovered he was having an affair. I was doing the laundry and found lipstick on his shirt but it wasn't mine. When I confronted him, he confessed, asked for my forgiveness and said it would never happen again. He actually blamed the fact that I was pregnant for his "need" to look elsewhere. We had two more children but he continued to cheat on me. He was so damn careless that I always found out. He would be remorseful, make all sorts of promises and on we'd go, but he was a charming, exciting man and apart from his philandering we had a good life together. He was an excellent father to the kids too, and the only man I ever loved. Divorce wasn't something that Catholics like me ever considered – it was a sin.

'When the children were in their teens I warned him many times that I wasn't prepared to go on accepting his behaviour, but he'd been doing his "cheating/forgive me" routine for so long he didn't take me seriously. All of a sudden something snapped in me. He had been seeing another woman for almost a year and their relationship seemed to be more serious then his previous liaisons. One weekend he didn't return home. So on the Monday, I packed his bags and sent them to his office telling him not to bother coming home ever again. I instigated divorce proceedings and my life has been miserable ever since because I've missed him. The children never really forgave me for breaking up the home. I now lead a pretty lonely life and often cry about my lot.'

Very few women expect to be alone in their middle age. Such a fate is never a part of their girlhood dreams. Annita Keating probably spoke for many middle-aged women when she talked to *The Bulletin* magazine's Jennifer Byrne in 2004 about the breakdown of her twenty-five-year marriage with former Prime Minister Paul Keating. She said, 'I never, ever thought that I would be on my own one day . . . because he and the children were my life.' Annita told Jennifer that she would prefer not to live alone and was ready to consider a relationship but, as many other 55-year-old mothers know, once a woman is over fifty a good man is hard to find. There are hundreds of lonely middle-aged women resigned to the fact that they will never find a mate because all too frequently 'available' men prefer younger females to women of their own age.

Getting older and losing her physical appeal can be a cruel period of adjustment for a woman. 'Women often complain of being invisible at this stage of their lives,' Ita says. 'I always tell them to head for Italy because Italian men seem to appreciate females of all ages and you don't need to have a relationship with anybody – although if that happens it's a bonus. Just to be noticed and admired as a sexual being does wonderful things for a woman's self-esteem. Nowadays, men never "ogle" me in Australia, but not long ago when I was in Italy those hot-blooded Italian men did. It made this mature woman feel like a girl again!'

There is no guarantee that if a mother does find a new partner, not necessarily a long-term one but just someone with whom she would like to enjoy a fulfilled sex life, her children will automatically approve. 'I finally found a man who appealed to me and we went to bed together. My teenage son was supposed to be out for a few hours but came home early, discovered us and was so angry at the very thought of me having sex with someone other than his father that I gave up the relationship. His hostility made life too difficult for me to do otherwise and I didn't want to upset him further because he was still trying to come to grips with my leaving his father. Maybe I'll try again in a few years when my son is older and perhaps in a sexual relationship himself, which might help him understand that, like him, I have emotional and sexual wants too.'

⁓

Relationship counsellors usually advise couples to seek professional help in trying to sort out their differences before consulting a divorce lawyer. But when feelings run high – as they so often do when marriages are floundering – more often than not many couples dismiss such suggestions as futile, believing they are past the point of no return. However, it cannot be assumed that divorce will bring them happiness. A 2002 University of Chicago survey found no evidence that unhappily married adults who divorced were typically any happier than unhappily married people who stayed married. Two-thirds of unhappily married spouses who stayed married reported their marriages were happy five years later. The most unhappy marriages reported the most dramatic turnarounds – among those who rated their marriages as very unhappy, almost eight out of ten who avoided divorce were happily married five years later.

No one would wish women or men to remain in relationships that brought them little joy but it is possible that the benefits of divorce are sometimes oversold. Relationships Australia research shows that many divorced couples wish they had stayed together, with 37 per cent of people regretting their divorce five years later and 40 per cent of divorced people believing their divorce could have been avoided.

Julie instigated her divorce after one of her husband's work colleagues informed her he was having an affair with a co-worker. 'When I confronted him he admitted it was true. I felt so let down. Then I got mad and hired a lawyer and she was so tough that whatever was left of our relationship was soon destroyed. In essence she told me we'd take him to the cleaners and we did. He begged me to give him another chance but I wouldn't. Now I think I was a bloody fool. We'd always had something of a tumultuous relationship but it suited us, and I realise now that we probably could have worked things out if I'd been prepared to give him a second go. I think I'd be much happier if I'd stuck with my husband for better, for worse – but it's not politically correct to admit such a thing is it?'

The theme of depriving children of a 'normal' family life is a common source of guilt for divorced mothers. When faced with the break-up of her marriage, Johanna Griggs had to accept that her ideal of marriage and the way she had always dreamed her children would grow up was not to be. 'All I ever wanted was a good healthy marriage, and to give up on that and at the same time handle the cold, hard realities of what goes on in a divorce, which is not pleasant for anyone, gave me a level of guilt. In the last couple of years I have well and truly reconciled myself to the fact it is probably the best thing that happened, and the boys definitely are better off the way things are now, but at the time I agonised hugely over the end of my marriage.'

The break-up of the family unit also troubled Amanda, a mother of three boys. 'I moved to the country, something I felt guilty about because I left my two older sons with my husband and his new wife, while the youngest lived with me. That's the really cruel thing about marriage breakdowns – separating the children, changing schools and making them lose touch with their friends. I could have stayed in Sydney but the cost of living is so high there that I decided to move to the country where financially I could survive a little easier. The older boys came to visit but I still felt I had abandoned them. No option felt right. It was a matter of choosing which of several bad ones was better.'

Sometimes, couples manage to find a 'civilised' arrangement that allows them still to enjoy a different kind of family life together. Actor Joy Smithers and her husband separated after seven years of marriage and were divorced two years later. 'I felt very guilty about breaking up the family home. We went to counselling for one whole painful year, not in an attempt to get back together, but to try to figure out how we could move on as parents and resolve some of the resentment and bitterness that had led us to hating each other. Things are great now. We have both happily remarried and have had children with our new partners. Our kids love each other and we share hand-me-downs and mind each other's brood. However, the decision to leave, then trying to repair the family unit and survive things like Christmas is full of guilt. All I can say is that if you really try then time does heal all wounds.'

Time does not necessarily make telling children the real reason behind a marriage break-up any easier though. In fact, many parents never tell their children the truth. Obviously, the age of the children involved is a major factor but sometimes coming clean can be too painful or even confronting – and sometimes both. Many parents also say they are reluctant to add further to their children's unhappiness and are not sure that emotionally they would be able to handle the truth. Whether it is good in the long term to shield children this way is debatable, because without knowing what really happened some go through life believing they were the reason their parents did not stay together.

'I don't know that I have ever been honest with my children about my own break-up,' Geraldine Doogue says. 'I haven't lied but I haven't contributed much information.' A Melbourne mother who prefers to remain anonymous sees no reason for children to know all the facts. 'Parents are entitled to their privacy. When they were little, I used to tell them that people change and that while we both loved them very much, we didn't love each other the right way any longer to live together. The truth was I had fallen in love with someone else and, when I left my husband, was in the middle of a raging affair. I had three years of amazing love and sensational sex and I've never known anything like it again. I wasn't able to sleep with two men at the same time and I wasn't prepared to give up my lover so I left my husband. I didn't tell him the real reason and he never guessed and I could hardly tell my kids, could I? They would have been shocked. Mothers are not supposed to have love affairs. I don't feel the slightest guilt about what I did.'

There is no simple right or wrong answer to the 'what to tell the children' dilemma. Christine's sons took the issue out of her hands. She had allowed her husband to have primary custody of their two sons while she had access rights. 'I felt he would be able to provide for them better than I could and consequently they would have more opportunities but I also wanted to be able to pursue my acting career. The day came when the boys said they had a right to know why I'd left them and kept on and on until they were satisfied with my answers. My sense of failure was thrown up in my face but their honesty in telling me how they felt about everything, while painful, was also a relief.'

Society judges mothers far more harshly than it does fathers. 'Good' mothers are not supposed to leave their children. Margot Cairnes' son was four and her daughter was six when her marriage ended. 'I actually left them with my husband for a year, which caused me unimaginable guilt. Our marriage was an abusive one and I left because I felt my life was in danger. My self-esteem was so low I actually believed the children would be better off with him. With my current level of confidence, it's almost inconceivable I could have thought such a thing, but back then I was convinced I was such a bad mother, such a terrible person, that the children should be with their father. At the end of the twelve months – and no longer having to put up with an abusive relationship – I realised my attitude was ridiculous, and when I asked for the children back, he was only too keen to return them.

'But they were quite damaged by the care they'd received when I wasn't with them. I'd tried to see them but their father did everything in his power to stop me. I was heartbroken. He made me feel so guilty by telling me I wasn't a good mother. The children were angry with me too because he told them I didn't love them. When they came back home, they were very keen on making me feel guilty and it was hard to fight against them. If anyone caught me with guilt, it was definitely the kids.

'About eight years ago I decided that I wasn't going to suffer any more guilt and today I don't. What helped me greatly was a friend who reminded me that children have two parents and asked me, "If you left them in the care of their father and bad things happened to them, how is it your fault?" Then I remarried and my second husband would tell me I was a loving mother and the family doctor told me he had never seen a mother fight for her kids like I'd fought for mine. And I thought to myself, "Perhaps I haven't done such a bad job after all."'

About half of Australia's divorced men and women remarry within five years. Jennie married again three years after her first divorce. It was her husband's second marriage also. Jennie's three children liked their new stepfather and, at first, everything was terrific. 'We all got on well and did family things, which pleased me because I wanted the children to be like other kids in normal families. Then I began to see a side of my husband that had never surfaced before. He liked a drink but there would be times when he'd had far too much and, when this happened, he would become aggressive towards me.

'One night he came in late from a business function with a few too many drinks on board, and he kept drinking while watching something on television. I got up to go to bed and I told him he was drinking too much and suggested he stop. He followed me up the corridor and we began to argue. My daughter woke up and came out to see what all the commotion was about and saw him hit me across the face. I was stunned. He'd never struck me before and he seemed to enjoy doing it but I never gave him the opportunity to do it again. I wasn't put on earth to be some man's punching bag. I packed up the kids and went to my sister's place. We were divorced twelve months later. I feel mortified my daughter saw this violent behaviour but I feel even worse that I let such a loser get close to my children.'

When divorce happens, it's not only the immediate family that is affected. It takes its toll on the extended family as well – especially grandparents – compounding the guilt of mothers who value this special relationship. 'I not only felt guilty about upsetting my daughters' relationship with their father, whom they loved dearly, but equally guilty about breaking up their close attachment to their grandparents,' Pru Goward says. 'Everything was made worse by the fact that I moved interstate, which meant the grandparents didn't see the girls except for school holidays. I knew how much they meant to these two special older people and I was stricken by that.'

Prime Minister Howard says he is concerned that many boys are growing up without the influence of male role models. This is due to divorce, mothers choosing to have children without a live-in partner, and female schoolteachers outnumbering their male counterparts throughout Australia. Opposition Leader Mark Latham shares the prime minister's concern and says that boys who have no father or male mentor in their lives often suffer throughout their youth. Many mothers also worry about their children having little interaction with men. 'I don't know how women solve this problem if they have boys,' Debbie says. 'My three boys never see their father – his choice, not theirs, and definitely not mine. I want my boys to know what a nice man is.'

Pru Goward thinks it is equally important for girls to have a strong male influence in their lives. 'There are stages in a young woman's life that she really can't move beyond unless she has a rich relationship with her father. We seem to be obsessed now about relationships between fathers and sons and fathers as role models to sons but if you're a girl, your father is the first person you flirt with and it is through him that you learn to trust a man. A girl learns how she should behave with the opposite sex from her father.'

'My biggest regret is that the children haven't seen enough

of their father and mother together as role models,' says Di Morrissey. 'Their father was very hurt at our break-up and I think he still finds it painful to be with me. They had two separate individuals as parents rather than one unit, and we both tried to lead fulfilled happy lives and guide and love our children. We both have partners and are happy, which pleases the children, but we are rarely together as a family unit and that saddens me.'

A question that often eats away at mothers is what kind of effect their divorce will have on their children. Studies show that women from divorced families report less trust and satisfaction in their relationships, and that adult children of divorced parents are more likely to get divorced than those who come from intact families. 'My daughter Penny feels it has made her and her friends whose parents are divorced much warier about marriage,' says Pru Goward. 'In a way that's not a bad thing. I plunged into marriage at twenty-one, which was a mite too young, but I was super-confident. I thought marriage would be easy and that we had a lot in common, but I had no idea about the many things we didn't have in common.'

Joy Smithers also worries that her marriage breakdown might affect her children's ability to sustain their future relationships. 'Whatever path I chose I was stuck guilt-wise. Should I stay for my child and let her grow up seeing her mother a defeated shadow that she would probably emulate, or should I go it alone and risk having no more kids and no normal family life as I'd always dreamed of having.'

It is sometimes extraordinary how mothers feel they must shoulder guilt. When her daughter's marriage broke down Caroline was sure that the fact that she was divorced 'and my mother before me' might have contributed in some way to her daughter's marriage breakdown. 'Perhaps it was my fault that she had not been able to maintain her relationship with her husband. I analysed the way I'd brought her up, the example I'd set, asked myself if I had vetted her husband well enough, should I have noticed there was something wrong sooner than I did. I made myself sleepless with guilt. I am sure I let her down in some way.'

When Johanna Griggs' parents divorced after more than thirty-two years of marriage she found herself in the unexpected role of helping her mother put her guilt feelings to rest. 'Mum was worried her divorce would affect the memories my sisters and I had of our childhood, and that it might have an ongoing effect on the way we remembered our growing up and rub off on her grandchildren. It was a revelation for me in a way that my mother, whom I thought of as an icon of strength, was actually quite vulnerable. All of us told her we had the most fantastic upbringing and that it was due to both her and Dad and nothing would ever change that for us.'

No matter how bad a relationship might become most couples start married life full of optimism, expecting to be together forever. Gabrielle Krieg had all kinds of dreams. 'I grew up in Adelaide and I was raised to be a mother with the white picket fence, kids and a dog, but I'm of the generation that got mixed messages. Before I had finished my education girls were being told that they could have careers and choices. I felt terribly torn. When my marriage broke up, my son was five and I felt guilty because I had to get a full-time job and I worried about being away from him. However, he loves his school and his after-school care, because all his mates go too and they have a great time together.

'To my surprise, I found I liked working full-time and that I liked myself better too. Now I've bought a business of my own and it is the best thing I've ever done. I have never been happier and I am able to chase my own dreams and challenges. For me, divorce, while painful, was not the end of the world but rather the beginning.'

16

Stepmothers are seldom wicked

Stepfamilies are a growing phenomenon in Australia with one-third of marriages involving at least one person who has been married before, and most of these second marriages include children from a previous relationship. Girls do not dream of becoming stepmothers when they grow up, nor do children dream of living with step-mothers. But it happens. Trying to work out the best way to handle stepchildren is often the most difficult part of a new relationship, and more often than not women find they have underestimated the emotional toll of being a stepmother.

A woman may love her partner's children but at the same time find she is unable to shake off feelings of resentment and jeal-ousy towards their mother and her prior relationship with their father. His children are also constant reminders of his past life. 'The way I saw it, my stepchildren were biological proof of my husband's life with someone else before me,' Cheryl says. 'I felt terribly guilty for thinking like this. I knew it wasn't the children's fault and yet I allowed my jealousy to get the better of me.'

Cheryl consulted a marriage counsellor and says it was the

best thing she ever did. 'The advice I got saved my marriage. I now accept that the kids will always be a part of the package he had with his former wife. I love him and I know he loves me, because if he didn't he probably would be with his first wife.'

While stepfamilies represent new beginnings they are almost never without difficulties. The lives of many people need to be combined and all kinds of adjustments will have to be made. A woman can feel like the ham in the sandwich, caught between trying to please her children – and sometimes his children – as well as her new partner. It is important not to rush this process. Relationships Australia's Anne Holland says there is no such thing as an instant adjustment and that it takes time and effort for everyone to feel comfortable in the new family. She says some children will never feel secure. 'The idea that the new stepmother and stepchildren will instantly love each other and recognise each others' strengths is unlikely to happen. Love cannot be forced upon anyone and the relationship may take time to develop.'

Women who become stepmothers know this only too well. 'Step-parenting has huge degrees of difficulty, not only because the parents have gone through the trauma of divorce but because someone new is being "imposed" in the children's lives,' says Sydney businesswoman Bev Dyke, who has three stepchildren and is doing private research on the issue. 'Children dream of their parents getting back together again and even when there is basically a communication breakdown between the parents, it is hard for them to shake off that dream. I've always tried to let the children have as much time as possible with their father, but at the same time felt it important to be very involved in the family in order to develop a relationship with them. I have endeavoured to be a friend and to give whatever I can, knowing that what I contribute is a bonus, above and beyond what the children receive from their two parents. I didn't feel my role was to direct them but to add value to

their lives. I never expected to be loved like a parent or to get recognition for my contribution – but then again, parents often don't
get thanked either.'

Bev was forty, and her stepchildren were seven, nine and
eleven, when she became involved with their father thirteen years
ago. 'It has been an amazing journey and if we knew then what we
know now, we would have done some things differently. As you'd
expect, there have been some problematic times, and if our love had
not been so strong I might not have stayed in difficult times. But it
has been very worthwhile, both in terms of our relationship and in
seeing the children grow to adulthood.'

Geraldine Doogue found stepmothering 'the hardest thing'
she has ever done in her life. Her experience has taught her that
a stepmother 'should start slowly with modest expectations and
almost characterise herself as the aunt/friend. You need to work at
the relationship gradually, and if the friendships develop and there
is compatibility there, go for it. I was on fallow ground and had to
learn as I went.'

Jean Claude Strong took on two stepchildren when she
married James and believes stepmothers should not be too directive.
'I've always believed in treating children as individuals, whether
they're your own or stepchildren.'

The common perception is that step-parenting is a 'no win' situation,
and when Kate announced she was getting married very few of her
friends thought it a good idea. 'When you tell people you are having
a baby everyone is excited and positive but when you tell them you
are marrying a divorcee and acquiring two stepchildren there is an
incredibly negative vibe. My friends asked me how I was going to
cope, was I sure it would work, wouldn't it be messy . . . They were
so pessimistic.'

Kate's husband is fourteen years her senior and has a son and daughter. 'When you get stepchildren, you're sort of dumped in at the deep end. With your own children there are the nine months of pregnancy, ante-natal classes, post-natal classes, and all sorts of support. There's plenty of advice for new mothers but little real help available for stepmothers. You move through the stages of development with your own children gradually, but when stepchildren arrive you don't know much about them at all.'

Kate says she feels guilty for not loving her stepchildren in the same way she loves her biological children. 'I have a good relationship with them though and I get on well with their natural mother. You have to put yourself in her shoes. I ask myself how I'd feel if my husband remarried and someone else was looking after my kids. We set a rigid routine right from the beginning and stuck to it. There were rules and jobs the children were expected to do.' Family therapists agree with this kind of approach and suggest that getting children involved in creating rules also helps in the smooth running of a blended household.

Kate's role does not include discipline. 'I might tell them to stack the dishwasher but I don't make decisions about what parties they can go to, for instance. I am a carer but without the full responsibility.' She believes her success as a stepmother is largely due to her initial acceptance of her husband's children. 'If you resent the kids then perhaps you shouldn't marry their father in the first place. You are marrying a package. His children will never "go away" and they don't disappear when they're sixteen either. You have to accept that, look for the pluses and take it one day at time.'

Sally never thought she would have any difficulties putting up with Bill's children. The couple had been living together for five years when they decided to marry. He had two daughters from his first marriage and she was fond of them both. 'When we told them we were going to marry, the older girl wasn't at all happy. I was hurt by her reaction but I thought I could handle it – as long as I was with Bill everything would work out. I should have spent more time thinking things through at the beginning but I've always been impulsive. Everything was more or less okay until their mother got a job posting overseas and, so that the girls' education wouldn't be disrupted, it was decided that they would live with us. It was the hardest thing I've ever had to do in my life. I resented having to share my space with them and my life with my husband's past.'

However difficult she found her role, Sally's Greek background had instilled in her a strong sense of motherhood duty. 'No matter how bad I felt I always put the girls' needs ahead of my own. I tried not to let them see how I felt and treated them with total respect. Now that I know something about being a stepmother, I've come to the conclusion that God didn't mean for children to be raised in stepfamilies. Everyone tries their best but it is the wrong situation for kids. I adore my husband. He is my soul mate and the greatest thing that ever happened to me but I've had to pay a high price. If I had my time over I would not have become a stepmother nor would I recommend it. Parents should not divorce. A woman is not meant to live in the same house as her husband and raise some other woman's children.'

Samantha also finds looking after another woman's child something of a struggle. She is thirty, her stepdaughter is twelve and she and her husband have a three-year-old daughter of their own. 'Being a stepmother is very different to being a biological mother because you do have to care for another woman's child but you don't have full control – you have to follow the value system of the child's mother. I've found it even harder since I've had my own daughter because I have to cope with two sets of different rules for two children.

'Now that my stepdaughter is entering adolescence, it's even tougher because she wants to develop her own set of rules.

Two sets of rules are hard enough but three really stretches the friendship. If she doesn't like what her mother decides, she comes to me. It's no point asking my husband for help because he just says, "What do you think?" In the end, I know she has to do what her mother wants but I hate being piggy in the middle. As she gets older, my stepdaughter has become very "creative" with conflict. If she doesn't want to do something with her mother's family, with whom she lives most of the time, such as going to her grandmother's birthday party, she will invent some problem and say she needs to be with her father. Kids are very smart and soon learn how to use their situation to avoid family responsibilities.

'I have the authority to make decisions that directly affect her safety but, because I don't have the ultimate veto, I often tell her to call her mother when it comes to deciding what she can or can't do. All the step-parenting books say that you shouldn't interfere with that power. If you do that's usually when you will have problems. I think it is important to work with the biological mother not against her. When it comes to school functions I only go if asked and I never push it. Step-parents and biological parents have to keep in constant communication. It is the only way it works for children.' The experts agree and say that maintaining a good relationship or at least a civil one with a former partner can have a very positive effect on the children and therefore the family.

While some stepmothers are unable to let go of their partner's past, many former wives want to hang on to their ex-partner's new future. The thought of another woman having anything to do with the upbringing of their children is so unacceptable to them that they are prepared to go to great lengths to make her life a misery. 'There is very little that you can do if you're a stepmum and the other mum is around because mothers *don't* want another woman in their children's lives,' Caroline Eburn says. 'My four stepchildren were horrible and terribly rude because their mother had told them I had stolen their father from them even though he was separated when I met him. She hated me and was very bitter and still is thirty-five years later. Whenever I'd ask the children to do something they'd say, "Bugger off, you're not our mother."

'When they went home, I'd always get a letter from my husband's ex-wife saying, "You are not my children's mother, *don't* . . . " I didn't want to be their mother, I just wanted to do the best I could and live peacefully. I took one of the girls to an art exhibition once and she introduced me to one of her friends as "the wicked stepmother" and she meant it. When their father and I had a child of our own, they were nice enough to her but, as they were much older, didn't really have much to do with her. When their father died unexpectedly, they went out of my life. I used to encourage my daughter to see them because, after all, they are her brothers and sisters. She would go out with them but when they had a few drinks, they'd start saying nasty things about me. My daughter used to protest – "That's my mum you're talking about!" – but they just kept on vilifying me. In the end, because the things they said were so vile, she stopped seeing them.'

When Margaret's ex-husband remarried she hated his new wife. 'I couldn't communicate with her. I wasn't jealous of her but I couldn't accept the fact that she had any influence over my kids. I remember my daughter returning after a weekend with them and her stepmother had cut her hair. I was livid, as if a violation of my rights as a mother had occurred. When I remarried, my first husband accused my new husband of wanting to take over his role as father and they almost came to blows. We had two more children and it was a constant balancing act. My eldest daughter was very jealous. She is a mother herself now and still feels aggrieved that my last two children – her siblings – had two parents who were happily married. Blended families need help to get over these hurdles. There should be some obligatory course or counselling before people with children marry, and it should continue during the first couple of difficult years when families are trying to reach agreement on the best way to live together.'

When emotions get tangled up with reason, children often suffer as mothers manipulate their feelings and use them as revenge to get back at their fathers. When Kerrie and Geoff had a baby, his four-year-old daughter Kim from his first marriage was thrilled. 'She thought he (the baby) was wonderful and when her friends came over she would bring them in to see him. It was lovely to watch and I thought we were on our way to becoming a truly happy, blended family. Kim and I had got on well from the start but now I could feel – or so I thought – a special bond developing between us.

'Then things changed,' Kerrie says. 'I came into my son's room one afternoon and heard Kim saying, "I hate you," and before I could stop her, she had pinched him and made him cry. When I remonstrated with her, she was defiant and stomped out of the room but not before saying she hated me too. When her father came in from mowing the lawn, I told him what had happened and he had a talk with her before lights out. "Kim thinks you don't love her any more now that you have your own baby." I was dismayed. "But who told her something like that?" "Guess," he said.

'I don't even know Geoff's first wife Jill and she doesn't know me either but she says the most appalling things about me to Kim, who is only five. One weekend when we were having lunch, Kim said, "My mum hopes you'll get run over by a bus because then you'll die. You won't, will you?" Then she burst into tears. Geoff cuddled her while we both did our best to reassure her that nothing was going to happen to me and that her mum didn't really mean it;

that she was probably angry about something when she said it. Kim was very upset and so was I.

'When Geoff took her home, I had a good howl but not for long because the phone rang. I knew who it would be. Jill always rang within half an hour of Geoff dropping off Kim. She'd go on with her usual diatribe of hate – "You're not Kim's mother and you have no right to tell her what to do!" – she would go on and on. Usually I let it wash over my head; this time I interrupted her to say I thought Kim was becoming distressed by some of the things she was saying about me and would she please stop. "I'll say whatever I like." She spat the words at me. After she'd slammed the phone down, I found myself wishing that Jill would get run over by a bus; I just couldn't help myself.'

How do children feel when they are caught in the cross-fire? Charlotte thinks both her parents and stepmother let her down. 'My mother hated my stepmother because she believed she had "stolen" Dad from her, and my stepmother hated me because she resented having to "share" my father with me. I could never please either of them and neither of them ever gave a damn about my feelings. When I spent time with Dad and my stepmother, my mother would be waiting to quiz me the moment I walked in the door. Her opening remark was usually, "How's darling Daddy and that bitch?"

'My stepmother treated me like shit from the word go. When I'd go and stay with her and Dad, she would start picking on me from the moment I walked in the door. My room wasn't tidy enough, I wasn't dressed neatly enough, I didn't help enough; nothing I did pleased her. One day I talked to Dad about it. Why did she always have to be so mean to me? I heard them talking about it later in the kitchen and she said, "Well you don't expect me to like her, do you?"

'A few years later Dad and my stepmother went to live in

London. I really missed him. I wrote to him every week and he did the same. My mother was convinced that my father was trying to turn me against her and would sometimes open my letters before I got home. I began hiding them but it didn't matter where I put them she always found them and then would pick an argument with me over something Dad had written. I tried to ring Dad once when he was overseas and, when I did, told the operator I wanted to reverse the charges. I heard Dad answer the phone, and when the operator asked if he'd pay for the call, I heard my stepmother's voice in the background saying, "Don't take it. Why should we have to pay?" and Dad told the operator he wouldn't take the call. My stepmother hated me so much that she turned Dad into a wimp, and she wonders why I loathe her.'

In many cases, a woman never overcomes her dislike of her stepchildren because they have caused her to change her expectations. Instead of having her man to herself she has to share him with them, and the knowledge that his former partner is always lurking somewhere in the background adds to her frustrations. Instead of starting a family with a man she loves, she inherits a ready-made one, and the only thing she has in common with the children is their father. Some women are not able to cross such a great emotional divide and, as a result, many second marriages fail. When this happens, everyone loses, but especially the children as their family unit is disrupted once again.

A second marriage is often a child's third family unit. The first is with the child's biological parents' marriage and the second is as a single-parent unit – usually it's the mother who sets up home on her own following the breakdown of her marriage. When the second marriage breaks down a child often has to break off relationships formed with the relatives of its step-parent. Thirty per cent of Australian children live in single, step or blended families, and one in ten live in stepfamilies.

'There are many more family relationships in stepfamilies,' Anne Holland says. 'There are likely to be grandparents, uncles, cousins, siblings and a parent living outside the family with no link with other members of the stepfamily.' The Stepfamily Association of Victoria says, 'Stepfamilies have family forests rather than family trees.'

There are so many things that need to be addressed – such as what the children will call their new step-parent. Usually they call them by their first name but some step-parents do not like this and alternative names need to be found. What do they call the new set of grandparents that come with their parent's new spouse? How are they expected to relate to them when they already have two sets of grandparents? Celebrations like Christmas can become complex and many children learn to dread what was once a much-anticipated family event.

'You try to do the right thing by your parents and usually fail and the person who suffers most is you,' Francine says. 'My mother always expects me to have Christmas lunch at her place and it's always lavish. Then I have to go to Dad's home and have another Christmas feast with him and my stepmother. One year I just couldn't manage my stepmother's brandied peaches with the pudding and she took it as some kind of personal insult and the evening was spoiled. I've suggested that we all have Christmas together but my parents don't want to do that – I wish they'd think of me sometimes and not be so self-centred. I hate Christmas.' Lots of children of divorced parents feel the same way.

⁓

'Blended families can work but it takes a lot of effort,' Penny says. She was married for five years and has one daughter, Diana, from her first marriage to Mike. When she married Ian they added a son and a daughter to the family. Mike married Lisa and they had three more sons. Penny thinks that all these changes were hard on Diana. 'She had seven years of being the only little star on the horizon with not two but four parents to fuss over her. Then before long five more siblings were added to her world. She was jealous at times and I don't blame her. I felt guilty about my first marriage breaking up but I was determined to make it all work.

'We now have a wonderful blended-extended family. In fact we all get on so well that friends and acquaintances often comment about this, but that doesn't mean we haven't had our moments. As the biological mother there have been times when I'd like to have strangled my own kids and when I had to remember how much harder it must have been for Lisa as a stepmother. She never tried to undermine my role as the mother, seeing herself as more of a friend and mentor to Diana. When I was trying to negotiate Diana's teenage years Lisa was a great source of support – someone for Diana to let off steam with and someone for me to occasionally do the same. We have become good friends. The men in this equation have worked hard too. Mike adores his only daughter but never showed any resentment towards Ian – whom Diana calls Poppy – as stepfather, and Ian has never treated Diana any differently to his biological children.'

Perhaps it is easier for a stepfather to be accepted into a blended family than a stepmother because there is no stigma connected to the man's role, while the term stepmother usually has the description 'wicked' attached to it – sometimes in jest, but often for real. 'It is so unfair that we are always labelled this way,' Carmel says. 'Several of my friends are stepmums like me and we want our stepfamilies to work, not just because we love our husbands and our kids – all of them, whose ever they are – but because our self-esteem as women is tied up in whether or not we are successful.'

No matter how well intentioned a stepmother might be, forming a relationship with her partner's children is stressful nonetheless. They are strangers to each other with little shared history and all of a sudden they are 'family'. Just how is a woman supposed to mother a child who already has a mother? Stepchildren are not sure how to react to their stepmother either. They feel a natural commitment to their own mother, and if she demands absolute loyalty and support from them they find it hard to be affectionate to their stepmother. Any friendliness shown by the child to her stepmother is often viewed as betrayal.

When a woman marries a man whose wife has died there are increased challenges for her as a stepmother because death has touched his children in a profound way. Women in this situation often say the biggest hurdle that has to be overcome is the extent to which their partners have overprotected their children. 'Since his wife died eight years ago my husband has more or less treated his daughter as an adult and she saw me as a threat to the changed relationship she'd enjoyed with her dad since her mother died.' Jackie says. 'She was also anxious that I'd hog her father's love and was very possessive of him. She'd never had grief counselling and, because he didn't want his daughter to be unhappy, he'd never encouraged her to talk about her grief either. Counselling had helped me greatly when my first husband died and I was able to persuade my second husband that it would help his daughter too. It didn't mean that all of a sudden our relationship was smooth sailing but it did help her get in touch with her feelings.'

Often a stepmother feels guilty for not bonding quickly enough with her stepchildren and suffers anxiety and anger when this fails to happen. She wants her family to be perfect and to seem like a 'normal' family. 'The expectation for the new family to appear like a first-time-round family with two natural parents and their children living in one household together can cause pain for everyone because it leads to a denial of the existence of other parents and relatives,' Anne Holland says. 'It is important to see the benefits of being in a stepfamily and to accept that it will never be the same as the first-time-round family.'

While working through these kinds of issues is not easy, over time most stepfamilies successfully find their way through them to form rich and lasting traditions of their own – but it would not happen without the stepmother. She is the 'glue' that holds the family together, a fact that is often overlooked even though there are plenty of stepchildren prepared to give glowing testimonials. 'My stepmother has been wonderful and I don't know what I'd do without her,' Jane says. 'She has helped me with everything ever since she came into my life – school, career, and now my two kids. She also helps me understand Dad. I love her very much.' Courtney says she can never thank her stepmother enough for the guidance she has given her. 'I have a mother but my stepmother has been my mum.'

There is nothing normal about a blended family and trying to keep things running smoothly and everyone happy requires considerable skill. Psychologists stress that the very best outcomes occur for children when there is a high degree of cooperation between the parents. Family psychologist and mediator Anne Bernstein, author of *Yours, Mine and Ours*, says that even though her relationship with her children existed before her relationship with her husband, a mother should not let her children come before him. 'This bond with her husband will give her support and strength in developing relationships with his children and, in turn, all of the children will gain a great deal of security from the strength of their marital relationship.'

In hindsight, the one mistake Penny thinks she made was interfering with her second husband's attempts to discipline her daughter. 'I couldn't bear him to chastise her because I thought it might damage their relationship. If she had to be disciplined, I thought it best I do it. If she became angry, I felt that as her mother I could make up with her more easily. It tended to undermine him somewhat.' Many mothers make this mistake when they marry a second time. Women see it as their right to discipline their children because they consider themselves the ultimate decision-maker in their lives. If the stepfather does try to discipline her children and the mother does not agree with his approach she often asks him to stop.

Experts say it is common for each parent to put the interests of their children first. They warn that there needs to be an agreement between couples about discipline and suggest that neither parent reprimand any child before discussing the issue together. It can take a while to make this work but couples who stick to this approach are able to develop parenting guidelines. Marriages often break up because couples put off making a decision about who disciplines the children.

Interestingly, although men claim they never feel guilt, when they are in blended families some fathers do admit to a change in sentiment. While Penny's husband says he has no guilt about his own two biological children, he does feel guilty about Penny's first child, his stepdaughter Diana. 'When Penny and I got together I saw her daughter as a bonus – two for the price of one. My speech at our wedding was about the two girls in my life. I love kids. After a seven-year gap we added two of our own in quick succession. We were so busy with the little ones that looking back I sometimes am guilty that I did not give my stepdaughter enough of my time. Of course, I might have behaved exactly the same way if she were my biological child.'

John Kench has two daughters in their twenties from

his first marriage and three children from his second marriage. 'I have no guilt over the three children from my current marriage but I do feel guilty about my two older daughters. As a consequence of my first marriage breaking up, I haven't had enough time with them. I feel guilty that I haven't been able to give them enough of a male role model and a male perspective from someone who is of their flesh and blood and who understands their make-up.'

For separated and divorced parents with children, guilt tends to be the number one issue. This is triggered primarily by the reduced time parents are able to spend with their children, limited financial resources, and sometimes distance because of new living arrangements. It is also possible that when men talk about guilt what they are really feeling is more a sense of regret for missed opportunities. It comes as a surprise to men to discover how much they enjoy their children the second time round. Usually because their careers are established they have more time to devote to their parenting role, something they were not able to do when they were younger and forging their way up the corporate ladder.

When Pru Goward introduced her partner David Barnett into her family unit she found that protocols for step-parenting needed to be developed. 'It wasn't just financial issues but everyday things that I hadn't really thought about. My nine-year-old daughter who was able to walk to the bathroom with no clothes on when her dad lived with us could no longer do this. There were also things about David that my daughters didn't expect, because he wasn't like their father and this man didn't make them. He wasn't like them; they didn't have his genes. When a new partner enters the family, kids do watch warily.

'In the beginning, David felt guilty about being a father to my two girls because he thought it took something away from his children and, as my children were younger, he was concerned that he might take even more away from them and their father. But over time, those kinds of worries subsided and both girls say David has been a wonderful stepfather. Their love for one another has grown naturally and has never been forced. They all feel incredibly comfortable together.'

Margot Cairnes' second husband Christian had strict rules that he expected her children to follow. 'He insisted they take their shoes off when they came into the house for instance, and there were certain things they could and could not do. Once we were all living together the kids resented this regime change. One day they came to me and said, "We hate Christian." I told them that was fair enough, that I had fallen in love with him, not them, and there was no requirement for them to like him; we all just had to live together. From that moment on there were no more arguments and they got on like a house on fire.'

Stepfamilies are all about second chances and there does come a time when stepfamilies stop thinking of themselves that way and become a family. It might not be anything like the traditional nuclear family but it is a family nonetheless. When Penny's daughter Diana was doing her Year Twelve exams her school held a special father–daughter dinner, so she asked her real father and her stepfather to come with her – and walked into dinner with two very proud dads, one on each arm.

The real rewards of being a stepmother often become more apparent as stepchildren grow older and become parents themselves, when they are better able to appreciate the role their stepmother played in their lives. Last Mother's Day Cherie received a card from her stepdaughter Elizabeth. In it she had written, 'Now that I'm a mother I understand what you did for me when I was growing up. I didn't appreciate it at the time. I do now. Thank you for caring for me and about me. Thank you for listening, sharing and counselling me, but most of all thank you for helping me become the person I am today.'

'It took me completely by surprise,' Cherie said. 'I cried when I'd read it. "Thank you" might have been a long time in coming but it was worth the wait.'

17

Learning to live with the loss of a child

There is no pain in the world worse than losing a child, and because a mother expects her children to outlive her, nothing prepares her for such a tragedy. A child's death is often sudden. There is no chance to say goodbye. In a single moment, all of a mother's dreams are wiped out. First she feels shock, then anger and disbelief, and finally guilt that in some way she was responsible. No matter how many years go by she never stops grieving. Sociologist Dianne McKissock, whose work includes bereavement counselling, says guilt is a part of every mother's grief and by keeping her grief alive she is able to stay connected to her child. 'As long as she feels guilt she is still a mother and by holding herself responsible she keeps the special bond she had with her child.'

When Rosalind Gillespie's daughter Alexia was seventeen, she died from a fall during an abseiling expedition in the Blue Mountains in New South Wales. She was an experienced abseiler and a strong, athletic young woman. Her mother found it easier to write down her thoughts about her loss rather than talk about them . . .

'Abseiling in fact was not the cause of Alexia's accident. She tripped while walking along a narrow rock ledge and fell 40 metres onto rock with her hands somehow caught behind her in her backpack. Because of the efforts of her brave companions who gave her continuous mouth-to-mouth resuscitation she lived somewhere between three to five hours during which time an emergency helicopter tried to gain access, ran out of fuel and had to return to base and try again. On the second attempt, the rescue team again failed to reach her, and finally someone was sent down the cliff by rope. By the time Alexia finally was lifted into the helicopter she had died of a brain haemorrhage and internal injuries.

'Learning of her death was a sudden and total shock. It was a cold Sunday night; we were preparing dinner to be eaten in the lounge and had set up a table in front of a cheering fire. It was a simple change of routine and a bit of a weekend treat. Alexia seemed later than she had promised and, as usual, I had my ear half-cocked waiting for the familiar slamming of car doors, the yells and the crunch of her return footsteps. When there was a knock at the door, I think my husband Ian opened it. I stood ready to mock-scold her for lateness but in the hallway were two young policewomen and the parents of her companion on the trip. I knew immediately something was very wrong.

'I probably heard them tell me she was dead and maybe I heard them say something about what had happened. I am not sure now. What I do remember is that her companion's mother tried to put her arms around me, and how my body felt peculiarly stiff and awkward. The mother was wearing a textured black wool shawl that pricked the skin of my face and I remember I struggled to escape her embrace. I know I tried to speak and I think I said something like, "Not my girl, not my beautiful girl," over and over again. I could hear my voice, it sounded utterly false, cracked and high, and as though someone else were saying the words. I did not cry but felt cold and distant and I desperately wanted these people, however nice they were trying to be, to go away.

'They went at last and in a numbed manner Ian and I and our son tried to organise ourselves. To me it felt as though my ears were blocked and we were puppets moving behind glass. Later that night a close friend drove us to Bathurst Hospital. We were directed to the mortuary where we asked to see our daughter. The staff was worried we would be upset and that our request breached their protocols. We prevailed and, after much cautioning, were allowed to enter the mortuary and sit next to Alexia who was lying covered on a narrow table. We took the sheet off her but put it back after seeing how badly she had been hurt. I uncovered the side of her face that was not so damaged and held her hand. They were big hands like my partner's and had always impressed me by their beauty. I sat there for a long time and whispered to her a great deal, about how I loved her. Somehow, I imagined she could still hear.

'We drove home the next day. Arrangements were organised for the required autopsy and then a week later for her burial. During this time, many people came by and flowers arrived. I was glad of this. The young people who had been on the climb with her came and talked to us one night and we in fact had what might have seemed a quite happy gathering. Provoked by me, jokes – some very black indeed – were made and I bustled about getting drinks and making tea. In fact, I did not feel that I was there. It was as though part of me was above looking down. I functioned adequately enough, in fact quite well. Much of the time I was busy, and spent a good part of the night ironing and cleaning despite being aware of the incongruity and uselessness of these tasks.

'As the long, long days wore on I had short periods when I was able to find time alone and fell into a desperate weeping, but it wasn't too bad. I was still watching myself and thought I would be able to cope. I was also very busy. Friends and relatives arrived from New Zealand and needed to have somewhere to stay. Friends organised the funeral and I made a short, heartfelt statement about what Alexia had meant to us. Her violin teacher played *Air on a G-string*, all her classmates came and I was impressed how the boys and girls all stood in mixed close groups holding hands or each other. Later the father of one of Alexia's friends brought his two daughters to our home and they sat for a long time up in her room with a lighted candle. This was uncomfortable but bearable.

'The wake was held in our house and the rooms were packed with young people. At one stage, they found a video I had made of Alexia and friends acting out a variety of Monty Python skits. It was well done, very funny and everyone was laughing. My own friends had come to be with me and we sat in the garden. From time to time, I made what I thought were amusing comments and people laughed, perhaps politely, and I would wonder what it was I was saying. As the time went on my attempts at humour seemed more and more repetitive, unreal and finally unsustainable. I felt incredibly tired but was unable to lie down or sleep properly. It was so much easier to do things.

'Then it was over. The flowers died and were thrown out and the friends stopped calling so often. At this stage grief hit me with such force I felt completely torn apart. From our backgrounds in hospitals – Ian in medicine, mine as a nurse – we supposedly knew something about grief. After all, we had had to deal a lot with death, either in assisting at the final stages, advising and hopefully comforting relatives and so on. We had also both lost our parents. What neither of us understood was the profound sense of loss we would feel at the death of our own child. This we discovered was something we knew nothing about at all.

'At this time I think both Ian and I experienced intense periods of heightened awareness. Certainly I did. We were aware of the need to keep a semblance of an organised life and so we exercised and kept up our usual walks. I remember still the way the trees were so intensely etched against the clear, impossibly blue sky. Rocks were fabulously grainy and marked with pits and lines; leaves, flowers, bees, dewdrops, the sparkle of the harbour water all took on hues of acute concentration and too-sharp lines. I seemed to see and take in everything. In fact, the light and incisiveness of objects was so painful I wanted to wear dark glasses. Sound too was particularly penetrating. A bird's song, for instance, would cut loudly and insistently through my brain. It was so sharp it scratched my brain unbearably. I do not drink and have not experienced hallucinatory effects from drugs but I imagine this is what it might feel like.

'The remembering of dreams is rare for me, but at this time they were very vivid and sometimes left such a strong impression of being real that I often needed to forcibly remind myself they were not in order to put them in perspective. They were usually something about a baby, which was not Alexia, or Alexia herself as a tiny child. Often they were very happy dreams that made me unhappy in realising their lack of reality.

'In this early period I walked home one afternoon, I think from a trip to the city from where I had returned on the ferry. I took a slightly different route back to the house. It was dusk and as I turned the corner into the lane behind our house, I saw a few young people straggling up the hill towards our garage. In the midst of them was Alexia, walking in that characteristic manner of hers, obviously joking and intent on pulling her friends' legs. My heart almost burst with relief and joy and then she turned her head and it wasn't her at all. Such visions occurred several times and, although only momentary, it was very disturbing. In the end I realised it was probably a form of déjà vu where the memory of her was so strongly imprinted in my brain that certain things triggered my seeing her.

'In the first few years there were many contradictions in my behaviour. I now worked professionally as a film-maker and production manager and also undertook a university course. I not only needed the intellectual stimulus but also needed to keep myself occupied with things outside myself. Even so, and despite being so incredibly busy, for several years I woke every morning to find I was crying. When no one was around I wept wildly and constantly for long periods. This wasn't pleasant as it left me feeling numb and battered. I did not want to cry this way but could not seem to stop. Sometimes I was so numb the crying would cease, and I would think, "Ah good, there are no tears left." In this numbed state, I would at least be able to do things. Nevertheless I would do them in a dream while all the time maintaining long rambling mental conversations with her. Then the crying would start all over again.

'Having always enjoyed being solitary for long periods I now found I quite desperately wanted to be alone most of the time. I wanted most of all to be able to cry in peace and hoped with enough time it would stop. Yet so often, I found such relief when someone did call or drop in and I was forced to stop. At such times I would put on what I hoped was a good face and do my best to be entirely normal. What dismayed me was to find that when I was with people I really had only one incessant topic of conversation and that was of Alexia. I found this very difficult but it really was all I could talk about because everything else was without interest. I could hear myself and knew how entirely self-centred and interminable it was and would make myself stop. However, the thoughts remained and would force themselves back into the conversation at any unguarded moment. I have since seen other people do the same thing and am now, hopefully, much more patient when it happens.

'When I was a young nurse, we learned about people whom it was said had died of a broken heart. At seventeen, strictly agnostic and keen on the scientific explanation for things, I was sympathetic but secretly thought at the time it was a romantic Victorian notion. No less agnostic now, I have learnt just what might have been understood by this idea. It was one of the most difficult things to deal with. I experienced an emotional pain in my chest in the area where my heart is. Despite the emotional dimension the pain was so strong as to feel physical and quite palpable. It was there and stayed there without let-up for seven or eight years, maybe longer. It faded finally but would come back in waves, and still does on occasions. It was exhausting, unexplainable and debilitating.

'I do not know if other people feel this pain so strongly. How could you in any case measure such a thing? I do know that it was more often than not so painful I wanted to somehow get my fingers into my chest and tear my heart – or whatever it was that caused it – out. Sometimes in my rage of grief, I wanted to pound the bloody thing with a stone to pulp so I could no longer feel. I have not lost my memory of this pain and still fear its return.

'Another physically felt pain is not so easily described. It is a feeling of having lost a part of yourself. It seemed to affect the very way I held my body. I felt utterly crushed. It was feeling as though my left arm had been cut off and the bloody stump was still there. Or my leg. It did not matter what. I felt like a wet, oil-soaked bird with broken wings dragging its way along a beach knowing I would never be able to fly again. Of course, there was a sort of truth in this as I realised that it was a large part of my life I had lost.

'One startling thing for someone so lacking in religious belief was I felt an almost biblical sense of having been punished. There was a sneaking superstitious thought that perhaps I had not been fully loving or attentive enough to my children. Or maybe it was some other unnameable sin, such as taking advantage of all the freedoms offered to women these days. At least I could argue with myself about these notions but they were strangely compelling and all consuming.

'Another part of this guilt was the torturous notion that maybe if I had just done this or maybe been firmer about that she would still be alive. Feeding into all of this was the memory of a fierce argument we had had the day before she left, where I got mad at the amount of time she was spending organising her very full social life and called her to task for not attending enough to her studies in the run up to the HSC. She was very bright and the schoolwork was easy but if she was to succeed at her ambitious career plans this was not the time to play so hard. This did not happen very often but this time I really was angry and unrelentingly critical and when she left the next day we had still not – as we had always done in the past – put the argument to rest or somehow made things right between us.

'Another of the contradictory things I (or we) did was to keep Alexia's room exactly as it was. She had left it in its usual untidy state. Her clothes were tossed in lumpy piles, the bed was unmade, her school notes stacked in collapsing piles, even her used, slightly blood-stained panties were left in a rolled twist on the floor near her bed. I could not bear to have anything shifted. Even though I knew it could not possibly be I had an almost metaphysical feeling the spirit of her was still there. I wanted her to be there so badly, I didn't care whether I believed it or not. I did not care either what the room was like or what other people might think. The grief of Miss Haversham distilled through Dickens' Victorian world made sense at last.

'As I moved through the months of grief that follow such a death, I became very aware of the wariness with which people viewed me. I became mindful that for most people I must temper my public expression of emotion. We found some people we knew, but perhaps not well, avoiding having to meet us by averting their eyes when passing and occasionally even crossing the road. It is totally forgivable behaviour in my book, and I knew that in the past I had unconsciously done such things myself. I could feel that for some people it was a terrible effort to ask me how I was and I often spent quite a bit of energy trying to reassure people I was just fine. Of course, I was not.

'When a close death like this happens, you often are strongly advised to have counselling. You sometimes wonder if the person giving such advice is using it as a way of protecting themselves from the confronting business of dealing with you so intimately. At the time of my daughter's death counselling was considered almost mandatory. Dutiful to the ideas of the time I did try it but found the counsellors to be of little help. They were unfailingly compassionate and concerned but obviously not experienced in loss of this kind. In fact, I felt I worried one so much I ended up saying things to try to comfort her. The other two I found were peculiarly out of touch. It seemed to me that I had to work out these things for myself. I suspect I simply was not ready for any form of advice or efforts to comfort anyway. As I remember, it was easier for me just to steel myself and get on through the days.

'One of the remarks a number of people made that I found truly disturbing was to be told how brave I was. Bravery is something you would hope to display if there had been a chance for you to save your child from her death. In a situation like this, there had been no choice. In the end, the most helpful thing people did was to simply ask how I was and then be patient enough to listen. As I have learnt, this is not an easy thing to do. To those who did listen I probably said quite desperate, emotionally over-the-top and miserable stuff. It could not have been pleasant to listen to, but somehow to say these things and for someone to hear it was something I felt did help me to accept what had happened.

'Some sort of acceptance does finally come. I learnt to articulate this understanding when I heard an Aboriginal woman speak on the radio about the rape, mutilation and murder of her daughter by a group of young men in the town where she lived. She said that in the end you actually do not get over the loss of a greatly loved child, you simply learn to live with it, and this is how it has proved to be. I have learned to live with my daughter's death and to continue with my life. Perhaps it is similar to the process of an old tree that has lost a limb. The tree remains in place but eventually uneven new growth in the shape of a grizzled knot covers the rawness of the site.

'Looking back, my story seems a God-awful muddle of moments of progress and huge regressions and confusion. It did not help that I was unlucky enough to have a couple of quite severe medical problems that inevitably got entangled with the feelings of loss. My partner – with whom I had always had a close and most loving friendship – and I drifted apart for some time. We both had such different responses to the loss. There was no dislike or anger towards each other, we simply thought it might be easier to be apart. Instead, as it turned out we meandered along separately in a cloud of grief and despair for some years before finally coming back to a closer and deeper understanding of each other.'

Dianne McKissock says it is normal and reasonable for a mother who has lost a child to go through the kind of grieving process that Rosalind experienced. 'When someone dies and a mother expresses her guilt, the person listening often tries to comfort her by saying, "You mustn't feel like that," or "You mustn't blame yourself." Well meaning though that advice is, it only makes the bereaved mother angry because she wants someone to hear she feels guilty. What she is saying is, "Can't you hear how *bad* I feel?"'

Donna was in the United States with her husband at a conference when their eighteen-year-old daughter Melissa called from Canberra, where she was a university student, and told her mother she was not feeling well. Donna told her to go to the doctor straight away, which she did. On the second day, Melissa rang her mother again to report that she was feeling a little better but that she thought she was yellow. 'Those words go through my head every night,' Donna says. 'She said, "I think I am going yellow but nobody else can see it." Her father and I both laughed as we imagined Melissa at the mirror thinking she was yellow but we thought nothing of it. I told her to keep taking her antibiotics and to be sure to take the whole course.

'We rang several times to see how she was and during one of those calls I told Melissa to get her medical records from her doctor and that as soon as I was back we'd go to see mine and get her sorted out. She told me she felt very tired and I remember thinking she sounded it too. When I phoned the next day, she said it had taken her forty minutes to get dressed. Something was very wrong and Graeme and I immediately decided to return home. I rang and told her we were on the way. We threw everything into a suitcase and flew from Orlando, Florida, to Los Angeles and from there back to Sydney, but within twelve hours everything had gone loop-the-loop.

'I rang from one of the airports – everything is so blurred – only to be told Melissa had been rushed from Canberra to Sydney where she was admitted to Royal Prince Alfred Hospital's Intensive Care Unit. Something was wrong with her liver; it was only functioning at 20 per cent. When we left Los Angeles, we knew she needed a liver transplant but by the time we'd reached the hospital Melissa was unconscious. Graeme's brother and his wife and our daughter Alena were with her for twelve hours before she slipped into the coma, which happened the day before we got home. She didn't know her aunt and uncle but she knew Alena and teased her and said the usual sort of nasty things that big sisters do.' Five days later Melissa died from acute liver necrosis – cause unknown.

'When you lose a child you are on your own and there is a sadness that never will go away,' Donna says. 'I can't go to Graeme because he is grieving. He can't help me and I can't help him and I can't go to Alena because she is grieving. I can't even go to Mum, although I know she is grieving for me as a daughter. I feel so lonely sometimes but I just can't open up and the nights are the worst. I feel guilty when people ask me how many children I have. If I say I have one daughter I feel desperately guilty – I don't want to lessen Melissa's memory but there are times when I think, "Oh shit, I don't want to go through all this." I feel guilty about outliving my child. Mothers take on the role of carers for their children and I couldn't deliver.'

This feeling of 'biological responsibility' perhaps helps to explain the different nature of grief and guilt responses between mothers and fathers. While fathers tend to have 'rational guilt' when their child dies, a mother's guilt is often described as 'irrational'. Psychiatrist Professor Beverley Raphael, the Director of the New South Wales Centre for Mental Health, says that even when a child has a prolonged illness a woman has the feeling that she hasn't been able to care enough to prevent the illness or to protect the child from being ill. 'There is the ambivalence involved in wishing to end the child's suffering and distress in prolonged illness and there is the everyday ambivalence that has to be confronted when there is a sudden death of a child. There are some times when we wish a person wasn't there, and when that person dies there are times when we fantasise in some way that it was our wish that did it. That is part of human nature. We search for meaning particularly in grief. We look for omens and understanding to make sense of what has happened.'

Katerina's son Mitch died of lymphoma, aged twenty-five. He had been unwell for two months and had seen several doctors but it was not until he collapsed and was finally admitted to hospital, breathless, that he was diagnosed with a tumour in his chest – lymphoma. In spite of the fact this diagnosis had eluded five well-trained doctors, Katerina felt guilty that she had not worked it out herself, sooner. 'If I'd found out what was wrong with him sooner maybe things would be different . . . If we had gone for help a bit earlier maybe he would still be alive now.'

Cathy's baby son was four months old when he died from Sudden Infant Death Syndrome (SIDS). Sixteen years later she holds herself responsible for her son's death. 'I know my guilt is very irrational and I've spoken to my husband about it. He has guilt too but his is rational. I'm sure mine comes from my maternal instinct, my belief that a mother has to be there to look after her child, no matter what happens. My husband's guilt is that he put him to bed, which is rational guilt and is totally different.'

Dianne McKissock has counselled parents who have lost babies to SIDS. 'Let's say you have a hypothetical situation of a father putting a baby to bed and he lies the baby on his tummy and that has contributed to its death. The mother is likely to tell herself, "I shouldn't have let him put the baby to bed – it's my fault." I think irrational guilt is caused by a mixture of biology and social expectation.'

Even when there is a scientific reason to explain the baby's death, a mother will irrationally accept responsibility. When Annette's unborn baby died at twenty-one weeks because of a clot on her placenta, she blamed herself, citing a host of possible misdemeanours. 'It has to be the alcohol . . . I had one or two drinks now and then . . . I shouldn't have exercised so much . . . If only I hadn't been so negative that it was a girl . . . I should not have been like that.'

When a mother is grieving the loss of a child, her pain is so consuming that she can think of little else. Often the dead child's siblings are neglected and have to cope with their grief on their own, even though it is just as real and painful as their mother's. Their family structure has changed and the relationship that children have with each other is special to them. They have shared secrets, hopes and dreams together and now that has ended. If they are going to come through the grieving period successfully, siblings need to be able to talk about their memories and their feelings too.

'It was some months after Melissa's death before Alena and I had a conversation about her,' Donna says. Alena instigated it. She talked about her guilt, which really threw me because I never expected her to feel this emotion. I think she feels guilty that she's alive and her sister isn't. I feel desperate sometimes because Alena is hurting so much. I am her mother, I am meant to make everything better – like I should have when Melissa needed me – but I can't.'

Grieving parents often unintentionally neglect their remaining children. Their grief overwhelms them so much that nothing is allowed to intrude, not even those closest to them. Donna keeps a copy of some words written by a 'bereaved sibling' by her bedside to remind her of how Alena feels.

> I know with all my heart that you are suffering, but in my own way *so am I*!!!!!
> Sometimes I just want to scream at you, 'What about me? Aren't I important anymore?'
> I often feel very insignificant – it seems that my sister has been elevated to 'sainthood'.
> You seem to forget that she wasn't perfect.
> My experience of life with my sister was different to yours so please understand that my 'memories' may be vastly different.
> I often feel that my life will never be as important as it should have been. That major milestones in my life, such as

sporting achievements, graduations, marriage, the birth of
my children, will always be tainted with sadness.
Life has lost its shine – there will *always* be sadness.
I really miss my sister too. And I miss who you used to be.
Sometimes I keep my sadness to myself so that I won't
upset you.
I don't know whether to let you see my pain or whether
I should hide it from you.

Siblings need to be encouraged to share their sorrow and
not feel they have to hide their grief from their parents. They do
grieve as intensely as their mothers – and fathers – even if they
don't seem to show it. If they want to go to their brother or sister's
funeral to say goodbye they should be allowed to do so. The same
rule should apply when a parent dies. When Marianne's husband
died suddenly from a heart attack at thirty-eight she did not allow
their two children to attend his funeral and now deeply regrets this.
'I allowed myself to be over-ridden by everyone. People kept telling
me a funeral was no place for children but they were both old enough
to come and over the years have been quite vocal in their condem-
nation of those who prevented this happening. I went "off the rails"
in the first two years after my husband's death and feel guilty that
I wasn't much, if any, help to the girls in their grief.'

It takes time for a mother to heal. The worst mistake people can make
is to encourage the grieving person to 'get over it', Dianne McKissock says. 'As a bereavement counsellor I try to listen to a mother's
guilt and understand it and to imagine how she might think in an
effort to understand why she feels so responsible for a child's death.
The more a mother is able to tell that story and to feel heard and
understood, over time the intensity of her guilt will decrease and it

will become more manageable. But even so, until the day she dies, a mother will still say she feels guilty.'

And she will never stop thinking about her lost child either.

18

Like mother, like daughter –
the unbreakable bond

A mother's influence on her daughter is powerful. While instructing her in the rituals of womanhood she shapes her daughter in her own mould, and sees in her the opportunity to realise her own unfulfilled dreams and expectations. The mother–daughter relationship is unique and at times complex, but nothing can break the bond. It can be severely damaged as mother and daughter journey through life together, but even at its most fragile the bond endures – for better, and for worse.

Although a mother knows that when her daughter becomes a mother she will not be perfect, there is a long period of time when a daughter expects her mother to be a model of perfection. Her thinking does not change until she becomes a mother herself, and when this does finally happen it marks an important change in their relationship. They are now both mothers and therefore equals. 'There is a crucial moment in a daughter's life when she realises that her mother is another woman,' researcher Karen Fingerman, PhD, says. 'Before that, a mother is a symbol. She's all knowing, all powerful – maybe the enemy, maybe the nurturer –

but suddenly her daughter is able to see her mother as another woman with similar problems and experiences.'

Fingerman, an assistant professor of human development and family studies at America's Pennsylvania State University, says mother–daughter relationships are among the most complicated interactions human beings experience, and often comprise many conflicting feelings such as love, anger, worry, resentment, envy and need. 'Each woman's large investment in the other is the primary force that complicates relations between mothers and daughters. This investment carries with it much potential conflict, but it is a good thing nonetheless. It means having someone who accepts you, no matter what, and wants what's best for you.'

When Fingerman studied the relationship between forty-eight pairs of ageing mothers and their adult daughters she found that although many aspects of the relationship change as daughters enter midlife, certain emotional qualities remain constant. In particular, mothers continue to influence the way daughters feel about themselves. Years after daughters are grown, they feel guilty and ashamed when their mothers criticise them and feel happy when their mothers are proud of them. 'The relationship between mothers and their adult daughters is one in which the participants handle being upset with one another better than in any other. Women should recognise the strength of their relationship with their mother and appreciate it more.'

Fingerman says daughters should not try to change their mothers because it is an impossible task. 'Try to focus on the positive side of your relationship and accept your mother as a person with faults. One of these may be that she can't understand you as well as you wish, but it doesn't change her love for you. No matter how old you become, your mother will tend to behave like a mother towards you. She'll keep trying to make you into the fantasy she has of you. Mothers and daughters do enjoy each other's company and maintain strong ties for a variety of reasons that stem from their shared experiences as women. And their relationship remains central in both women's lives.'

⤴

Some daughters have such a love/hate relationship with their mothers that they not only dislike being compared to her but also dread the thought of becoming anything like her. However, it is just not possible to shake off a mother's influence because, deep down inside, daughters have absorbed her conditioning and it affects how they feel as women and as mothers. As Oscar Wilde once said, 'All women become like their mothers' and ultimately, it seems this is true. They laugh just like their mothers, they teach their children the same kinds of things their mothers once taught them, and they often have the same sense of humour. When they reprimand their children or are just chatting to a friend the thought crosses their minds that they sound exactly like their mother! There are times when they even physically emulate them.

'One evening Kate and I were having dinner with one of my oldest girlfriends,' Ita says. 'Evelyn was saying something and we were both listening when suddenly she stopped and said, "It's amazing, you two are both sitting exactly the same way." And we were – leaning forward, our right hands under our chins, our left hand resting on the table, even our legs were crossed the same way – it was quite uncanny. Now that it has been drawn to our attention we realise we often do this.

'I'm also amazed at how much my handwriting now resembles my mother's,' continues Ita. 'It didn't always. I went to a school where we were taught a uniform way to write and every girl who went to my school recognises the handwriting, but as I've become older my handwriting has become more and more like my mother's. One of my brothers commented on it when I sent him a card for his birthday. He was quite taken aback when he saw the handwriting on the envelope because Mum has been dead for ten years.'

It is not only a mother's good habits that rub off on daughters; her bad habits can also leave their mark. For instance, daughters frequently follow their mother's example and marry an alcoholic or an abusive man, subjecting themselves to lives of sadness just as their mums did. 'I couldn't believe it when my husband had his first affair and then another and another,' Leonie says. 'He turned out to be a serial philanderer just like Dad. Mum wasn't surprised though. "There was something about him that reminded me of your father," she said. I just wish she'd mentioned it to me before I got married.'

Germaine Greer once asked if motherhood was a privilege or a punishment and caused considerable debate. The thought of women being 'punished' for becoming mothers was considered provocative, but some mothers do not enjoy their role and it cannot be taken for granted that mother love automatically gets switched on when a woman has a baby. Jean was twenty-one when her daughter was born. 'I didn't like her much because she made my life a misery. I used to belt the hell out of her when she dirtied her nappy, which I feel bad about now. She was difficult when she was small; all my friends were going overseas and having a good time and I was stuck with this rotten baby. I hated her at times. I feel guilty now because I feel I loaded her up with the resentment I felt. The fact that she is not part of my life now is my fault, I know that, but she hasn't turned out how I hoped she would. She's not like a relation. She's like a nothing person.'

Mothers often criticise their daughters, which daughters expect and accept, but sometimes that criticism is so harsh and unloving that withdrawal is the only option. Margot Cairnes says there was a period of time when she did not see her mother very often because her behaviour was unbearable. 'She has always been critical of me. My first husband was abusive and when I left him my mother thought I'd made the wrong decision and condemned me for leaving. When my daughter had a serious asthma attack and nearly died my mother said it was my fault and wrote me a letter saying it was obvious I was an incompetent mother and that I should give up my daughter for adoption. Distancing myself from her was very painful, but ultimately I decided I didn't need to read letters like hers and I made a conscious decision to cut myself off from her.

'Initially, I felt guilty about this and I sought therapy to help me resolve it. I'd discuss how I felt about the things my mother had said to me, and the therapist would say, "It's not okay for your mother to talk to you like that. Why do you accept your mother laying all this nonsense on you? It only encourages you to feel guilty." Without the therapist's support I doubt I'd have been able to make the choice of taking out of my life people like my mother, who were giving me guilt messages, and put into my life people who give me supportive messages, like my current husband who tells me I am wonderful. I don't feel at all guilty about my mother now. I think we get what we dish out.'

The bond Margot has with her mother may be brittle but it still goes on. 'We have a relationship but you would hardly say it was warm. She is in a nursing home up the coast and I visit her every couple of months as it takes the whole day to get up there and back, and I talk to her once a week on the phone. I think of her as my birth mother. If I could have chosen my mother I'd have selected someone who was more caring or affirming, who would have said, "Darling, how terrible," when my daughter was ill. I modelled my own mothering on what not to do. Sometimes I look at my children and wish I'd had a mother like they have. I'm not saying I haven't made mistakes but when I look at the level of love, care and support that I give my children, I'd love to have had the same in my own life.'

~

One of a mother's principal objectives is to prevent her daughter making the same mistakes she did, and during the teenage years – which sometimes are the most volatile period in the entire mother–daughter relationship – she applies herself diligently to this task. Mothers and daughters can push each other to the limit during this time. Their frequent arguments often end with a daughter telling her mother, 'I hate you,' because she feels her mother does not know or understand her. 'Maybe we are tougher on our daughters,' Jean Kittson says. 'They are going to be women and we have to pass on the rites to them and let them know that life is tough. We want our daughters to be perfect and to not have any flaws that will prevent them from doing anything . . . We want their lives to be smooth.'

On average, mothers and teenage daughters argue for fifteen minutes every two and a half days, and mothers often complain of feeling emotionally drained. But the news is not all bad. At the 2004 British Psychological Society's annual conference, Cambridge University academic Dr Terri Apter told delegates about new research that showed arguing may be good for a mother's relationship with her moody offspring because teens use arguing as a communication tool. 'Daughters often use arguments to update mothers about what they are doing and what is important to them. Arguments sometimes keep the relationship going.'

Sue, who has two teenage daughters – Natalie, fourteen, and Annaliese, sixteen – thought their teenage years might be a nightmare but says they haven't been. 'They have been surprisingly good. You can avoid arguing if you just talk to them, keep the dialogue going and try to find out where their trigger points are,' she says. 'When I say no they usually kick up and I get the pouting drama queen act and "You're trying to rule my life," and "It's unfair," and "All of my friends are allowed to do it and I'm not." But then you need to remind them of the bonuses and you do have to concede sometimes and meet them halfway. If they want to stay overnight at a friend's place and I know it is going to be inappropriate, rather than stopping them from going, I say, "You can go but I will pick you up from there at 11.30." Prohibition never works.'

Sue says her relationship with her own mother was on a par with the relationship she has with her daughters, although she kept her mother in the dark about what she did and how she felt just to keep her happy. I've fostered the reverse with my girls and have always encouraged them to be open, and they are. Sometimes I wish they didn't tell me all the stuff that they tell me but then I think there is no rulebook. My mother was horrified to find out, as an adult, what I had been doing and sometimes I'm shocked knowing what the girls are doing and wish I was like my mother, happily oblivious.

'My children come and tell me things that take my breath away and I have to respond calmly and say, "Oh, that's nice, dear. Do you really think that is appropriate?" If I judge my daughters it is to their face. They can tell me things but they don't expect me to agree with it, but they still tell me. I'm a great believer in "knowledge is power". There is nothing they can tell me that I can't deal with, but if they don't tell me I can't deal with it. I do worry sometimes that they unwittingly will put themselves in situations and then find they can't get out of them. I love our mother–daughter relationship and we do lots of things together. We are all heavily involved in karate and we go away for weekends as fellow team members rather than as mother and daughters.'

Lucie, the mother of Anna, thirteen, and Katherine,

fifteen, sees her role as helping her daughters deal with some of the complex situations they might encounter and encouraging them to establish their own independence by making their own decisions. 'I guess it is more guidance. I wasn't prepared for them to be so opinionated. They often challenge things I say and I always have to give a reason why. We argue a lot, and probably because we are very similar in personality. Sometimes things can be a bit fraught in the household but we seem to thrive on it.

'I try to have discussions with them and turn them around so they're the ones who make the decisions, not me, and although we argue, in the end they always listen. I would like to think as they get older that they will look back and see that perhaps Mum may have been right.

'I worry they might encounter something in life that is stressful or that some situation might arise that is beyond their ability to deal with, and I hope that I will give them the skills to handle such things. I would like to think my kids are more open with me than I was with my mother. There were a lot of things I didn't tell my mother because I was very protective of her – but really I don't think she'd have been able to understand a lot of the things I wanted to talk about.'

A mother is the primary role model and teacher of cultural values for all children. She teaches her daughter the rules of femininity and the expectations of womanhood and motherhood. Some daughters believe their mothers have been less than honest about motherhood, that they have glossed over the difficulties and talked only about the incredible wonders and delights of being a mother, as if that makes everything right.

'I think certain mothers are dishonest,' Rebecca Wilson says. 'Our own, as well as friends who are mothers. There are things a mother will admit but other secrets never pass their lips. Most women go through incredibly dark times when they have a baby for instance, and the main reason it is so dark is that they won't admit it, and sometimes the pressure on a woman to be a perfect mother can turn them into another person.'

Miriam sometimes thinks her mother was too honest. 'She told me so often how difficult it was to be a good mother that I was almost scared of motherhood. I didn't have my son until I was thirty-nine and he is simply the most wonderful part of my life. Perhaps my mother was too tired and busy looking after all of us – there were five of us – to enjoy being a mother.'

Mothers never stop worrying about their daughters. 'I often tell my kids that it is a mother's role to worry and they just laugh at me,' Ita says. Fiona is thirty-five, her mother Diana is sixty-two. 'There I was at the office, frantic with a deadline, when Mum rang,' Fiona says. 'She got straight to the point. "I think you should go and see the bank manager and fix your mortgage rates before they go up. I'm worried that if they do, your budget is going to be affected . . . Of course, you don't have to take my advice but I think you should at least talk it over with your bank."

'I laughed and without thinking said, "You sound like a mother." "I am and always will be a mother," she retorted.'

When a national television show asked a group of daughters if they thought there was a special bond between daughters and mothers they all answered in the affirmative, but each of them defined it differently. For one it was her mother's willingness to love unconditionally, others said it was closeness, another thought it was being able to talk to each other about anything, while one girl nominated friendship – her mother, she said, was her best friend. They were all in agreement on one point, however; the relationship with their mothers was something they cherished.

'When I need my mother she is always there for me,'

Robyn says. 'When I was in my teens, she used to listen to all my problems and try to help me sort them out. I can see now how constructive her advice was. When my marriage broke down and I spent most of my weekends and evenings around at her house crying she comforted me. I never would have survived the first miserable year without her love and support. She was amazing. I guess the fact that she has been divorced herself helped her understand what I was going through, but sometimes I didn't have to say anything because she seemed to be able to read my mind.

'She has a busy career but never once has she said she didn't have time for me or told me not to come round, although there must have been times when I played havoc with whatever she had planned. Mum never once complained. Now that I am in my mid-thirties our relationship has broadened into a deep friendship where we understand each other even better. I not only continue to confide in Mum but now she sometimes shares confidences with me. I love it when this happens because I feel as if I've been admitted to some kind of secret circle. She has a great relationship with my brother but I know she never talks to him about her intimate feelings like she does with me. I enjoy her company so much.'

'The thing I always remember about Mother was the way she talked to her mother,' Janie says. 'They called each other every day and laughed a lot together. I liked to sit and listen. Now I'm a mother I try to do the same with my mum but because we both have outside jobs there isn't always time for a daily phone chat. However, two days never go by without one of us phoning the other. I feel guilty if I don't talk to her.'

In the same way daughters know how to push their mother's guilt buttons, mothers are experts at doing the same thing to their adult children. 'When Kate was little my mother would ring at six o'clock every evening and ask, "Isn't that child in bed yet?"' Ita says. 'Usually I'd reply, "No, Mum, things are done differently now because women go out to work." It wasn't as if I kept Kate up until midnight. She was always in bed by seven but Mum seemed to take delight in making me feel guilty. I could set my watch by her nightly phone calls. Sometimes I didn't bother to answer but that only meant when she rang the next night and I did answer she'd give me a lecture for keeping Kate out late the evening before!'

Some daughters regret not telling their mothers how much they admired them and how they appreciated all the things they did for them. Often the realisation of their mother's contribution to their lives only happens after she dies, when a daughter's guilt can be immense. 'Now that I'm fifty-nine and looking after my grandchildren sometimes two and three at a time, I can't believe how much I imposed on my mother,' Jan Murray says. 'I now realise women my age shouldn't have to do this. I've always said that behind every successful woman there is an exploited woman – and I know I exploited my mother. She looked after my five kids when I went to university; then when my husband John (former Federal Tourism Minister John Brown) was in Canberra and I was with him, she'd sometimes have them for a week. I couldn't have done it all without my mother, but at the time I didn't appreciate it. I used to take it for granted that she would help. I didn't feel at all guilty then, but I do now.'

Ros Kelly feels guilty about all the things her mother did for her too. 'I couldn't have done everything I have without her. She helped me at home so much but when I look at the relationship she had with my children, especially my daughter, I think they were some of Mum's happiest days. For our arrangement to work there could be only one boss in the home and my husband and I delegated this role to my mother. The fact that my children have turned out so well is a great credit to her.'

'As you get older you realise how wise mothers are and, now that mine is dead, I feel guilty that I spent so little time with her acknowledging her many abilities,' Mary Lou says. 'It's not until you become a mother yourself that you get some idea of how much your mother had to put up with, and that what she was trying to do was share not only her wisdom but also her mother's and her grandmothers'. It was generous, loving advice and I'm sorry I didn't understand this and thank her before she died.'

Time-poor mothers always seem to feel guilty about not seeing enough of their mothers – and fathers. 'After I left home my husband and I moved away from where my parents lived for a time and I saw them only once a year,' Dianne McKissock says. 'It wouldn't have taken much for me to phone or write to them more often – why didn't I? My father died before my mother and now I think how lonely she might have felt all the years when she was on her own. I wish that I had done more.'

Dianne says her mother never made her feel guilty but some mothers who feel neglected occasionally do take forceful action. 'I don't mean to be awful to my mother but I get so busy at the office that somehow my day seems to slip away,' Phoebe says. 'We have the same greengrocer and when I went shopping last weekend he said my mother had asked him to pass on her best wishes and to say she hoped I was well. Ouch!'

Sally Loane says she feels guilty when she realises she hasn't rung her mother for a couple of weeks. Rabbi Allison Conyer says that although she speaks to her mother almost every day and has an amazing relationship with her, it is not guilt-free by any means. 'My two children are her only grandchildren so I have to deal with criticisms such as, "How could you abandon the family and live in another country in another hemisphere?"'

A mother protects and teaches her daughter and then has to push her from the nest so she can become a person in her own right. This constant 'push–pull' between a mother's desire to always nurture her child and her understanding that the 'umbilical cord' must be severed at some stage is easier said than done. Until her own mother was diagnosed with breast cancer eight years ago, Penny wasn't aware of her struggle to do this. 'The day her breast cancer was diagnosed she came round to my place and for the next five nights we sat up talking and drinking. She confessed that she had loved the fact that her "successful doctor daughter" was so dependent on her and found it flattering, but when my first marriage broke down she realised this wasn't a healthy set-up and went through a stage of actively "cutting the cord". I remember when she did this. It was the first time I couldn't seem to get on well with her and I didn't understand why. Mum cried as she told me how painful it was for her to break those ties. I did become more independent and her insight and honesty made me love her even more.'

‿

There is an old Chinese saying that if the mother-in-law and the daughter-in-law are on intimate terms, the whole family will be happy. It's certainly true that when a son marries, the balance of feminine influence changes. The mother–daughter-in-law relationship is one of the most complicated of all: two women who love the same man are suddenly 'family' and the relationship is not always a happy one. Psychologists say that serious strife between a mother and a daughter-in-law usually signals an immature relationship between the mother and her son.

Maria, who comes from a large Italian family, finds her relationship with her mother-in-law infuriating because, 'She always tries to make me feel guilty about the way I look after my daughter. When I first came home from hospital, she smothered my baby with attention and wouldn't even let me hold her because she wanted the baby to herself. She finds fault with everything

I do. I had learnt to do things a certain way at the baby classes but my mother-in-law declared it was wrong and did the opposite. She always knows what's best for my baby. After a day with my mother-in-law, I feel like I need a week of counselling.'

But some mothers-in-law get on so well with their daughters-in-law that lasting friendships are formed. Joy Smithers is very fond of hers. 'When I am busy with a fourteen-hour day plus travel, Vera flies down from Brisbane and takes over and I become one of the kids. She organises all the after-school classes, drives the children everywhere, shops, cooks, cleans, mends and reads stories. She even folds and irons my underwear. I only ever hear supportive words from her mouth. What's more, if I do have any spare time, she sends Tony and me out on a "date".'

Di Morrissey has great affection for her first mother-in-law, too. 'I recently went to her ninetieth birthday. I flew to America especially because I wanted to tell her once more how grateful I've always been for her support and how much I love her. She never criticised me and was always encouraging, interested and approving. If I asked what she thought or how she would do things, she'd tell me. Because my husband's job meant we lived overseas most of my contact with her was through letters. She used to say, "Be nice to your family first and treat them as you want to be treated – just because they're family doesn't mean you can treat them any old way." When Peter and I divorced, she told me that, sad as she was, she would not be taking sides but would always love me and as the mother of her grandchildren her door and her heart would be always open to me.'

The mother–daughter relationship is a sequence of coming together and drawing apart experiences. There is the separation of birth, the dependence of childhood, the challenges of adolescence, and the reunion of adulthood when mothers often become dependent on their daughters. 'When my mother was in her seventies and not well I went round to make sure she took her medicine and I found myself tucking her up into bed,' Ita says. 'It was an odd feeling doing for her what she had once done for me.'

'I treasure the bond I share with my daughter,' Barbara says. 'It means so much to me because my relationship with my mother was flawed and I've always felt there was an emotional void in my life. I wished many times that my mother had been different. I tell myself she loved me, but most of my life I haven't felt loved at all and at times nothing but lonely. Mothers are supposed to be the strength you rely on, mine wasn't. When I had problems I had to cope with them on my own.'

Barbara's mother was an alcoholic. 'She wasn't always but I do have great difficulty remembering her ever sober. When I was little, she seemed like other mums or she does in my memory. She always smelt nice and wore pretty dresses and I used to love trying on her evening gowns when she was out. I can still remember how lovely it was to come home after school and find her there, but that's about the extent of my good mother memories. By the time I was eleven, she had become a heavy drinker. Her habit got progressively worse and was the reason why Dad left her. As I grew up she was never there for me when I needed her and now I am in my sixties I feel an enormous void in my life. I hated coming home and I avoided bringing friends to our house because I never knew what state she'd be in.

'I used to hope she'd change, that somehow a miracle would happen and she would snap out of it. I'd look at my friends with their mothers and envy them. There was always an emptiness in my life – even now I still feel it – but there was still a somewhat battered and bruised bond between us nonetheless. My mother came over for lunch one day and when she was leaving her handbag wasn't shut properly. "Your bag is open," I said. "Let me fix it for you, someone will rob you." "Don't worry," she replied, hugging it to her chest. As I took the bag from her, it opened to reveal a bottle of gin that she had taken from our bar.

'My mother's inadequate mothering has inspired me to try to be the best mother possible. I vowed I'd never be like her. My daughter was never going to feel she hadn't been well mothered. I'm not silly enough to think that I am a perfect mother; I know such a creature doesn't exist. But I do think I am a good enough mother, and my daughter is secure in the knowledge that wherever she goes a piece of my heart always goes along with her.'

Like mother, like daughter – the unbreakable bond

19

Like mother, like son – the resilient relationship

The birth of a son brings with it a once-in-a-lifetime opportunity to create the perfect man – although surely if such a thing were possible some clever female would have done so by now. However, as mothers eventually come to realise, this is an impossible dream. Not only is a man shaped by centuries of conditioning and inbred qualities, but his genetic wiring is so strong that he is able to resist all attempts to mould him in any other way than his instincts dictate. This is not deliberate resistance on his part but something that comes naturally to him.

No one should underestimate a mother's influence on her son, however, because it is just as powerful as the one she exerts on her daughter. Whether her son acknowledges it or not, his mother will have an effect on his life forever. The things she has – or has not – taught him will never go away and will shape not only the way he thinks about himself but also the way he views women generally. Of course, it is essential for their development that boys have positive male role models in their lives, but the development and ultimate success of a man's future relationships with women is usually dependent on his mother's response to his sexuality.

The subject of raising boys has been a hot topic since the nineties when it became apparent that girls were forging ahead of them in the education stakes, not only at school but also at university. Studies also showed that girls were more articulate and confident, that boys were being left behind, had low self-esteem, and often resorted to anger and violence in their frustration. As a result, their future was looking somewhat bleak. Psychologists and family therapists – mostly male – quickly jumped on the 'save our boys' bandwagon and a plethora of books on the matter appeared. Many of them share the common theme that too much mothering is not good for boys.

In his best-selling *Iron John: A Book about Men*, American author Robert Bly said that over-mothering results in sons becoming 'mummy's boys' who are too tied to women as children and, on reaching adulthood, are then too tender, too empathic and too interested in women's issues. A mother might well ask what is wrong with having such attributes. They might also argue that while females do have these softer skills – which are nothing to be ashamed of – they are also assertive and confident about achieving their goals. Twenty-first century women do not recognise the stereotypical descriptions that are all too often levelled at them in an attempt to pressure mothers to distance themselves from their sons.

Bly also blames mothers for getting in the way of boys' relationships with their fathers. Australian family therapist Steve Biddulph, author of another bestseller *Raising Boys*, believes mothers often turn sons against their fathers but is prepared to concede that men can be at fault too, and is critical of dads who give priority to their jobs. 'If you work fifty-five to sixty hours each week, including the time it takes to travel to your workplace, you cannot succeed as a father,' Biddulph says.

It is well documented that men are their own worst enemies when it comes to forging relationships with their kids, both boys and girls. Many are prepared to leave parenting to their wives and partners, and often put their jobs ahead of their family interests. Since the nineties it has become apparent that some dads have been rethinking their fathering role and changing their working hours to spend more time with their children. Like working mothers, they are agitating for workplace reform and more family-friendly practices that recognise that fathers want time with their kids just as much as mothers do. Other changes are slowly taking place too; for instance stay-at-home dads are no longer considered a novelty.

Some of the male critics of mothers seem to think that parenting should be seen as some kind of competition between men and women. The authors know from their own experience that, just like girls, boys benefit from having a close relationship with both parents. It is shared parenting that usually produces well-rounded sons and daughters. Children raised this way are often less dependent on one parent over the other. Biddulph says that boys learn through relationships and by building trust in a person. 'They learn the person, not the subject. Therefore they dislike change and disruption.' He also says that because boys are more prone than girls to separation anxiety they should, if possible, be kept out of childcare before the age of three.

'Boys need more mothering than girls because they are much more immature,' says Nanette Moulton, who thinks boys are about two years behind girls in their development. Biddulph says that boys have an intelligence delay of one year in comparison with girls.

Nevertheless, he believes that by the time a boy is fourteen he must distance himself from his mother so that he can reach a more adult image of women. Most mothers say this happens quite naturally and therefore there is no need to hasten the separation.

Why Biddulph and other male psychologists feel boys must break away from their mothers at this age is puzzling. 'Robert Bly comes across as a bit of a woman-hater to me,' Ita says. 'Encouragingly for mothers, there are plenty of well-qualified experts who think mothers should reject the patriarchal motherhood model.'

Family therapist Olga Silverstein believes, 'What is done to little boys is inhuman. They are not the "big boys" they are told they are. They need to cry, to express their true feelings, but they are not allowed. They need to maintain a love and connection with their mothers as they are growing up.' In her book *The Courage to Raise Good Men*, she urges mothers to shun what she describes as the 'outmoded culture of masculinity' and allow boys to be themselves. 'Because of the way men are raised and the emotional shutdown that is required of them, it becomes all but impossible for them to reach out or to be reached.'

'I would argue that boys do not need to repress closeness with their mothers to become masculine, and that it is important for men to acknowledge the strong influence of mothers and women,' says Bob Pease, an Associate Professor from Melbourne's RMIT Social Science and Planning Department. He has been involved in anti-sexist men's politics since the seventies and specialises in men, masculinities and gender relations. Pease believes that men need to understand their mothers as women with their own life histories, expectations and needs. 'Such analysis can enrich their perception of women as a whole. Many men have difficulty seeing their mothers as women with separate lives before and apart from motherhood.'

'For a lot of sons their relationship with their mothers is their safest relationship,' says Charlie Kreiner, board director of America's National Organization of Men against Sexism. He believes mothers need to be celebrated and appreciated. 'A boy loves his mother, she loves him. He has a relationship with her that in most cases is protective, secure and safe. Men would never choose to split from their mothers. They are humiliated into leaving – sometimes by their father, sometimes by older boys, but usually it's within the school system as an institution.'

'If Ben was misbehaving when he was in his early teens, the worst thing I could threaten him with was that I would kiss him goodbye at the school gates,' says Ita. 'He was instantly good!' Most boys go through this stage of denying their closeness to their mothers. Other boys make them feel embarrassed, even ashamed of their relationship with their mother. 'A mother is made to feel ashamed too,' Kreiner says. 'If her son doesn't push away first she often does because she's been conditioned with the same stuff about "mummy's boys". So they both push away from each other. Mothers are afraid if they stay close to their sons they'll raise "sissies" and sons worry they'll be "sissified".' A boy quickly learns that he will not be accepted into male society unless he turns his back on his mother.

'The result is a son who is disconnected, isolated and thrown into the world within that isolation,' Kreiner says. 'He is left to build relationships with other males and females based on gender roles rather than closeness, safety and love; and then conditioned to use sex as the way out of this isolation, which has nothing to do with sex but the lack of real human closeness. You don't have to break away from one relationship to have another.'

William Pollack, the Assistant Professor of Psychiatry at America's Harvard Medical School, has done extensive research on boys, some of which has formed the basis for his book *Real Boys: Rescuing our Sons from the Myth of Boyhood*. He writes about the need for boys to be with their mothers for as long as possible to develop their emotional intelligence and stability. 'Boys need to be allowed to separate at their own pace. Boys cannot be made weak by warm, loving relationships with either their mother or their father. This only makes them into loving, caring and strong young men who become fine members of our society.'

'When boys are ready they do gradually pull away,' says Frances Jay, whose three sons – Hugh, nineteen, Andrew, sixteen, and Philip, thirteen – are all close to her. 'When they have a problem or are worried about things the boys come to me, and with their dad they do "fun" things like going to football. Both my older boys began "detaching" themselves when they were about fourteen and began to challenge me. Hugh used to do this by shouting, until I explained this wasn't the way to speak to women. I also tell my sons they should never walk away from a woman and they should always listen to what she has to say. I've told them that because I am a strong woman they need to stand up to me if they feel they are right or have something to say, but that I expect them to deliver their opinions in a respectful manner.

'I believe that if boys learn how to communicate through their mother they will be better able to communicate with women when they grow up. I think boys should be raised to be independent. My sons know how to clean and cook. Andrew made his first cake yesterday complete with butter icing! They know they're expected to do well at school and go to university. I've taught them how to be sensitive to other people's needs too. For instance, if I come home cranky and tired after a day at the office they need to work out why I might be feeling this way.'

Not all that long ago it was considered 'a woman's duty' to produce a son and heir to continue on the family name. While it would be nice to think the pressure on women to do this no longer exists in the twenty-first century, there is still a certain kudos that comes with producing a son. A woman who is the mother of all boys is often elevated to 'star' status. 'It happens to me all the time,' Nannette Moulton says. 'People, especially Europeans and Asians, tell me how lucky I am to have three boys, how proud I must be. It's always assumed that my sons will have good careers and that ultimately they will become my protectors. I don't think this way at all. I'm just happy to have three healthy kids.'

Marg Malkin says the expectation that a son's first priority is to look after his mother is widespread. She is the mother of Nick, twenty-nine, Miranda, twenty-seven, and Stephie, twenty-six. 'It is almost an ownership thing, as if a mother has the right to expect her son to one day fulfil a protectionist role for her. But I think children's lives have to be free and that you're lucky if they want to see you.' How did she feel when the doctor told her she'd had a boy when Nick was born? 'Pretty clever and it was a weight off my shoulders too, because having a boy does please the father.'

'I can remember being so relieved to hear "It's a boy!" when my first child was born because I knew how much it meant to my husband,' Camille says. 'My sister has three sons. When the first one was born my husband told the proud father, "Well done, mate, you won." When their second son came along my husband said, "Well done, you won both times." And when their third son arrived, he said, "I can't believe you've won three times in a row."'

It is not only fathers who place a high value on sons. Society also holds them in high regard too. 'My first child was a girl and I was just thrilled,' Wendy McCarthy says. 'People were pleased for me. But when I had my next child – a son – the first thing I noticed was the general approval of family and friends who told me it must be so wonderful for my husband to have a son to carry on the family name, that kind of thing.'

Many women do secretly admit to wanting their first child to be a boy. Sally, now fifty-five, has two girls and two boys. 'My first child was a girl and although I've never said it out loud I was disappointed she wasn't a boy.' Joanne remembers feeling much the same way when her first child was a girl. 'When my parents came to see me, Dad said, "I guess you're disappointed you didn't have a boy." Although I told him not to be so silly, he was right – I was! Later I felt guilty that although I had a beautiful, healthy baby girl I had this let-down feeling because she wasn't a boy.'

While most women say they wish only for their babies to be born healthy such feelings often vanish once they give birth to a son, and women often admit to being surprised by the emotions they feel. 'When Tom was born it was instant love at first sight,' Penny says. 'It was different with the girls. I loved them of course and bonded with them but I was totally "in love" with my son. Other mothers I have seen as patients often ask if it is "normal" to feel differently when they have boys and girls, as many of them have felt this "in love" phenomenon. I assure them that, even though I did too, it is well and truly balanced by the joy of a daughter whom you love just as much – perhaps in a different way – and who ultimately becomes your friend.'

'I don't remember feeling a different kind of love for Ben when he was born but rather a kind of deep contentment that I had been blessed with a child of each sex,' Ita says. 'I was equally besotted with both my children from the moment I set eyes on them and very happy to have a girl first because I longed for a daughter. As the only girl among three brothers I'd often wished for a sister, and when Kate arrived I thought all my Christmases had come at once – as she was born on Christmas Eve this was probably an appropriate reaction! But when Ben was just a few weeks old I received a letter from his uncle in Scotland congratulating me on having a son and for continuing on the name of the Clan Macdonald, and it's possible I felt a little smug on receiving such praise.

'Right from the start Ben was so different from his sister. It wasn't just the way he ate and slept but how he demanded my attention. Kate used to lie quietly in her cot in the mornings and give me a big smile when I went in. Ben would be thumping around in his cot, not crying but certainly making himself heard by banging his rattles. When he was crawling I'd often find him closely examining power points with his fingers, an activity that had never commanded his sister's attention!'

~

Contemporary research into gender studies still debates the nature–nurture argument but one thing is certain: being a boy is not simply the opposite of being a girl. Boys are different in a host of complex ways. Steve Biddulph says many studies show that not only boys' hormone systems but also their brains are not the same as girls'. Mothers have never required scientific proof of this undeniable fact. They know how unlike girls boys are because they spend more time at the coalface than anyone else.

'With the boys I always had to be alert to what they were doing all the time. The girls were very straight down the line and easier to handle,' says Carolyn Steele, mother of two boys and two girls. Cindy Crosthwaite, who has four sons, discovered how much more energetic boys can be. 'My sons are all very physical and need physical activity. They are also very physically affectionate. Girls may be physically affectionate but the ones I know are quite happy to spend the day colouring or doing quiet things whereas boys are loud and noisy – but I wouldn't change them for the world!'

'A boy's social maturity is about two years behind girls',' says Marg Malkin. 'We raised our kids while running a lodge at Mount Hotham in the Victorian snowfields. It used to concern me that Nick didn't seem as comfortable in what was pretty much an adult atmosphere. He often hid in the roof squirting people in the restaurant with his water pistol through cracks in the ceiling rather than socialising with our guests and staff. The girls were butter-flies who knew how to set up the bar. They'd be out in the kitchen chatting up the chef or washing glasses, and automatically did such things from when they were six or seven. Nick was more quietly observant. I found it much easier to raise a son. Boys' hormones don't run as wild as they do with females.'

Marie Beatson, a mother of five boys and one girl, agrees. 'Rachel did everything earlier than the boys. She talks more than the boys did – and still does. She read earlier too.'

But opinions seem to differ on whether boys are more or less affectionate than girls, and whether they're easier or harder to raise. For Marg McCallum, mother of two girls and one boy, her son Ian 'was definitely different from the girls – not nearly as temperamental – but the girls are much more affectionate and ring all the time. I would be lucky if I heard from Ian week in, week out. But he is living a long way away in Tom Price in Western Australia in a different time zone and is married. He has always been much more independent than the girls, not unaffectionate but different.'

Anne Stephens finds that even though her daughter Rebecca is only seven, she appears 'more intuitive towards women and what their needs are' than her two older sons, Ben and Josh. 'I expect more from Ben because he is the eldest, which is unfair I know, and I have told him this. I don't mean to put this pressure on him and every now and then I have to stop myself.'

In contrast, Jan Rossington found it more difficult to raise girls 'because although boys can be quite nasty and revolting when they are younger, Deborah (Jan's daughter) was much more difficult mentally. She could be quite horrible really . . . Boys aren't bitchy in the way girls are.'

Lucie Paterson, mother of three girls and one boy, remembers, 'It was actually quite enlightening for me to discover how different boys and girls are. I expected that it was all linked to the way a child was brought up and you could direct them a certain way. But Joseph definitely shows different ways of behaving and I can only put this down to the fact that he is a boy. For instance, I've never bought him a gun but there must be about ten or fifteen toy guns in the house. Joseph doesn't get as caught up in things as the girls do either, such as worrying about what their friends think. He is very affectionate towards me. He'll come over and say, "I love you, Mum," more than his sisters ever would.'

~

For all the advances women have made in so many aspects of their lives, mothering of sons still occurs within a male-defined and dominated culture. Although most modern mothers reject patriarchy they understand that their sons have to be initiated in its way or risk being isolated from the accepted male culture. Few mothers would willingly inflict such a 'fate' on their son but, even so, many of them are prepared to have a go at changing their son's inherent male conditioning.

Wendy McCarthy's children are all adults – Sophie is thirty-six, Hamish is thirty-four, and Sam is thirty-one – 'and old enough for me to say that as a young feminist mother I seriously tried to organise a family environment where everyone could do everything. They all played with the same blocks, toys, teddy bears and dolls – although I must say that in my household dolls weren't all that popular. I wanted to raise sons who saw the world differently. I encouraged them to explore their feelings, to be kind and gentle and, although I probably wouldn't have acknowledged this then, it very quickly emerged that the boys' genetic wiring was different. They were more interested in building toys than talking to dolls, perhaps quietly mother-resistant to being the same as their sisters. It was more an individual difference.'

'When I was first married I used to ask my mother-in-law why she hadn't done a better job raising my husband and she'd always say, "I tried, darling." Veronica Fordham has two sons, both in their twenties, and a thirty-year-old daughter. 'Now when I look at my boys I understand how it is so conditioned in them to be male – but that doesn't mean they aren't sensitive; although boys don't have anything like the sensitivity of girls, it is buried deep inside them. Sometimes you have to search to find it and just when you think they don't have a sensitive bone in their bodies, all of a sudden they tune in.'

So, do women mother their sons and daughters differently? The consensus is yes. Indeed it is often said that mothers raise their daughters and mother their sons. 'I don't deliberately set out to mother them differently,' says Melanie, who has a pigeon pair, 'but I find that sometimes I do. I seem to forgive my son more often when he is naughty than I do my daughter because he gets so worried if I'm upset.'

Sarah, a mother of four, also admits to being more lenient with her sons than her daughters. 'The girls say I have two sets of rules – one for them and another for their brothers.'

'My mother used to forgive my three brothers everything and anything,' Ita says. 'She'd tell me, "Your brother is going through a difficult stage," and whichever one it was would get away with blue murder. I used to think it was so unfair.'

Sons are only too well aware of their mother's double standards. 'My mother was eternally supportive and always there for me – to a fault,' says 46-year-old Rick. 'If I ever had a problem that I would discuss with her, it was never my fault. I could do no wrong in her eyes. I could have been an axe murderer and she would have found some way to forgive me. She wasn't the same with my sister and was more balanced in her perspective with her.'

'My mother always expected me to do things in the house like washing the dishes and making dinner often every day, but my two brothers only had to take out the garbage bins and sometimes help mow the lawn once a week, if that,' Catherine Rodgers says. 'I didn't make that mistake with my kids. Both my son and daughter were expected to cook dinner a couple of times a week and do whatever chores needed to be done inside and outside the house. I don't think mothers should make excuses for boys over girls because it simply sends out the wrong messages about equality.'

Mothering of sons changes at different stages in boys' lives. All mothers of sons know the amazing 'physicality' of young boys. Joselyn remembers how differently little boys and girls played when she used to take her twin boys to playgroup picnics. 'The see-saw was a classic example. The girls would go up and down gently, talking and laughing. For boys, the best thing to do on a seesaw was to jump off quickly and without warning, so their mate on the other end would come crashing down with a clunk. Every park has a tap and under every tap is a puddle and boys always managed to sit in it. If they came near the picnic rug boys would send all the food flying and drinks were always spilt. Boys would climb every tree – and anything not nailed down, they would pick up and throw. The mothers of boys were always on the go retrieving a son, whereas the mothers of girls were able to sit and chat because their daughters were usually nearby, skipping, or collecting flowers or chatting too. Of course we mother boys differently – we have no choice!'

'Boys convert feeling into movement. They need space and the opportunity to move when faced with issues or problems and when dealing with emotions and anxieties,' Penny says. 'When parents take part in action-oriented activities with their sons, boys often open up and talk. If I want to find out what's worrying my daughters I take them to a café for coffee or a meal. If I ask Tom, who is now fourteen, anything he usually grunts. But when we go for a run together, he opens up about all sorts of things. When mothers bring their sons to see me at the surgery I tell them it's important for them not only to talk with their boys but also to listen to them. Because boys are not good at communicating we often let them get away with saying very little while we encourage girls to talk.'

'Ben went through that stage of not talking much – from about fourteen to twenty,' Ita says. 'I'd ask him something and he'd say "yep" or "nope". Then one day he starting "talking" again – it was an overnight transformation. I could scarcely believe my ears. I've learned that it's best to wait for your son to talk to you – he has to choose the time, not you.'

'As my sons entered their teens, they craved male attention,' Margi says. 'There are a couple of my husband's friends whom they seek out in particular. Interestingly, their favourite is a guy who has three daughters. I think he loves doing "boy things" with my sons that he doesn't get to do at home and they pick up on his enthusiasm. My friends who are single mothers work hard at bringing positive male role models into their sons' lives – coaches, uncles, grandfathers, male friends.'

This is not just important in a social context but also in the education of boys. Dr Peter West, Head of the Research Group on Men and Families at the University of Western Sydney, told the *Sydney Morning Herald* in April 2004 that, 'Schools will fail boys until they hire men who can lead them and laugh with them.' Boys have a 'masculine energy', which means they need to run around and be physical. West believes that male teachers can better understand this behaviour and recognise it as normal and useful, rather than naughty and loud. In understanding and, what's more, enjoying boys' physicality and their need for this to be praised, male teachers help boys develop their masculinity.

Many of the mothers interviewed for this book are aware that boys generally need more praise than girls, because they have a more concrete way of thinking and learning about the world and therefore need more obvious, tangible confirmation of doing well at something. It is not enough to simply show praise, as mothers can do for daughters; mothers of sons need to say it as well.

It is often not until middle age that sons fully realise how deep their mother's love is for them. Forty-year-old Robert possibly speaks for many men when he admits, 'I never realised how much my mother loved me until I was looking for something in the garage one day and came across a box marked "Mum's treasures". In it I found a photograph that had been taken at the hospital a few hours after I was born, my first pair of walking boots, my first footy jumper, every card I had ever made her, a paper Easter bunny, homemade Christmas decorations, and a plaster impression of my hand when I was three years old. She had even kept all my school reports and photographs of me with my school mates taken at end of year photography sessions . . . and a baby album detailing my first twelve months.'

If sons feel guilty about their mothers – and many do not – it comes later in life after they have established their own families and better appreciate just how much their mother did for them and how much she cared. As they get older, a 'softness' develops in many men in their feelings towards their mother. Although mothers invariably become friends with their daughters as they both age, and while they can and do have a close relationship with their sons, a boy's mother always remains 'Mum'.

'Because my mother was so blindly supportive, there was a period of time when I rather took her for granted,' Rick says. 'Looking back, I now see that I didn't put in the effort with her that I should have. This realisation came with the birth of my first child, when I had a much greater understanding of all my mother had done for me. She is now in the advanced stages of Alzheimer's and in a baby-like state. I have incredible love for her mixed with sadness. I'm not looking after her physically because she's in a nursing home and I'm pragmatic enough to know I can't do that, so I don't feel guilty. But, because we can't communicate on any sort of intellectual level, when I visit her I have these amazing periods of reflection. The memories flood back.

'In the past there were times when I had "unhealthy" attitudes towards women because they were condoned by my mother. I now realise that it's critical for a mother to condition her sons about what is acceptable thinking and behaviour towards women. Recently, my boss – who is a woman – told me, "You have everything going for you except you are such a chauvinist." Her remarks really hit home, but it took my boss to tell me something that I think my mother should have told me. It occurred to me that my mother had built in me a very giant but fragile ego that I had to carry through life, so that every knock hit me so much harder. Thankfully, I have a strong wife, who has not only helped me enormously but has also been a big influence on our three sons.

'I love my mother for her unconditional love; however, I now know that it's not healthy. Although I accept that men are important to their son's upbringing I think a mother has a critical role in socialising the male.'

Dorothy Johnson's son is forty-two. 'My experience is that sons are more open than daughters. My son talks to me about everything from his sex life to his job. I had a strong bond with my daughter, who was a year older, but I think girls are more internalised. (Dorothy's daughter died in September 2004 after a car accident.) When a son marries he breaks away and goes his wife's way by spending more time with her parents – my son hasn't done that yet because he isn't married.'

Occasionally, a man's love for his mother can make it hard for him to find someone to love. In 2003, singer Justin Timberlake told *New Idea* that his love for his mum was affecting his relationships. 'You search for someone as good as your mother and that's a losing battle.' This maternal attachment might also explain why many women often feel men are looking for a partner who will 'mother' them. 'When my brother's marriage broke up, I asked his wife what caused their split,' says Mick. 'She told me the problem was Mum – "Your brother thinks she can do no wrong."'

Mothers do have firm views on their son's future partners. Marg Malkin says she wants her son to marry someone who will allow him to be what he is. 'I've brought our kids up to have life skills and respect for other people but not to take things for granted. I don't want to see that unravelled by Nick finding someone who is really going to push him around. I wouldn't like him to marry someone like his eldest sister because she expects her boyfriend to iron her shirts and criticises him when he doesn't do the job to her satisfaction. She is pushy and demanding and just the sort of person I wouldn't want Nick to marry. I wouldn't like to see him having to do every single thing in the house because he is totally domesticated and I don't want anyone to take advantage of that. I want him to have an equal relationship. I've taught him how to be self-sufficient and I would be so cross – and sad – to see him taken advantage of . . . I just hope his character is strong enough.'

Michael, who is in his early fifties, had his first and only major conflict with his mother over his choice of marriage partner. 'I am first-generation Australian – my parents are Greek – and anyone who wasn't Greek, was considered a second-class citizen. I was very shy with girls but, in the traditional Greek way, three girls had been selected from whom I was expected to choose a wife. But when I met Karen, an Australian, she just knocked me out. Several months after we started going out, Karen went overseas and I chased her. When I told my mother we were engaged, she really got into me. It was terrible. Up until then, my mother had been the most important woman in my life and now Karen was going to fill that role. I felt as if I was doing something that hurt my mother and I worried about making her suffer this way.

'It resolved itself over the years, as my mother watched what an amazing job Karen did in mothering our children. Recently, my mother told me that she was ashamed of how she had treated Karen, and told me that she now looked on my wife as a daughter.'

The relationship between mothers and their sons is a secretive one because boys are not encouraged to talk about their feelings, especially their love for their mums. The irony is that mothers understand this but sometimes yearn for an acknowledgment of their love, which they know in their hearts (or at least like to believe) is returned, even if it is never expressed. Yet a man's relationship with his mother is the first important relationship in his life. Her smile, her voice, her hugs make him happy as a baby and give him confidence. The mother–son bond strongly influences the way a son thinks about himself. As he goes through boyhood he observes the way his mother interacts with other men in her life – not just her partner, but her father, her siblings, her uncles and family friends. She is his role model for his future relationships with the opposite sex. 'Before I married I checked out how Matthew got on with his mother because my own mum always told me, "like mother, like son",' Cathy says. 'The two of them got on famously and it was obvious that he respected his mother and that she had raised him well.'

These days a great many men admit to being confused about relationships with women and complain that they just do not know what females want or expect of them. Maybe their confusion has much to do with the outmoded male code by which sons are raised. As William Pollack points out, 'The Boy Code imposes a gender straightjacket on them, often leaving boys without the experience or the tools to express their emotions safely.' The Boy Code no longer works because modern society no longer values traditional codes of manhood. On the one hand boys are pressured to be tough, but on the other, society demands they be more sensitive.

The reality is that men have failed to keep up because they have failed to embrace change the way women have. The Women's Liberation movement of the twentieth century brought with it sweeping changes in attitudes to what women wanted out of life, as well as to the way girls were educated and reared and their expectations generally, but men and boys did not come along for the ride. This 'new' woman frightened men and consequently they have lagged behind, still following a rigid code that was developed centuries ago and that is totally unsuited for today's world.

Instead of blaming mothers for loving their sons, men need to acknowledge their positive influence on their lives and develop a new code that allows them and boys to express their feelings and, when necessary, their sadness. Mothers have always understood the male need to be able to do this and perhaps are at fault, and should even feel guilty, for not speaking out sooner. This does not mean boys should be raised as girls – perish the thought. Boys must be always allowed to be boys but without the emotional constrictions currently foisted on them.

20

Motherguilt has no place in the twenty-first century

It makes no sense at all why perfectly sane women feel the need to berate themselves over what they consider to be their supposed shortcomings as mothers. Being a mother is an honourable calling and one most women take seriously. It can have its tough moments but, in spite of everything, most women are prepared to do whatever it takes to be the best mother possible and to live up to what is expected of them. It is society's unrealistic expectations of their maternal role that makes this nigh on impossible and causes Motherguilt. It is unfair that being a mother carries with it far greater cultural expectations for the responsibility of the emotional development and happiness of children than fathering does – especially as men and women are supposed to be equal. Under such circumstances, if something goes wrong it is only natural that mothers suffer feelings of guilt – or blame themselves. But they should not be made to feel like this.

Women's need to please others makes them vulnerable to criticism, whether real or imagined. Consequently they often keep their opinions to themselves and do not express their feelings for fear of what others will think. If only they could get over this particular insecurity their lives would be so much easier, but it is a constant worry. Even as little girls, women torment themselves wondering what their friends might think about what they say or how they dress, perform at school, play sport – there is no end to their list of worries. Their underlying fear is they might offend or harm others if they express their feelings of disappointment and anger about anything – a trait not shared by the opposite sex, and one which perhaps in some way explains why women constantly put themselves down and are so self-critical.

Women place similar kinds of restrictions on themselves in pursuit of their careers. No matter how talented they might be it is generally not in the female psyche to admit to being overly ambitious. Even if women outperform men in the workplace they downplay their abilities; brushing aside compliments and suggesting their achievements are a matter of luck. A successful woman often insists, 'I was lucky enough to be in the right place at the right time,' no matter if she has worked her butt off – which is usually the case – to make sure she was precisely in the right place by design, not luck, when opportunity knocked.

'As a long-time employer of women, I regularly find it necessary to tell them that they are really good at what they do,' Ita says. 'Many's the time I've had to encourage women to seek a promotion or reassure them they are able to do a particular job. Once, I spent considerable time convincing a highly talented Churchill Scholarship winner that she was more knowledgeable than men in her chosen field, knew in practice what many of them knew only in theory, and had no need to feel nervous about speaking to them. But as any astute employer would – or should – know, women don't like to blow their own trumpet and rarely do in the way that comes so naturally to men. I don't say this as a criticism but merely a statement of fact.'

It is also a fact that guilt and self-esteem are linked. The latter is fundamental to the health and wellbeing of every woman and to the way in which a person values their worth and importance. Lack of self-esteem produces anxiety and fear and therefore guilt. Because women need to be liked and to please others they run themselves ragged taking care of the family and the house – and more often than not also working outside the home. The ability to get more done in less time is one of today's most respected skills, and women pride themselves on being able to do this better than men. They rarely take time off for rest and relaxation. Even if they are sick women soldier on, as they do not want to be seen letting down their bosses, their work colleagues or their families.

'I used to think I was proving something – what, I'm now not exactly sure – by struggling to the office when I was ill and a young working mother,' Ita says. 'I would sit at my desk with my bottle of antibiotics nearby, proudly wearing my "sacrifice" for all to see but wishing I was at home in bed. I must have been nuts.' Ita is not the only woman who has done this to herself. Most women feel they must take care of everyone and everything else before looking after themselves. Wrong!

'Until I started writing this book I hadn't realised how widespread Motherguilt was and how many women undervalue their self-worth, not just in mothering but in so many areas of their lives,' says Ita. 'Doing things for others seems to be the way we bolster our self-esteem. We tell ourselves that people will like us, something that doesn't necessarily equate but women have been raised this way. We like to be "needed".

'I remember a woman who worked for me once saying she wanted to be "needed". This was after her husband – to whom she'd been married for more than twenty-five years – had traded her in for a younger model. "You mean you want to be loved,"

I said. "No, I need to be needed," she replied. I had a long talk with her about discovering her sense of self.

'Women wear themselves out by taking on too much, and because we are good at giving we have this strange belief that the more we give, the more we'll get. I have a sign in my office: 'Say NO', but when people ring and ask me to do something – usually for nothing – I can be staring at the sign but will still say yes. Then I sometimes have to struggle to get everything done because I have taken on too many commitments. I tell myself I'm crazy but I keep on doing it. There have been times when I have not been in control of my life because the demands of the many jobs I was juggling were controlling me, which is not a good way for any woman to lead her life. And I know I am not the only woman who feels compelled to do this.'

'Mothers find it hard to simplify their lives and put themselves first because they've been indoctrinated for so many years that to do so is being selfish,' Penny says. 'When they come to see me at the surgery I tell them they must take better care of themselves because if they go on neglecting their own needs they will burn themselves out and run the risk of suffering from irritability, low self-esteem and depression. Many of them give me a knowing look as if to say, "Look who's talking," and they're right. I don't give myself enough time either. Just about all women seem to have a habit of putting themselves last, although we talk about the need to include doing something just for ourselves on our priority list. Sometimes I do find it hard to practise what I preach.

'I advise my patients to try and keep some of the interests they had before children. They may not be able to devote as much time to them, but they don't have to completely sacrifice themselves just because they're mothers. If they keep their hand in, they will be able to increase their involvement in such activities when their children are older.'

Wherever one cares to look there are examples of women taking on too much and putting other peoples' needs above their own. Beth, a young mother with three children under five, was pressured to volunteer to find prizes for her son's school fete, even though she has her hands full with the kids – one of whom is still a baby and a bad sleeper – and works one day a week for her dad. At this stage of her life, Beth has no time for anything extra and none at all for herself. 'I knew I should have said no but I didn't want to be seen as letting the school down. I was a new mum at the school and I wanted people to like me and not do anything that might reflect badly on my son,' Beth says.

Stay-at-home mums are notorious for taking on all kinds of extra roles at their kids' schools, to the extent that their voluntary work can become a 'career' and often so consuming that, after their kids have gone to bed, mothers work late into the night to get everything done. No one would suggest that women stop volunteering – the community would grind to a halt if they gave up the many voluntary roles they fulfil. Volunteering also provides vital services and, in many cases, much-needed funds for schools and welfare organisations. However, wherever women work and in whatever capacity, they have a habit of taking on too much and of exhausting their personal energy and resources on others. They need to learn to step back and keep something in reserve for themselves.

When a woman becomes a mother the accepted cultural definition of womanhood dictates that her maternal role takes precedence over any of her other needs. Women are generally expected to be caretakers. They expect it of themselves too. After all, women have been conditioned this way for centuries and are trained from infancy to take on the bulk of this work. They unquestionably make themselves available to their children, partners, parents, friends and co-workers.

Women set very high standards for their parenting role and also assume they will be responsible for most of it. If she fails at one of her tasks, a mother rarely confides her sense of failure to anyone, but instead tells herself that she must have done something wrong. Women are supposed to be competent at everything they do – to be good mothers, good partners, good household managers, good employees – and, if necessary, to forsake their personal needs.

'Society is very tough on women,' Margot Cairnes says. 'We allow ourselves to be bombarded by external voices that dictate and judge our mothering abilities and then, after absorbing all this "advice", we judge ourselves by other people's unachievable standards. We need to reject them and pay attention to our inner voice, which says to us – if only we'd listen – "I am a person. What matters to me? What are my values? Am I true to them?" If we judge ourselves by our own criteria, it is nurturing and very empowering.'

It is no good women saying they no longer wish to be Superwomen unless society changes its Superwoman expectations of them. In order to conquer Motherguilt a woman has to see herself not just as a mother but as a person. So does everyone else. 'It is almost necessary for a woman not to be a person when she is a mother,' Carla Zampatti says. 'She is expected to forgo who she is, what she is, what she feels, and just be a good mother – that is what human nature expects in terms of the continuation of the species.'

A woman's need to follow individual dreams and fulfil aspirations does not vanish just because she is a mother. Recognising herself as a person, and insisting her partner, children and other family members do too, increases a woman's self-esteem and gives her the confidence to rationalise guilt and to value her many talents. 'I'd like to see every mother take a leaf out of Mohammed Ali's book,' Ita says. 'When they get up in the morning they should look at themselves in the mirror and shout, "I AM THE GREATEST!"'

Women must stop being so modest about their abilities. They are good at what they do.'

'Women talk a lot about choices and they can make a choice about guilt too,' Penny says. 'When situations arise that would normally make a woman feel guilty she needs to pause and reflect – "Will I do guilt or give it a miss?" She actually needs to talk to herself and make that choice. Psychologists and psychiatrists call it cognitive behavioural therapy. With a little practice women can get very good at doing this. It is not denial but a conscious decision to drop the emotion of guilt.

'Time-out therapy can also be an effective guilt-buster. When toddlers are being naughty we give them time out by removing them from the situation so they can calm down and think about things. Time-out therapies come in all different sizes. Not long before Mother's Day last year I was listening to talkback radio and one woman rang to say all she wanted for Mother's Day was to go to the bathroom without someone else in the room. I tell mothers to give themselves permission to lock the bathroom door. Time out can be going to the movies – provided there is no mention of Disney in the credits – going to the gym or having lunch with the girls. Anything, just as long as a mother is doing something for herself.

'The ultimate form of time-out therapy is the weekend away with women friends. I've been doing this for several years now. Ten of us take a beach house for a weekend of eating, sleeping, drinking and talking. This kind of group therapy is sheer bliss and I recommend it to all Motherguilt sufferers.'

As the twenty-first century gathers momentum there are indications that women are re-evaluating their choices yet again. Having embraced equality – imperfect though that still is – and made impressive gains in the workplace, the big challenge for humankind will be for men to embrace equality in the home. Women cannot keep going the way they are. As the Women's Rights movement guru Gloria Steinem says, 'Having it all doesn't mean doing it all. Men have always had it all and not done it all. With Women's Liberation the leap of consciousness we made was that women can do what men can do. The next leap of consciousness we need is that men can do what women can do.'

Geraldine Doogue agrees. 'We have to get men more involved as nurturers. Men, individually and as a group, need to reassess their responsibilities towards modern family life.' Most women, particularly mothers, think the same way. They are fed up at having to handle more than their fair share of household tasks, while holding down a job in the paid workforce.

But this will not happen successfully unless mothers are prepared to give up some of their authority and allow fathers to learn on the job – without criticising them for any shortcomings. It does not really matter if men do things differently, only that their tasks get done. Women will need to remember their anxious moments and early insecurities when they were new mums, and the mistakes they made when acquiring their mothering skills. Fathers will need to be allowed to learn by trial and error too. There will be resistance. Men have been told for so long that they were not necessary to raise children. Why should they believe women now? Their nurturing transformation will not be an overnight miracle.

Meanwhile, women are thinking through new possibilities in the workplace and trying to come up with wider interpretations of equality and success that better balance the demands of career and family life. The next stage for women is to compose their lives in a way that feels right for them and not by current male definitions. But any kind of move towards a new equality in the workplace means that the role of women and men in the home will have to change. More men will be expected to cook dinner, clean the house, bath the kids, and involve themselves fully in the invisible work done by women.

Other changes are afoot. In June 2004, *60 Minutes*' Tara Brown reported on 'the new wife', an emerging women's movement in the United States promoting 'old-fashioned priorities'. Generation Y women, the daughters of the Baby Boomers and aged eighteen to twenty-four, have watched their mothers' attempts to be Superwomen and are deciding they do not want to lead similar lives. They want to have their children when they are young and to take at least five years off their careers to be with them. They are looking for – and finding – husbands who will be sole providers, young men who have also watched their crazy, busy lives and had to cope with tired mothers. They want settled family lives too, where there is time to enjoy their relationships with their family.

The new wife is educated and articulate. She is a woman who wants to enjoy life and feels secure in the knowledge that she is making the right choice about her life. There is no question of guilt in her making this choice either. This is her choice and no apology will ever be necessary.

Change always takes its time and it may take until the end of this century before women and men are equal in every sense of the word. It is heartening that women are challenging their options, although it is too soon to predict where this might lead them. Perhaps the most encouraging aspect is that women have the courage and confidence to question their roles at home and in the workplace – this bodes well for the future. In the meantime, one of a mother's first priorities must be getting rid of Motherguilt. There are a number of Positive Action Steps a woman can take to help her do this.

> ✦ **Enjoy saying no.** This has to become the most important word in a mother's vocabulary. Most women are guilty of saying yes even when they are emotionally

spent. Learn to say no. Practise saying it every day, along with, 'I haven't the time because I have other plans.' Do not apologise for this. Never say no now and then yes later. Suggest someone else to do whatever is being asked of you. The only person who should utter the words, 'Leave it to me, I'll take care of it,' is another woman.

→ **Enjoy time with your children** and remember that a tidy house is a sign of a wasted mind. Unimportant tasks can wait. Take time out to have fun with your kids. It is important children see this side of you. They like to have fun with their mothers and see them laugh. A child's humour makes a mother feel good and is unbelievably infectious. Their funny anecdotes continually delight children in the 'telling' and become the basis of family folklore as they are passed on by mothers over the generations.

→ **Enjoy the precious moments** that come when a mother least expects them. The shy good morning smiles when children sneak into your bedroom and want to get into bed with you; the first ballet concert or football match; eating ice-creams and seeing things through kids' eyes; listening to children's conversation about their day . . . Even from a very young age children have their own sets of values and personality.

→ **Enjoy being sick occasionally.** Be kind to yourself when you are unwell. Stay in bed until your temperature is back to normal. Your family will be able to manage without you. If your children are very young enlist the aid of your support network. Accept all offers of casseroles willingly. Allow the family to wait on you for a change and relish the rare opportunity to do nothing. It may be hard for you to believe but when you get up you will discover that everyone will have survived, including the dog.

→ **Enjoy being like other mothers** – with whom you may be surprised to discover you have much in common. For instance, there are few mothers who have never had mean thoughts about their children or occasionally smacked or yelled at them. Kids enjoy seeing their mothers blow a fuse because they like to brag to their school friends about the most effective ways they have found to cause this to happen. Most first-time mums have difficulty breastfeeding. Few mothers have homes that look like the ones in *Vogue Living*. A dirty refrigerator is not a crime nor is an overflowing basket of clothes waiting to be ironed. There are times when most women worry that they are no longer as attractive to their partners as they once were. All mothers suffer from tiredness.

→ **Enjoy time for yourself.** Whether it is only an hour or a night off, just do it. Taking a couple of minutes daily to do something for yourself is not selfish. If a babysitter is beyond your budget develop an exchange system with friends and neighbours. Have a bubble bath, go to bed early and read a book. Or even better, put the kids to bed early and have a romantic dinner with your partner. Go for a walk. Simple pleasures are the most enjoyable and relaxing.

→ **Enjoy being a mother.** Never be afraid to praise yourself for a job well done. Tell yourself you are doing a good job as a mother. Tell other mothers the same thing. No one tells mothers this often enough. When you are coping with a number of jobs it is easy to think that none of them is being done the way you would like. Being a good mother does not mean you have to make life perfect for your children. If something goes wrong, do not blame yourself or hold yourself responsible. You can only do your best and cannot and never will be able to make everything okay for everyone.

→ **Finally, rethink that word guilt**. Is guilt related to anger? Most mothers would say yes. So, if you feel guilty, what are you angry about? It is hard to clarify guilt but anger can be resolved. Every time you feel guilty substitute the word anger. Now handle that anger. But the most effective solution would be to feel regret, not guilt. There is no blame associated with regret, nor the slightest hint of guilt. Regret requires no explanation, simply the realisation that a mother did the best she could in a situation – which is what all women do from the moment they give birth.

All too often, mothers are taken for granted and their many qualities, especially those relating to leadership, completely overlooked. Yet a mother is possibly the world's most powerful and effective leader. Without her expert guidance her children would flounder. She shapes them and colours their beliefs, and her influence lasts a lifetime. She constantly offers encouragement and gives them the confidence to tackle the challenges and detours they will encounter throughout their life's journey. She is a role model for her daughters and sets an example to her sons as well. Her imagination inspires her children. It is through her eyes that their curiosity about the world is stirred. She will love them forever – and worry about them too. It could be argued that mothers are supreme beings. There is an old saying that brilliantly reinforces this line of thought: 'God could not be everywhere, so he made mothers.' Well, of course!